Problem Solving

in

Analytical Chemistry

A Practical Handbook Containing
Over 1000 Worked Examples, Problems and Answers

Themistocles P. Hadjiioannou
University of Athens

Gary D. Christian
University of Washington

Constantinos E. Efstathiou
University of Athens

Demetrios P. Nikolelis
University of Athens

SOLUTIONS MANUAL

PERGAMON PRESS
OXFORD · NEW YORK · BEIJING · FRANKFURT
SÃO PAULO · SYDNEY · TOKYO · TORONTO

U.K.	Pergamon Press plc, Headington Hill Hall, Oxford OX3 0BW, England
U.S.A.	Pergamon Press, Inc., Maxwell House, Fairview Park, Elmsford, New York 10523, U.S.A.
PEOPLE'S REPUBLIC OF CHINA	Pergamon Press, Room 4037, Qianmen Hotel, Beijing, People's Republic of China
FEDERAL REPUBLIC OF GERMANY	Pergamon Press GmbH, Hammerweg 6, D-6242 Kronberg, Federal Republic of Germany
BRAZIL	Pergamon Editora Ltda, Rua Eça de Queiros, 346, CEP 04011, Paraiso, São Paulo, Brazil
AUSTRALIA	Pergamon Press Australia Pty Ltd., P.O. Box 544, Potts Point, N.S.W. 2011, Australia
JAPAN	Pergamon Press, 5th Floor, Matsuoka Central Building, 1-7-1 Nishishinjuku, Shinjuku-ku, Tokyo 160, Japan
CANADA	Pergamon Press Canada Ltd., Suite No. 271, 253 College Street, Toronto, Ontario, Canada M5T 1R5

First edition 1988

ISBN 0–08–036972–3

Printed in Great Britain by A. Wheaton & Co. Ltd., Exeter

CHAPTER 1

1-1. On the basis of the data we have the following table:

Sample, g	KCl, g		Error (absolute), g
	Theor.	Exp.	(Exp. - Theor.)
0.4000	0.1000	0.0978	- 0.0022
0.3600	0.0900	0.0878	- 0.0022
0.3800	0.0950	0.0927	- 0.0023
0.4400	0.1100	0.1079	- 0.0021

There is a constant determinate error equal to - 0.0022 g.

1-2. (a) Exp. $= (5.84 + 5.77 + 5.65 + 5.66)/4 = 5.73$ mg Fe/mL

$$\text{Theor.} = \frac{2.6450\text{ g} \times 1000\text{ mg/g} \times 0.5351}{250\text{ mL}} = 5.66\text{ mg Fe/mL}$$

$$\%\text{ error} = \frac{5.73 - 5.66}{5.66} \times 100 = +1.24\%$$

$\therefore$ the accuracy of the method is not satisfactory.

(b) $$s = \sqrt{\frac{(0.11)^2 + (0.04)^2 + (0.08)^2 + (0.07)^2}{3}} = 0.09$$

1-3. Maximum uncertainty in determining weight w of precipitate M_2A is 0.2 mg

$\therefore$ $(0.0002/w)\,1000 = 1$, or $w = 0.2000$ g

$A / M_2A = A / [(2 \times 3.5\,A) + A] = 1/8$, hence weight of $A = 0.2000$ g$/8 = 0.0250$ g.

If $S =$ minimum size of sample, $0.25\,S = 0.0250$ g or $S = 0.1000$ g

1-4.

$(x_i - \bar{x}_A)^2$	$(x_i - \bar{x}_B)^2$	$(x_i - \bar{x}_C)^2$
0.00002	0.00152	0.00022
0.00000	0.00026	0.00020
0.00010	0.00084	0.00007
0.00002	0.00004	0.00006
$\Sigma = 0.00014$	$\Sigma = 0.00266$	$\Sigma = 0.00055$

$$s_p = \sqrt{(0.00014 + 0.00266 + 0.00055)/(12 - 3)} = 0.0193 \text{ absorbance units}$$

1-5. $$\text{error} = \frac{23.17 - 23.24}{23.24} \times 1000 = -3.0 \text{ ppt}$$

1-6. (a) 1. $\bar{x} = (55.10 + 55.30 + 55.50)/3 = 55.30$ mg

$$s = \sqrt{[(0.20)^2 + (0.00)^2 + (0.20)^2]/2} = 0.20$$

From Table 1-1 at the 95% confidence level and $\nu = 2$, $t = 4.303$

$\therefore$ 95% confidence limits $= 55.30 \pm (4.303 \times 0.20)/\sqrt{3} = 55.30 \pm 0.50$ mg

2. For $\sigma = 0.24$ mg, 95% conf. limits = $55.30 \pm (1.960 \times 0.24)/\sqrt{3} = 55.30 \pm 0.27$ mg

(b) $|\bar{x} - \mu| = 0.40$ mg > 0.27 mg, hence $\bar{x}$ is significantly different from μ.

(c) If $|\bar{x} - \mu|$ were 0.27 mg, the conclusion that $\bar{x}$ is significantly different from μ would have a 5% probability of being incorrect. Actually, $|\bar{x} - \mu| = 0.40$ mg > 0.27 mg, hence the probability of the conclusion being incorrect is smaller than 5%.

$$z = \frac{|\bar{x} - \mu|}{\sigma/\sqrt{N}} = \frac{0.40}{0.24/\sqrt{3}} = 2.89,$$

which corresponds to an error probability between 0.1% ($z = 3.291$) and 1% ($z = 2.576$) (Table 1-1).

1-7. Gravimetric : $\bar{x} = 26.47$, $s = 0.055$, $\nu = 4$

$\therefore$ 90% conf. limits = $26.47 \pm (2.132 \times 0.055)/\sqrt{5} = 26.47 \pm 0.05$

95% conf. limits = $26.47 \pm (2.776 \times 0.055)/\sqrt{5} = 26.47 \pm 0.07$

99% conf. limits = $26.47 \pm (4.604 \times 0.055)/\sqrt{5} = 26.47 \pm 0.11$

Volumetric : $\bar{x} = 26.50$, $s = 0.074$, $\nu = 4$

$\therefore$ 90% conf. limits = $26.50 \pm (2.132 \times 0.074)/\sqrt{5} = 26.50 \pm 0.07$

95% conf. limits = $26.50 \pm (2.776 \times 0.074)/\sqrt{5} = 26.50 \pm 0.09$

99% conf. limits = $26.50 \pm (4.604 \times 0.074)/\sqrt{5} = 26.50 \pm 0.15$

1-8. (a) $21.32 - 21.17 = 0.15\% \equiv \sigma$, $21.47 - 21.32 = 0.15\% \equiv \sigma$

From statistical tables, or less accurately from Figure 1-3, for $21.17 < x < 21.47$, that is, for $\mu - \sigma < x < \mu + \sigma$, probability $P = 68.3\%$.

(b) $21.32 - 21.00 = 0.32\% \equiv (0.32/0.15)\,\sigma = 2.13\,\sigma$, $21.50 - 21.32 \equiv (0.18/0.15)\,\sigma = 1.20\,\sigma$

From tables, for $21.00 < x < 21.32$, that is for $\mu - 2.136\,\sigma < x < \mu$, $P = 96.6/2 = 48.3\%$, whereas for $21.32 < x < 21.50$, that is, for $\mu < x < \mu + 1.20\,\sigma$, $P = 77.0/2 = 38.5\%$

$\therefore$ for $21.00 < x < 21.50$, $P = 48.3 + 38.5 = 86.8\%$.

1-9. (a) For $N = 2$, $\sigma_{\bar{x}} = 3/\sqrt{2} = 2.12$. Hence, 2 mg/dL is $(2/2.12)\,\sigma_{\bar{x}} = 0.943\,\sigma_{\bar{x}}$. From statistical tables, or less accurately from Figure 1-3, the probability of a mean falling within the range $-0.943\,\sigma_{\bar{x}}$ to $+0.943\,\sigma_{\bar{x}}$, is 65.5%.

For $N = 4$, $\sigma_{\bar{x}} = 3/\sqrt{4} = 1.50$. Hence, 2 mg/dL is $(2/1.50)\,\sigma_{\bar{x}} = 1.33\,\sigma_{\bar{x}}$, and $P = 81.6\%$.

For $N = 9$, $\sigma_{\bar{x}} = 3/\sqrt{9} = 1.00$. Hence, 2 mg/dL is $(2/1.00)\,\sigma_{\bar{x}} = 2.00\,\sigma_{\bar{x}}$, and $P = 95.5\%$.

(b) From part (a), the probability of the mean of 4 determinations falling within the range 0 to +2 mg/dL of μ is $81.6/2 = 40.8\%$. Hence, the probability that the mean of 4 determinations is at least 2 mg/dL larger than μ is $50.0 - 40.8 = 9.2\%$.

(c) For $N=2$, $\sigma_{\bar{x}}=2.12$. From tables, 95% of the means of 2 determinations fall within the range $\pm 1.960\,\sigma_{\bar{x}}$, that is, within $\pm 1.960 \times 2.12 = \pm 4.16$ mg/dL.

For $N=4$, $\sigma_{\bar{x}}=1.50$ $\therefore$ range is $\pm 1.960 \times 1.50 = \pm 2.94$ mg/dL.

For $N=9$, $\sigma_{\bar{x}}=1.00$ $\therefore$ range is $\pm 1.960 \times 1.00 = \pm 1.96$ mg/dL.

(d) For $P=99\%$ and a range of ± 6 mg/dL, $|\bar{x}-\mu| = 6 = 2.58\,\sigma_{\bar{x}} = 2.58\,\sigma/\sqrt{N} = (2.58 \times 3)/\sqrt{N}$.

Hence, $N = [(2.58 \times 3)/6]^2 \simeq 2$.

For $P=99\%$ and ± 3 mg/dL, $N = [(2.58 \times 3)/3]^2 \simeq 7$

For $P=99\%$ and ± 1 mg/dL, $N = [(2.58 \times 3)/1]^2 \simeq 60$

1-10. (a) $\mu = \bar{x} \pm z\sigma/\sqrt{N}$, hence $N = \left(\frac{z\sigma}{\mu-\bar{x}}\right)^2$

For 95% confidence level, $z=1.960$ (Table 1-1) $\therefore$ $N = [(1.960 \times 0.025)/0.050]^2 \simeq 1$

(b) $N = [(1.960 \times 0.025)/0.020]^2 \simeq 6$

(c) $N = [(1.960 \times 0.025)/0.010]^2 \simeq 24$

(d) For 99% confidence level, $z=2.576$ $\therefore$ $N = [(2.576 \times 0.025)/0.050]^2 \simeq 2$

(e) $N = [(2.576 \times 0.025)/0.020]^2 \simeq 11$

(f) $N = [(2.576 \times 0.025)/0.010]^2 \simeq 42$

1-11. (a) From Table 1-1, for $\nu=3$ and $P=95\%$, $t=3.182$. $t_{exp} = \frac{|10.21-10.39|\sqrt{4}}{0.078} = 4.62 > 3.182$.
Hence, a negative determinate error is indicated at the 95% confidence level.

(b) For $\nu=3$ and $P=99\%$, $t=5.841 > 4.62 = t_{exp}$. Hence, it can not be concluded that there is a determinate error.

1-12. From Table 1-2, for $\nu_1=5$, $\nu_2=4$, and $P=95\%$, $F=6.26$. $F_{exp}=(0.14)^2/(0.05)^2 = 7.84 > 6.26$.
Hence, s_A and s_B are significantly different at the 95% confidence level.

1-13. From Table 1-1, for $\nu=9$ and $P=90\%$, $t=1.833$, whereas for $P=99\%$, $t=3.250$.
$t_{exp} = \frac{|21.24-21.20|\sqrt{10}}{0.12} = 1.05 < 1.833 < 3.250$. Hence, there is no significant difference between $\bar{x}$ and μ at the 90% and 99% confidence levels.

1-14. $\bar{x}_A = 40.02$, $\bar{x}_B = 39.75$. From Table 1-1, for $\nu=5$ and $P=95\%$, $t=2.571$.

Equation (1-19) : $s_{1-2} = \sqrt{[(0.05)^2+(0.03)^2+(0.02)^2+(0.03)^2+(0.05)^2+(0.03)^2+(0.02)^2]/(3+4-2)}$
$= 0.0412$

Equation (1-18) : $t = [(40.02-39.75)/0.0412]\sqrt{(3 \times 4)/(3+4)} = 8.58 > 2.571$. Since $t_{exp} >$ t_{theor}, the results are significantly different at the 95% confidence level.

1-15. Fluorimetry : $s_1^2 = \frac{\Sigma(x_i-\bar{x})^2}{N-1} = 6.514/6 = 1.086$

AAS : $s_2^2 = 1.668/5 = 0.334$

$F_{exp} = s_1^2/s_2^2 = 1.086/0.334 = 3.25$

From Table 1-2, for $\nu_1 = 6$, $\nu_2 = 5$, and $P = 95\%$, $F = 4.95$. Since $F_{exp} = 3.25 < 4.95 = F_{theor}$, there is no significant difference in the precision of the two methods (at the 95% confidence level).

1-16. From Table 1-2, for $\nu_1 = 3$, $\nu_2 = 5$, and $P = 95\%$, $F = 5.41$. $F_{exp} = 0.0089/0.0039 = 2.28 < 5.41$. Hence the t test can be applied.

$\bar{x}_1 = 10.28$, $\bar{x}_2 = 10.41$. From Table 1-1, for $\nu = 8$ and $P = 95\%$, $t = 2.306$

$s_{1-2} = \sqrt{(0.0267 + 0.0194)/(4 + 6 - 2)} = 0.0759$ and $t = (|10.28 - 10.41|/0.0759)\sqrt{(4 \times 6)/(4 + 6)}$ $= 2.65$. Since $t_{exp} > t_{theor}$, the two samples are significantly different at the 95% confidence level.

1-17. The results are arranged in order of increasing magnitude as follows :

Results	N = 8 Suspected result = 6.02	N = 7 Suspected result = 7.92	N = 6 Suspected result = 7.02	N = 6 Suspected result = 7.32
6.02	x_1	Rejected	Rejected	Rejected
7.02	x_2	x_1	x_1	x_1
7.12	x_3	x_2	x_2	x_2
7.22	x_4	x_3	x_3	x_3
7.28	x_5	x_4	x_4	x_4
7.31	x_6	x_5	x_{N-1}	x_{N-1}
7.32	x_{N-1}	x_{N-1}	x_N	x_N
7.92	x_N	x_N	Rejected	Rejected

The smallest result, $x_1 = 6.02$, is the first suspected result. $Q_{exp} = (7.02 - 6.02)/(7.92 - 6.02)$ $= 0.53 > 0.47 = Q_{0.90}$ (for N = 8, Table 1-4) ∴ 6.02 is rejected. The remaining results are relabeled, and the largest result is tested :

$Q_{exp} = (7.92 - 7.32)/(7.92 - 7.02) = 0.67 > 0.51 = Q_{0.90}$ (N = 7). ∴ 7.92 is rejected, and the next suspected result, 7.02 is tested :

$Q_{exp} = (7.12 - 7.02)/(7.32 - 7.02) = 0.33 < 0.56 = Q_{0.90}$ (N = 6). ∴ 7.02 is retained, and the next suspected result, 7.32 is tested :

$Q_{exp} = (7.32 - 7.31)/(7.32 - 7.02) = 0.03 < 0.56$ ∴ 7.32 is retained.

1-18. $$\% CaCO_3 = \frac{\text{meq } CaCO_3 \times \text{mg } CaCO_3/\text{meq}}{\text{mg sample}} \times 100 = \frac{(\text{meq HCl} - \text{meq NaOH}) \times \text{mg } CaCO_3/\text{meq}}{\text{mg sample}} \times 100$$

$$\text{meq } CaCO_3 = \underbrace{(50.00 \pm 0.05)(0.2250 \pm 0.0002)}_{\text{meq HCl}} - \underbrace{(26.47 \pm 0.02)(0.2872 \pm 0.0003)}_{\text{meq NaOH}}$$

$$s_{r,\text{meq HCl}} = \sqrt{(0.05/50.00)^2 + (0.0002/0.2250)^2} = 1.34 \times 10^{-3}$$

$$\therefore \text{ meq HCl} = 11.250 \pm (1.34 \times 10^{-3})\, 11.250 = 11.250 \pm 0.015$$

$$s_{r,\text{meq NaOH}} = \sqrt{(0.02/26.47)^2 + (0.0003/0.2872)^2} = 1.29 \times 10^{-3}$$

$$\therefore \text{ meq NaOH} = 7.602 \pm (1.29 \times 10^{-3})\, 7.602 = 7.602 \pm 0.010$$

$$\text{meq } CaCO_3 = (11.250 \pm 0.015) - (7.602 \pm 0.010)$$

$$s_{\text{meq } CaCO_3} = \sqrt{(0.015)^2 + (0.010)^2} = 0.018 \quad \therefore \text{ meq } CaCO_3 = 3.648 \pm 0.018$$

$$\%\, CaCO_3 = \frac{(3.648 \pm 0.018)(50.05 \pm 0.00)}{212.5 \pm 0.1} \times 100$$

$$s_{r,\%\, CaCO_3} = \sqrt{(0.018/3.648)^2 + (0.1/212.5)^2} = 0.0050$$

$$\%\, CaCO_3 = 85.92, \quad s_{\%\, CaCO_3} = 85.92 \times 0.0050 = 0.43 \quad \therefore \%\, CaCO_3 = 85.9 \pm 0.4$$

1-19. Maximum uncertainty in determining smaller volume V of titrant is 0.002 mL

$\therefore$ $(0.002/V)\, 100 = 0.5$, or $V = 0.400$ mL

1-20. 6.0×10^{-4}

1-21. (a)

N	x_i	y_i	x_i^2	$x_i y_i$
1	1.0	0.240	1.00	0.240
2	2.0	0.460	4.00	0.920
3	3.0	0.662	9.00	1.986
4	4.0	0.876	16.00	3.504
	$\Sigma x_i = 10.0$	$\Sigma y_i = 2.238$	$\Sigma x_i^2 = 30.00$	$\Sigma x_i y_i = 6.650$

Substituting the values of the table in Equations (1-27) and (1-28),

$$a = \frac{(4 \times 6.650) - (10.0 \times 2.238)}{(4 \times 30.00) - (10.0)^2} = 0.2110, \quad b = \frac{(30.00 \times 2.238) - (10.0 \times 6.650)}{(4 \times 30.00) - (10.0)^2} = 0.0320$$

$\therefore$ the equation of the regression line is $y = 0.2110\,x + 0.0320$,

that is, $A = 0.2110\, [Fe]_{ppm} + 0.0320$

(b) $0.452 = 0.2110\, [Fe]_{ppm} + 0.0320 \quad \therefore \quad [Fe]_{ppm} = 1.99$.

1-22.

Spect. method, x_i	Enz. method, y_i	d_i	$d_i - \bar{d}$	$(d_i - \bar{d})^2$	$x_i y_i$	x_i^2	y_i^2
90	75	15	−6	36	6,750	8,100	5,625
182	155	27	+6	36	28,210	33,124	24,025
175	143	32	+11	121	25,025	30,625	20,449
142	122	20	−1	1	17,324	20,164	14,884
110	90	20	−1	1	9,900	12,100	8,100
101	85	16	−5	25	8,585	10,201	7,225
122	98	24	+3	9	11,956	14,884	9,604
100	86	14	−7	49	8,600	10,000	7,396
$\Sigma x_i = 1{,}022$	$\Sigma y_i = 854$	$\Sigma d_i = 168$		$\Sigma = 278$	$\Sigma x_i y_i = 116{,}350$	$\Sigma x_i^2 = 139{,}198$	$\Sigma y_i^2 = 97{,}308$

$\bar{d} = 21$

$$s_d = \sqrt{\Sigma(d_i - \bar{d})^2/(N-1)} = \sqrt{278/7} = 6.30 \quad , \quad t_{exp} = \bar{d}\sqrt{N}/s_d = 21\sqrt{8}/6.30 = 9.43$$

From Table 1-1 , for $\nu = 7$ and $P = 95\%$, $t = 2.365 < t_{exp}$. Hence, there is a significant difference between the two methods. Substituting in Equation (1-29b),

$$r = \frac{8(116{,}350) - (1{,}022)(854)}{\sqrt{[8(139{,}198) - (1{,}022)^2][8(97{,}308) - (854)^2]}} = 0.995$$

CHAPTER 2

2-1. All couples agree with the data.

2-2.
$$[Cu + 4\,HNO_3 \rightarrow Cu(NO_3)_2 + 2\,NO_2 + 2\,H_2O] \times 5$$
$$[3Cu + 8\,HNO_3 \rightarrow 3Cu(NO_3)_2 + 2\,NO + 4\,H_2O] \times 2$$

$$11Cu + 36\,HNO_3 \rightarrow 11Cu(NO_3)_2 + 10\,NO_2 + 4\,NO + 18\,H_2O \quad \text{total reaction}$$
$$\therefore\ 5\,(36 \times 63.01)/(11 \times 63.55) = 16.2\ \text{g}\ HNO_3$$

2-3.
(a) $4\,MnO_4^- + 5\,N_2H_5^+ + 7\,H^+ \rightleftharpoons 4\,Mn^{2+} + 5\,N_2\uparrow + 16\,H_2O$
(b) $[I_3]^- + 2\,N_3^- \rightleftharpoons 3\,N_2\uparrow + 3\,I^-$
(c) $2\,Fe^{3+} + 2\,NH_2OH \rightleftharpoons 2\,Fe^{2+} + N_2\uparrow + 2\,H^+ + 2\,H_2O$
(d) $3\,OBr^- + 2\,NH_3 \rightleftharpoons N_2\uparrow + 3\,Br^- + 3\,H_2O$
(e) $NH_4^+ + NO_2^- \rightleftharpoons N_2\uparrow + 2\,H_2O$
(f) $NH_4^+ + 5\,NO_2^- + 4\,H^+ \rightleftharpoons 6\,NO\uparrow + 4\,H_2O$
(g) $HNO_2 + 2\,SO_2 + 3\,H_2O \rightleftharpoons H_3\overset{+}{N}OH + 2\,HSO_4^- + H^+$
(h) $N_2H_5^+ + 12\,NO_3^- + 11\,H^+ \rightleftharpoons 14\,NO_2 + 8\,H_2O$

2-4.
$Zn + 2\,NO_3^- + 4\,H^+ \longrightarrow Zn^{2+} + 2\,NO_2 + 2\,H_2O$
$Zn + NO_3^- + 3\,H^+ \longrightarrow Zn^{2+} + HNO_2 + H_2O$
$3\,Zn + 2\,NO_3^- + 8\,H^+ \longrightarrow 3\,Zn^{2+} + 2\,NO + 4\,H_2O$
$4\,Zn + 2\,NO_3^- + 10\,H^+ \longrightarrow 4\,Zn^{2+} + N_2O + 5\,H_2O$
$5\,Zn + 2\,NO_3^- + 12\,H^+ \longrightarrow 5\,Zn^{2+} + N_2 + 6\,H_2O$
$8\,Zn + 3\,NO_3^- + 19\,H^+ \longrightarrow 8\,Zn^{2+} + HN_3 + 9\,H_2O$
$3\,Zn + NO_3^- + 8\,H^+ \longrightarrow 3\,Zn^{2+} + H_3\overset{+}{N}OH + 2\,H_2O$
$7\,Zn + 2\,NO_3^- + 17\,H^+ \longrightarrow 7\,Zn^{2+} + N_2H_5^+ + 6\,H_2O$
$4\,Zn + NO_3^- + 10\,H^+ \longrightarrow 4\,Zn^{2+} + NH_4^+ + 3\,H_2O$

2-5.
(a) $CH_3COCOCH_3 + 2\,Ce(IV) + 2\,H_2O \rightleftharpoons 2\,CH_3COOH + 2\,Ce(III) + 2\,H^+$
(b) $CH_2OHCHOHCH_2OH + 2\,IO_4^- \rightleftharpoons 2\,HCHO + HCOOH + 2\,IO_3^- + H_2O$
(c) $CH_3CHOHCH_2OH + IO_4^- \rightleftharpoons CH_3CHO + HCHO + IO_3^- + H_2O$
(d) $C_6H_5OH + 3\,Br_2 \rightleftharpoons C_6H_2Br_3OH + 3\,HBr$
(e) $BrO_3^- + 2\,Cr^{3+} + 4\,H_2O \rightleftharpoons Br^- + Cr_2O_7^{2-} + 8\,H^+$

2-6.
$2\,MnO_4^- + 5\,H_2C_2O_4 + 6\,H^+ \rightleftharpoons 2\,Mn^{2+} + 8\,H_2O + 10\,CO_2$
$2\,MnO_4^- + 15\,I^- + 16\,H^+ \rightleftharpoons 2\,Mn^{2+} + 5[I_3]^- + 8\,H_2O$
$Cr_2O_7^{2-} + 6\,Fe^{2+} + 14\,H^+ \rightleftharpoons 2\,Cr^{3+} + 6\,Fe^{3+} + 7\,H_2O$

$7\,Cr_2O_7^{2-} + 3\,CH_2OHCHOHCH_2OH + 56\,H^+ \rightleftharpoons 14\,Cr^{3+} + 9\,CO_2 + 40\,H_2O$

$[Ce(SO_4)_3]^{2-} + [Fe(CN)_6]^{4-} \rightleftharpoons [Ce(SO_4)_3]^{3-} + [Fe(CN)_6]^{3-}$

$6\,Ce(IV) + HOOCCH_2COOH + 2\,H_2O \rightleftharpoons 6\,Ce(III) + 2\,CO_2 + HCOOH + 6\,H^+$

$[I_3]^- + 2\,S_2O_3^{2-} \rightleftharpoons 3\,I^- + S_4O_6^{2-}$

$[I_3]^- + 2\,C_2H_5SH \rightleftharpoons 3\,I^- + C_2H_5SSC_2H_5 + 2\,H^+$

$IO_4^- + 2\,H^+ + 3\,I^- \rightleftharpoons IO_3^- + [I_3]^- + H_2O$

$IO_4^- + HOCH_2CH(NH_2)COOH \rightleftharpoons IO_3^- + HCHO + OHCCOOH + NH_3$

$S_2O_3^{2-} + 4\,[I_3]^- + 10\,OH^- \rightleftharpoons 2\,SO_4^{2-} + 12\,I^- + 5\,H_2O$

$5\,I^- + 2\,Cu^{2+} \rightleftharpoons 2\,CuI + [I_3]^-$

$5\,Br^- + BrO_3^- + 6\,H^+ \rightleftharpoons 3\,Br_2 + 3\,H_2O$

$6\,Br^- + Cr_2O_7^{2-} + 14\,H^+ \rightleftharpoons 3\,Br_2 + 2\,Cr^{3+} + 7\,H_2O$

2-7. (a) $2\,AsH_3 + 12\,AgNO_3 + 3\,H_2O \rightleftharpoons As_2O_3 + 12\,HNO_3 + 12\,Ag$

(b) $3\,Mn^{2+} + 2\,MnO_4^- + 2\,H_2O \rightleftharpoons 5\,MnO_2 + 4\,H^+$

(c) $Pb + PbO_2 + 2\,H_2SO_4 \rightleftharpoons 2\,PbSO_4 + 2\,H_2O$

(d) $Cd + Ni_2O_3 + 3\,H_2O \rightleftharpoons Cd(OH)_2 + 2\,Ni(OH)_2$

2-8. (a) $2\,AlCl_3 + 3\,Na_2S_2O_3 + 3\,H_2O \rightleftharpoons 2\,Al(OH)_3 + 3\,S + 3\,SO_2\uparrow$

(b) $Na_2B_4O_7 + 12\,CH_3OH + H_2SO_4 \rightleftharpoons 4\,(CH_3)_3BO_3 + Na_2SO_4 + 7\,H_2O$

(c) $2\,Fe^{3+} + 3\,CO_3^{2-} + 3\,H_2O \rightleftharpoons 2\,Fe(OH)_3 + 3\,CO_2$

(d) $Na_2B_4O_7 + CuO \rightleftharpoons Cu(BO_2)_2 + 2\,NaBO_2$

(e) $[SbCl_4]^- + H_2O \rightleftharpoons SbOCl + 2\,H^+ + 3\,Cl^-$

(f) $Zn + SCN^- + 3\,H^+ \rightleftharpoons Zn^{2+} + HCN\uparrow + H_2S\uparrow$

(g) $3\,S + 6\,OH^- \rightleftharpoons SO_3^{2-} + S^{2-} + 3\,H_2O$

(h) $3\,C_2H_5OH + Cr_2O_7^{2-} + 8\,H^+ \rightleftharpoons 3\,CH_3CHO + 2\,Cr^{3+} + 7\,H_2O$

(i) $8\,HMnO_4 + 5\,AsH_3 + 8\,H_2SO_4 \rightleftharpoons 5\,H_3AsO_4 + 8\,MnSO_4 + 12\,H_2O$

(j) $10\,P_2I_4 + 13\,P_4 + 128\,H_2O \rightleftharpoons 40\,PH_4I + 32\,H_3PO_4$

CHAPTER 3

3-1. (a) ew = MW/3

(b) ew = 2 MW

(c) ew = MW/6

(d) ew = MW/2

(e) ew = MW/2

(f) ew = MW/2

(g) ew = MW/2

(h) ew = MW

(i) ew = MW/4

(j) ew = 2 MW

3-2. 1.14×10^{-4} mol Pb^{2+}/L $\times$ 207.19 g/mol $\times 10^{6}$ μg/g $\times 10^{-3}$ L/mL = 23.6 μg Pb^{2+}/mL

3-3. Series A :

1) Let y g be the required weight of salt. Then,

$$y\ g\ Hg_2(NO_3)_2 \cdot 2H_2O \times \frac{2 \times 200.59\ g\ Hg}{561.23\ g\ Hg_2(NO_3)_2 \cdot 2H_2O} = 500\ mL \times 0.0100\ g/mL = 5.00\ g\ ,$$

from which y = 6.99 g $Hg_2(NO_3)_2 \cdot 2H_2O$

2) Similarly,

$$y\ g\ SbCl_3 \times \frac{121.75\ g\ Sb}{228.10\ g\ SbCl_3} = 5.00\ , \quad y = 9.37\ g\ SbCl_3$$

3) $$y\ g\ Fe(NO_3)_3 \cdot 6H_2O \times \frac{55.85\ g\ Fe}{349.97\ g\ Fe(NO_3)_3 \cdot 6H_2O} = 5.00\ , \quad y = 31.3\ g\ Fe(NO_3)_3 \cdot 6H_2O$$

4) $$y\ g\ NH_4NO_3 \times \frac{18.04\ g\ NH_4^+}{80.05\ g\ NH_4NO_3} = 5.00\ , \quad y = 22.2\ g\ NH_4NO_3$$

Series B :

1) $$y\ g\ Na_2C_2O_4 \times \frac{88.02\ g\ C_2O_4^{2-}}{134.00\ g\ Na_2C_2O_4} = 5.00\ , \quad y = 7.61\ g\ Na_2C_2O_4$$

2) $$y\ g\ KNaC_4H_4O_6 \cdot 4H_2O \times \frac{148.07\ g\ C_4H_4O_6^{2-}}{282.23\ g\ KNaC_4H_4O_6 \cdot 4H_2O} = 5.00, \quad y = 9.53\ g\ KNaC_4H_4O_6 \cdot 4H_2O$$

3) $$y\ g\ Na_2SO_4 \times \frac{96.06\ g\ SO_4^{2-}}{142.04\ g\ Na_2SO_4} = 5.00\ , \quad y = 7.39\ g\ Na_2SO_4$$

4) $y\ g\ K_3[Fe(CN)_6] \times \dfrac{211.97\ g\ [Fe(CN)_6]^{3-}}{329.27\ g\ K_3[Fe(CN)_6]} = 5.00,\quad y = 7.77\ g\ K_3[Fe(CN)_6]$

3-4. See Example 3-5 .

$M_{Ni(NO_3)_2} = (2.00\ g\ Ni/L)\,/\,(58.71\ g\ Ni/mol) = 0.03407\ mol/L$

$\therefore\ M_{KCN} = 0.03407\ mol\ Ni/L \times 4\ mol\ KCN/mol\ Ni \times (100/30) = 0.454\ mol/L$

$N_{KCN} = (0.454\,mol/L)/(2\ mol/eq) = 0.227\ eq/L$

3-5. (a) Let y mL be the required volume of water. Then

$(24.5 + y)\ mL \times 0.500\ meq\ H_2SO_4/mL = 24.5\ mL \times 4.0\ mmol/mL \times 2\ meq\ H_2SO_4/mmol$,

from which $y = 368\ mL\ H_2O$

(b) Similarly,

$(120 + y)\ mL \times 0.0500\ mmol\ Ba(OH)_2/mL = 120\ mL \times 0.120\ meq/mL \times 0.500\ mmol\ Ba(OH)_2/meq$,

$y = 24.0\ mL\ H_2O$

(c) $M_{concd\ HCl} = \dfrac{1.095\ g\ soln}{mL} \times \dfrac{20.0\ g\ HCl}{100\ g\ soln} \times \dfrac{1\ mmol\ HCl}{0.03646\ g\ HCl} = 6.007$

$\therefore\ (50.0 + y)\ mL \times 1.00\ mmol\ HCl/mL = 50.0\ mL \times 6.007\ mmol\ HCl/mL$, or $y = 250\ mL\ H_2O$

3-6. Upon mixing, we have

$25.0\ mL \times 0.100\ mmol\ H_2SO_4/mL \times 2\ meq\ H^+/mmol + 10.0\ mL \times 0.200\ meq\ H^+/mmol = 7.00\ meq\ H^+$, and

$45.0\ mL \times 0.120\ meq\ OH^-/mL = 5.40\ meq\ OH^-$

At equilibrium, there is an excess of $7.00 - 5.40 = 1.60\ meq\ H^+/80.0\ mL$

$\therefore$ the mixture is acidic

3-7. $1000\ L \times 0.00100\ g\ F^-/L = 1.00\ g\ F^- \equiv 1.00\ g\ F^- \times \dfrac{41.99\ g\ NaF}{19.00\ g\ F^-} = 2.21\ g\ NaF$

3-8. (a) $M_{CH_3COOH} = \dfrac{1.05\ g\ soln}{mL} \times \dfrac{99.5\ g\ CH_3COOH}{100\ g\ soln} \times \dfrac{1\ mmol\ CH_3COOH}{0.06005\ g\ CH_3COOH} = 17.4 = N_{CH_3COOH}$

One liter of solution weighs 1050 g and contains $1050 \times 0.995 = 1044.75$ g $CH_3COOH/5.25\ g\ H_2O \equiv 199{,}000\ g\ CH_3COOH/1000\ g\ H_2O$. Hence ,

$$m = \frac{199{,}000\ g\ CH_3COOH/1000\ g\ H_2O}{60.05\ g\ CH_3COOH/mol} = 3314\ \frac{mol\ CH_3COOH}{1000\ g\ H_2O}$$

(b) $M_{NH_3} = \dfrac{0.898\ g\ soln}{mL} \times \dfrac{28.0\ g\ NH_3}{100\ g\ soln} \times \dfrac{1\ mmol\ NH_3}{0.01703\ g\ NH_3} = 14.8 = N_{NH_3}$

One liter of solution contains 898 X 0.280 = 251.44 g NH_3/(898 - 251.44) g H_2O ≡ 388.9 g NH_3/1000 g H_2O. Hence,

$$m = \frac{388.9 \text{ g } NH_3/1000 \text{ g } H_2O}{17.03 \text{ g } NH_3/\text{mol}} = 22.8 \ \frac{\text{mol } NH_3}{1000 \text{ g } H_2O}$$

(c) $$M_{HCl} = \frac{1.18 \text{ g soln}}{\text{mL}} \times \frac{35.6 \text{ g HCl}}{100 \text{ g soln}} \times \frac{1 \text{ mmol HCl}}{0.03646 \text{ g HCl}} = 11.5 = N_{HCl}$$

One liter of solution contains 1180 X 0.356 = 420.08 g HCl/(1180 - 420.08) g H_2O ≡ 552.8 g HCl/1000 g H_2O. Hence,

$$m = \frac{552.8 \text{ g HCl}/1000 \text{ g } H_2O}{36.46 \text{ g HCl/mol}} = 15.2 \ \frac{\text{mol HCl}}{1000 \text{ g } H_2O}$$

(d) $$M_{HNO_3} = \frac{1.41 \text{ g soln}}{\text{mL}} \times \frac{67.5 \text{ g } HNO_3}{100 \text{ g soln}} \times \frac{1 \text{ mmol } HNO_3}{0.06302 \text{ g } HNO_3} = 15.1 = N_{HNO_3}$$

One liter of solution contains 1410 X 0.675 = 951.75 g HNO_3/(1410 - 951.75) g H_2O ≡ 2076.9 g HNO_3/1000 g H_2O. Hence,

$$m = \frac{2076.9 \text{ g } HNO_3/1000 \text{ g } H_2O}{63.02 \text{ g } HNO_3/\text{mol}} = 33.0 \ \frac{\text{mol } HNO_3}{1000 \text{ g } H_2O}$$

3-9. $M_{H_2SO_4} = F_{H_2SO_4} = 4.83$ (Example 3-6a). Let y L be the volume of 0.500 N (0.250 M) H_2SO_4 and (10.0 - y) L the volume of 4.83 M H_2SO_4. Then,

y L X 0.250 mol/L + (10.0 - y) L X 4.83 mol/L = 10.0 L X 1.00 mol/L,

from which y = 8.36 L ∴ 8.36 liters of 0.500 N H_2SO_4 should be mixed with 1.64 liters of 4.83 M H_2SO_4.

3-10. See Example 3-7.

Let y mL be the volume of H_2SO_4 and (1000 - y) mL the volume of water. Then,

$1.85\,y \times 0.980 = [1.85\,y + 1.00(1000 - y)]\,0.660$, or y = 527 mL.

The normality of the initial solution is equal to

$$N_i = \frac{1.85 \text{ g soln}}{\text{mL}} \times \frac{98.0 \text{ g } H_2SO_4}{100 \text{ g soln}} \times \frac{1 \text{ meq } H_2SO_4}{0.04904 \text{ g } H_2SO_4} = 37.0 \text{ meq/mL}$$

3-11. (a) $$M_{HNO_3} = \frac{1.42 \text{ g soln}}{\text{mL}} \times \frac{70.0 \text{ g } HNO_3}{100 \text{ g soln}} \times \frac{1 \text{ mmol } HNO_3}{0.06302 \text{ g } HNO_3} = 15.8 \text{ mmol/mL}$$

(b) Let y mL be the volume of acid

$$\frac{\text{g HNO}_3}{\text{mL soln}} = \frac{1.42 \text{ g soln}}{\text{mL}} \times \frac{70.0 \text{ g HNO}_3}{100 \text{ g soln}} = \frac{0.994 \text{ g HNO}_3}{\text{mL}}$$

$$\therefore y = \frac{9.94 \text{ g HNO}_3}{0.994 \text{ g HNO}_3/\text{mL}} = 10.0 \text{ mL}$$

(c) 500 mL X 0.1580 mmol/mL = z mL X 15.8 mmol/mL

z = 5.00 mL concentrated HNO_3

3-12. Mole fraction of $H_2SO_4 = x_{H_2SO_4} = 0.097$ (Example 3-6d).

1 L NH_3 solution contains 1000 X 0.898 X 0.280 = 251.44 g NH_3

and 898 - 251.44 = 646.56 g H_2O

$$\therefore \text{Mole fraction of } NH_3 = x_{NH_3} = \frac{\text{mol } NH_3}{\text{mol } NH_3 + \text{mol } H_2O} =$$

$$\frac{(251.44/17.03) \text{ mol}}{(251.44/17.03) \text{ mol} + (646.56/18.02) \text{ mol}} = 0.292$$

Hence, $x_{H_2SO_4} < x_{NH_3}$

3-13. Let y g be the required amount of $KHC_2O_4 \cdot H_2C_2O_4$ and V L the volume of the solution. Then,

$$\frac{\dfrac{y \text{ g } KHC_2O_4 \cdot H_2C_2O_4}{(218.16/4) \text{ g/eq}} + \dfrac{1.000 \text{ g } Na_2C_2O_4}{(134.00/2) \text{ g/eq}}}{V \text{ L}} = 3.10 \times \frac{\dfrac{y \text{ g } KHC_2O_4 \cdot H_2C_2O_4}{(218.16/3) \text{ g/eq}}}{V}$$

or y = 0.614 g $KHC_2O_4 \cdot H_2C_2O_4$.

3-14. The normality of the initial H_2SO_4 solution is equal to

$$\underline{N}_i = \frac{1000 \text{ mL/L} \times 1.835 \text{ g soln/mL} \times 0.931 \text{ g } H_2SO_4/\text{g soln}}{(98.08/2) \text{ g } H_2SO_4/\text{eq}} = 34.84 \text{ eq/L}$$

Let y mL be the required volume of concentrated H_2SO_4. Then,

y mL X 34.84 meq/mL = 1000 mL X 1.000 meq/mL, or y = 28.7 mL.

3-15. Let y mL be the required volume of water. Then,

990 mL X 0.1038 meq/mL = (990 + y) mL X 0.1000 meq/mL, or y = 37.62 mL H_2O

3-16. Let $\underline{N}$ be the normality after mixing and $\underline{N}'$ after diluting to 100.0 mL. Then,

$$\underline{N} = \frac{(32.40 \text{ mL} \times 0.0980 \text{ meq/mL}) + (34.40 \text{ mL} \times 0.1080 \text{ meq/mL})}{(32.40 + 34.40) \text{ mL}} = 0.1031 \text{ meq/mL}$$

$\underline{N}' = (0.1031\ \text{meq/mL})\left[(32.40 + 34.40)/100.0\right] = 0.0689\ \text{meq/mL}$

3-17. (a) 20.00 meq NaCN X 2 mmol/meq NaCN X 0.04901 g NaCN/mmol = 1.960 g NaCN

(b) 50.00 mL X 0.1000 meq/mL X (0.1340/2) g $Na_2C_2O_4$/meq = 0.3350 g $Na_2C_2O_4$

(c) 5.00 meq X 0.2120 g $[Fe(CN)_6]^{4-}$/meq = 1.060 g $[Fe(CN)_6]^{4-}$

(d) 50.00 mL X 0.2000 meq/mL X (0.10599/2) g Na_2CO_3/meq = 0.5300 g Na_2CO_3

3-18. (950.0 + 50.00) mL X 1.4633 g soln/mL = 1463.3 g solution

50.00 mL X 0.7961 g CH_3OH/mL = 39.805 g CH_3OH

∴ weight of $CHCl_3$ = 1463.3 - 39.805 = 1423.5 g

$$m = \frac{\dfrac{39.805\ \text{g } CH_3OH}{1423.5\ \text{g } CHCl_3}}{32.04\ \text{g } CH_3OH/\text{mol}} \times 1000 = 0.8727\ \frac{\text{mol } CH_3OH}{1000\ \text{g } CHCl_3}$$

$$M_{CH_3OH} = \frac{(50.00\ \text{mL} \times 0.7961\ \text{g } CH_3OH/\text{mL})/(32.04\ \text{g/mol})}{(0.9500 + 0.0500)\ \text{L}} = 1.242 = F_{CH_3OH}$$

3-19. The volume of the mixture is 50.0 mL.

$M_{Ca^{2+}} = (20.0\ \text{mL} \times 0.100\ \text{mmol/mL})/50.0\ \text{mL} = 0.0400\ \text{mmol/mL}$

$M_{Na^+} = (30.0\ \text{mL} \times 0.200\ \text{mmol/mL})/50.0\ \text{mL} = 0.120\ \text{mmol/mL}$

$$M_{Cl^-} = \frac{\left[20.\ \text{mL}\left(0.100\ \dfrac{\text{mmol } CaCl_2}{\text{mL}}\right)\left(2\ \dfrac{\text{mmol } Cl^-}{\text{mmol } CaCl_2}\right) + \left(30.0\ \text{mL} \times 0.200\ \dfrac{\text{mmol } Cl^-}{\text{mL}}\right)\right]}{50.0\ \text{mL}} =$$

0.200 mmol/mL

The ionic strength is equal to

$$\mu = \frac{1}{2}\left[(0.0400)(2)^2 + (0.120)(1)^2 + (0.200)(1)^2\right] = 0.240$$

Using Equation (3-16), we have

$-\log f_{Ca^{2+}} = (0.51 \times 2^2 \times \sqrt{0.240})/(1 + \sqrt{0.240}) = 0.6708$ or $f_{Ca^{2+}} = 0.213$,

$-\log f_{Na^+} = -\log f_{Cl^-} = (0.51 \times 1^2 \times \sqrt{0.240})/(1 + \sqrt{0.240}) = 0.1677$ or $f_{Na^+} = f_{Cl^-} = 0.680$.

3-20. Let y mL be the required volume of $KMnO_4$.

1 mmol $KMnO_4$ ≡ 5 meq $KMnO_4$ ($MnO_4^- + 5e \rightarrow Mn^{2+}$)

∴ N_{KMnO_4} = 0.200 mmol/mL X 5 meq/mmol = 1.00 meq/mL

Since meq $KMnO_4$ = meq $Na_2C_2O_4$, we have

y mL X 1.00 meq/mL = 10.00 mL X 0.2500 meq/mL, or y = 2.50 mL.

3-21. The same amount of base is required to neutralize HCl or CH_3COOH. Let y mL be the required volume of NaOH, whereupon

y mL X 0.2500 meq/mL = 100 mL X 0.1000 meq/mL, or y = 40.0 mL.

3-22. (a) 0.654 g $KHC_2O_4 \cdot H_2C_2O_4$ ≡ 0.654 g/(0.21816 g/mmol) = 2.998 mmol $KHC_2O_4 \cdot H_2C_2O_4$ ≡ 11.99 meq $C_2O_4^{2-}$ ≡ 11.99 meq $KMnO_4$ ≡ 11.99 meq $KMnO_4$/(0.2500 meq/mL) = 48.0 mL

(b) 32.7 mg $KHC_2O_4 \cdot H_2C_2O_4$ ≡ 32.7 mg/(218.16 mg/mmol) = 0.1499 mmol $KHC_2O_4 \cdot H_2C_2O_4$ ≡ 0.450 meq H^+ ≡ 0.450 meq NaOH ≡ 0.450 meq NaOH/(0.1000 meq/mL) = 4.50 mL

(c) 5.88 g $K_2Cr_2O_7$ ≡ 5.88 g/(0.29419 g/mmol) = 19.99 mmol $K_2Cr_2O_7$ ≡ 119.9 mmol KI ≡ 119.0 mmol KI/(0.5000 mmol/mL) = 239.8 mL .

3-23. $$\underline{F} = \frac{0.604 \text{ g } Cu(NO_3)_2 \cdot 3H_2O/20.0 \text{ mL}}{0.2416 \text{ g/mfw}} = 0.125 \text{ mfw/mL}$$

$\underline{N}$ = 0.125 mfw/mL X 2 meq/mfw = 0.250 meq/mL

weight of CuS = 2.0 mL X 0.125 mfw/mL X 95.61 mg CuS/mfw = 24 mg

3-24. (a) $M_{H_2SO_4} = \left[2.1015 \text{ g } BaSO_4/(0.2334 \text{ g/mmol})\right] /50.00 \text{ mL} = 0.1801 \text{ mmol/mL}$

(b) Let y mL be the required volume of concentrated H_2SO_4.

$$M_{H_2SO_4} = \frac{1.84 \text{ g soln}}{\text{mL}} \times \frac{95.9 \text{ g } H_2SO_4}{100 \text{ g soln}} \times \frac{1 \text{ mmol } H_2SO_4}{0.09808 \text{ g } H_2SO_4} = 18.0 \text{ mmol/mL}$$

∴ y mL X 18.0 mmol/mL = 1000 mL X 0.1801 mmol/mL , or y = 10.0 mL

3-25. (a) Let y mL be the required volume of water. We have

(50.0 mL soln)(1.10 g soln/mL soln)(0.200 g HCl/g soln) =

(50.0 + y) mL soln (1.04 g soln/mL soln)(0.0816 g HCl/g soln), or y = 79.6 mL H_2O

(b) Let z mL be the required volume of $Ba(OH)_2$ solution.

$$N_{HCl} = \frac{1.04 \text{ g soln}}{\text{mL}} \times \frac{8.16 \text{ g HCl}}{100 \text{ g soln}} \times \frac{1 \text{ meq HCl}}{0.03646 \text{ g HCl}} = 2.328 \text{ meq/mL}$$

∴ z mL X 0.1250 mmol $Ba(OH)_2$/mL X 2 meq/mmol = 8.00 mL X 2.328 meq/mL,

or z = 74.5 mL $Ba(OH)_2$.

3-26. 8.67 mg CdS ≡ 8.67 mg/(144.5 mg/mmol CdS) = 0.0600 mmol CdS

51.4 mg Bi_2S_3 ≡ 51.4 mg/(514.2 mg/mmol Bi_2S_3) = 0.1000 mmol Bi_2S_3

CdS and Bi_2S_3 react with HNO_3, as follows :

$$3CdS + 8H^+ + 2NO_3^- \rightleftharpoons 3Cd^{2+} + 2NO\uparrow + 4H_2O + 3S$$

$$Bi_2S_3 + 8H^+ + 2NO_3^- \rightleftharpoons 2Bi^{3+} + 2NO\uparrow + 4H_2O + 3S$$

$\therefore$ $\left(0.0600 \text{ mmol CdS} \times \frac{8 \text{ mmol } HNO_3}{3 \text{ mmol CdS}}\right) + \left(0.1000 \text{ mmol } Bi_2S_3 \times \frac{8 \text{ mmol } HNO_3}{\text{mmol } Bi_2S_3}\right) = 0.960 \text{ mmol } HNO_3$ is required for the dissolution of the precipitate. 1.0 mL 4 M HNO_3 contains 4 mmol HNO_3. Hence, (0.960/4)100 = 24% of the acid will be consumed for the dissolution of the precipitate.

3-27. 0.10 mL X 50 mg NaClO/mL = 5.0 mg NaClO

$$NaClO + 2I^- + 2H^+ \rightleftharpoons Na^+ + Cl^- + H_2O + I_2 \qquad (1)$$

$$5NaClO + I_2 + H_2O \rightleftharpoons 5Na^+ + 5Cl^- + 2H^+ + 2IO_3^- \qquad (2)$$

74.44 X 4.0/253.81 = 1.173 mg NaClO are consumed in Reaction 1

$\therefore$ 5.0 - 1.173 = 3.827 mg NaClO react according to Reaction 2 and oxidize (253.81 X 3.827)/(5 X 74.44) = 2.61 mg I_2 to IO_3^-. Hence, 4.0 - 2.61 = 1.4 mg of iodine remain in the I_2 form.

3-28. Let y = mg $CaCO_3$, $\therefore$ 769.0 - y = mg $MgCO_3$ in the sample.

$$\frac{y \text{ mg } CaCO_3}{(100.09/2) \text{ mg/meq}} + \frac{(769.0-y) \text{ mg } MgCO_3}{(84.31/2) \text{ mg/meq}} = 40.00 \text{ mL} \times 0.4000 \text{ meq/mL, or } y = 599.52$$

$$\therefore \% CaCO_3 = \frac{599.52}{769.0} \times 100 = 77.96, \quad \% MgCO_3 = 100.00 - 77.96 = 22.04$$

3-29. Mass balance (M.B.):

(Cd) : $0.100 = [Cd^{2+}] + [Cd(NH_3)^{2+}] + [Cd(NH_3)_2^{2+}] + [Cd(NH_3)_3^{2+}] + [Cd(NH_3)_4^{2+}]$

(N) : $0.400 = [NH_4^+] + [NH_3] + [Cd(NH_3)^{2+}] + 2[Cd(NH_3)_2^{2+}] + 3[Cd(NH_3)_3^{2+}] + 4[Cd(NH_3)_4^{2+}]$

(Cl) : $0.200 = [Cl^-]$

Electroneutrality (E.N.):

$$2[Cd^{2+}] + [H^+] + 2[Cd(NH_3)^{2+}] + 2[Cd(NH_3)_2^{2+}] + 2[Cd(NH_3)_3^{2+}] + 2[Cd(NH_3)_4^{2+}] = [Cl^-] + [OH^-]$$

3-30. (a) E.N. : $[H^+] = [NO_2^-] + [OH^-]$, $\therefore$ $[NO_2^-] = [H^+] - [OH^-]$

(b) M.B. : $0.2 = [CH_3COO^-] + [CH_3COOH] \qquad (1)$

E.N. : $[H^+] = [CH_3COO^-] + [OH^-]$ (2)

Combining Equations (1) and (2) : $[CH_3COOH] = 0.2 - [CH_3COO^-] = 0.2 - ([H^+] - [OH^-]) = 0.2 - [H^+] + [OH^-]$

(c) M.B. : $0.1 = [H_2C_2O_4] + [HC_2O_4^-] + [C_2O_4^{2-}]$ (3)

E.N. : $[H^+] = [OH^-] + [HC_2O_4^-] + 2[C_2O_4^{2-}]$ (4)

Combining Equations (3) and (4) : $[H_2C_2O_4] = 0.1 - ([HC_2O_4^-] + [C_2O_4^{2-}]) = 0.1 - ([H^+] - [OH^-] - [C_2O_4^{2-}]) = 0.1 - [H^+] + [OH^-] + [C_2O_4^{2-}]$

(d) M.B. : $0.1 = [CN^-] + [HCN] = [K^+]$ (5)

E.N. : $[K^+] + [H^+] = [OH^-] + [CN^-]$ (6)

Combining Equations (5) and (6) : $[HCN] = 0.1 - [CN^-] = 0.1 - (0.1 + [H^+] - [OH^-]) = [OH^-] - [H^+]$

(e) M.B. : $0.1 = [H_3PO_4] + [H_2PO_4^-] + [HPO_4^{2-}] + [PO_4^{3-}]$ (7)

E.N. : $[Na^+] + [H^+] = 0.3 + [H^+] = [OH^-] + [H_2PO_4^-] + 2[HPO_4^{2-}] + 3[PO_4^{3-}]$ (8)

or $0.3 = [OH^-] - [H^+] + [H_2PO_4^-] + 2[HPO_4^{2-}] + 3[PO_4^{3-}]$ (8a)

Multiplying Equation (7) by 3 and combining the result with Equation (8a),

$$3[H_3PO_4] + 3[H_2PO_4^-] + 3[HPO_4^{2-}] + 3[PO_4^{3-}] = [OH^-] - [H^+] + [H_2PO_4^-] + 2[HPO_4^{2-}] + 3[PO_4^{3-}]$$

or $$[H_2PO_4^-] = \frac{[OH^-] - [H^+] - [HPO_4^{2-}] - 3[H_3PO_4]}{2}$$

(f) M.B. : $0.1 = [HSO_4^-] + [SO_4^{2-}]$ (because $[H_2SO_4] = 0$) (9)

E.N. : $[H^+] = [OH^-] + [HSO_4^-] + 2[SO_4^{2-}]$ (10)

Combining Equations (9) and (10), we have

$[HSO_4^-] = 0.1 - [SO_4^{2-}] = 0.1 - ([H^+] - [OH^-] - [HSO_4^-])/2$

or $[HSO_4^-] = 0.2 - [H^+] + [OH^-]$

3-31. If S is the molar solubility of BaF_2, then

$S = [Ba^{2+}]$

$2S = [F^-] + [HF] + 2[HF_2^-]$ $\therefore$ $[F^-] + [HF] + 2[HF_2^-] = 2[Ba^{2+}]$

3-32. $2[Ba^{2+}] = 3([PO_4^{3-}] + [HPO_4^{2-}] + [H_2PO_4^-] + [H_3PO_4])$

CHAPTER 4

4-1. (a) See Example 4-1.

$v = k[A][B]^2$ (1)

Hence, the reaction is third order.

(b) Substituting the data for experiment 1 in the above Equation (1), we have

$k = 4.0 \times 10^{-4}/(0.25)(0.25)^2 = 0.0256$

Hence, the initial rate is equal to

$v = (0.0256)(2.0)(1.0)^2 = 5.1 \times 10^{-2}$ $\underline{M}$-min^{-1}

(c) If the volume of the flask in experiment 3 is doubled, the initial concentrations are halved $\therefore$ $v = (0.0256)(0.25)(0.25)^2 = 4.0 \times 10^{-4}$ $\underline{M} \cdot min^{-1}$

4-2. See Example 4-2.

$K = (2/3)^2 / (1/3)^2 = 4$

$$CH_3COOH + C_2H_5OH \rightleftharpoons CH_3COOC_2H_5 + H_2O$$

$1 - x \qquad 2 - x \qquad x \qquad x$

$x^2/(1-x)(2-x) = 4$

$x = 0.845$. Hence, at the new equilibrium state the mixture will contain 0.845 mol $CH_3COOC_2H_5$, 0.845 mol H_2O , $1 - 0.845 = 0.155$ mol CH_3COOH, and $2 - 0.845 = 1.155$ mol C_2H_5OH.

4-3. (a) None

(b) The equilibrium is shifted to the right

(c) The equilibrium is shifted to the right

(d) None

4-4. Let x be the number of moles of D. Then,

$$K = \frac{[D]^4}{[A][B]^2[C]^3} = \frac{(8.0/10)^4}{(2.0/10)(4.0/10)^2(6.0/10)^3} = 59.26 = \frac{(x/10)^4}{(4.0/10)(4.0/10)^2(4.0/10)^3}$$

$x = 7.0$ mol D

4-5. $v = k[A][B]^2[C]$ (1)

Hence, the reaction is fourth order. Substituting the data for any experiment in the above Equation (1), we find the value of k. For example, from experiment 1 we have

$k = (4.8 \times 10^{-4})/(0.20)(0.20)^2(0.20) = 0.30$ $\underline{M}^{-3} \cdot s^{-1}$

4-6. (a) At equilibrium, let x be the number of moles of HI dissociated. Then,

$[HI] = (5.0 - x)/5.0 = (1.00 - 0.200\,x)\,\underline{M}$, $[H_2] = [I_2] = (x/2)/5.0 = 0.100\,x\,\underline{M}$

$$K = \frac{[H_2][I_2]}{[HI]^2} = \frac{(0.100\,x)^2}{(1.00 - 0.200\,x)^2}$$

$x = 1.403$ mol $\therefore$ degree of dissociation $= \frac{1.403\text{ mol}}{5.0\text{ mol}} = 0.281$

(b) $[HI] = (5.0 - 1.403)$ mol/5.0 L = 0.72 mol/L , $[H_2] = [I_2] = (1.403/2)$ mol/5.0 L = 0.140 mol/L

(c) Yes

4-7. Initially, $[Br_2]$ = 0.50 mol/5.0 L = 0.100 $\underline{M}$. At equilibrium, $[Br_2]$ = (0.100)(1.000-0.030) = 0.0970 $\underline{M}$, $[Br]$ = 2 X 0.100 X 0.030 = 0.0060 $\underline{M}$. Hence,

$$K_c = \frac{[Br]^2}{[Br_2]} = \frac{(0.0060)^2}{0.0970} = 3.7 \times 10^{-4}$$

4-8. $$K = \frac{(0.999)(1.998)^2}{(0.001)(0.002)^2} = 1.00 \times 10^9$$

4-9. Substituting the data in Equation (4-21), we obtain

$$0.00100 = \left(\frac{10.0}{5.00 \times 10 + 10.0}\right)^n$$

$n \simeq 4$

4-10. Substituting the data in Equation (4-20), we obtain

$$0.1 = \left(\frac{50.0}{10.0\,D + 50.0}\right)^4 \times 100 \quad \text{or} \quad \frac{50.0}{10.0\,D + 50.0} = \sqrt[4]{0.001} = 0.1778$$

$D = 23.1$

CHAPTER 5

5-1. Substituting in Equation (5-12), we obtain

$$1.8 \times 10^{-5} = \frac{(0.10)^2 C}{1 - 0.10}\ , \quad \text{from which } C = 1.6_2 \times 10^{-3}\ \underline{M}$$

5-2. We have

$$B + H_2O \rightleftharpoons BH^+ + OH^-\ , \quad K_b = [BH^+][OH^-]/[B] \qquad (1)$$

Mass balance : $C = [B] + [BH^+]$ (2)

Electroneutrality : $[OH^-] = [H^+] + [BH^+]$ (3)

from which $[BH^+] = [OH^-] - [H^+]$ (3a)

Combining Equations (2) and (3a), we have

$$[B] = C - [BH^+] = C - [OH^-] + [H^+] \qquad (4)$$

Substituting the values of $[BH^+]$ and $[B]$ from Equation (3a) and (4) into (1) and taking into account Equation (5-9), in the form $[H^+] = K_w/[OH^-]$, we have

$$K_b = \frac{[OH^-]\,([OH^-] - K_w/[OH^-])}{C - [OH^-] + K_w/[OH^-]} = \frac{[OH^-]^3 - K_w[OH^-]}{C[OH^-] - [OH^-]^2 + K_w}$$

or $[OH^-]^3 + K_b[OH^-]^2 - (CK_b + K_w)[OH^-] - K_wK_b = 0$

5-3. We have

$$NH_4^+ + H_2O \rightleftharpoons NH_3 + H_3O^+\ , \qquad K_h = \frac{[NH_3][H_3O^+]}{[NH_4^+]} = \frac{[NH_3][H^+]}{[NH_4^+]} \qquad (1)$$

Mass balance : $C = [NH_3] + [NH_4^+] = [Cl^-]$ (2)

Electroneutrality : $[H^+] + [NH_4^+] = [Cl^-] + [OH^-]$ (3)

from which $[NH_4^+] = [Cl^-] + [OH^-] - [H^+] = C + [OH^-] - [H^+]$ (4)

Combining Equations (2) and (4), we have

$$[NH_3] = C - [NH_4^+] = [H^+] - [OH^-] \qquad (5)$$

Substituting the values of $[NH_4^+]$ and $[NH_3]$ from Equations (4) and (5) into (1), and taking into account that $[OH^-] = K_w/[H^+]$, we have

$$K_h = \frac{[H^+]\,([H^+] - K_w/[H^+])}{C + K_w/[H^+] - [H^+]} = \frac{[H^+]^3 - K_w[H^+]}{C[H^+] - K_w - [H^+]^2}$$

or $[H^+]^3 + K_h[H^+]^2 - (CK_h + K_w)[H^+] - K_wK_h = 0$

5-4. $A^- + H_2O \rightleftharpoons HA + OH^-$,

$$K_h = \frac{K_w}{K_a} = \frac{\alpha^2 C}{1 - \alpha} \qquad \left[\text{text, Equations (5-99) and (5-101)}\right]$$

$$\therefore\ K_w = \frac{\alpha^2 C}{1-\alpha} \times K_a = \frac{(7.5 \times 10^{-5})^2\,(0.100)}{1 - 7.5 \times 10^{-5}} \times 1.80 \times 10^{-5} = 1.01 \times 10^{-14}$$

5-5. $NH_4^+ + H_2O \rightleftharpoons NH_3 + H_3O^+$

$$K_h = \frac{[NH_3][H_3O^+]}{[NH_4^+]} = \frac{\alpha C \cdot \alpha C}{(1-\alpha)C} = \frac{\alpha^2 C}{1-\alpha} \qquad (1)$$

$$K_h = \frac{[NH_3]\,[H_3O^+]}{[NH_4^+]} \cdot \frac{[OH^-]}{[OH^-]} = \frac{K_w}{K_b} \qquad (2)$$

Combining Equations (1) and (2) and substituting the data, we obtain

$$K_w = \frac{\alpha^2 C}{1-\alpha} \times K_b = \frac{(7.5 \times 10^{-5})^2\,(0.100)}{1 - 7.5 \times 10^{-5}} \times 1.80 \times 10^{-5} = 1.01 \times 10^{-14}$$

5-6. $$K_a = \frac{[H^+]\,[A^-]}{[HA]} = \frac{10^{-5.14} \times 8.0}{40.0 - 8.0} = 1.8 \times 10^{-6}$$

5-7. $$K_a = \frac{[H^+]\,[A^-]}{[HA]} \simeq \frac{[H^+]^2}{C - [H^+]} = \frac{(10^{-3.20})^2}{(0.25 - 10^{-3.20})} = 1.6 \times 10^{-6}$$

5-8. $$K_a = \frac{[H^+]\,[A^-]}{[HA]} = \frac{10^{-5.70} \times 10.0}{30.0 - 10.0} = 1.00 \times 10^{-6}$$

5-9. Let HA ≡ benzoic acid. Then

$$C_{HA} = \frac{360.0 \text{ mg HA}}{122.12 \text{ mg/mmol} \times 200.0 \text{ mL}} = 0.01474\ \underline{M}$$

$[NaOH] = [A^-] = (10.00 \text{ mL} \times 0.0869 \text{ mmol/mL})/200.0 \text{ mL} = 0.004345\ \underline{M}$

$$\therefore\ [HA] = C_{HA} - [A^-] = 0.01039, \text{ and } K_{HA} = \frac{10^{-3.82} \times 0.004345}{0.01039} = 6.3 \times 10^{-5}$$

5-10. $$K_a = \frac{[H^+]\,[A^-]}{[HA]} = \frac{10^{-4.30}\,(37.20 - 18.60)}{18.60} = 5.0 \times 10^{-5}$$

5-11. After the addition of 17.5 mL of base, the solution contains 17.5 mL X 0.200 mmol/mL = 3.50 mmol NaA, and 50.0 mL X 0.120 mmol/mL - 3.50 = 2.50 mmol HA

$$\therefore\ K_a = \frac{10^{-4.80}\,(3.50/67.5)}{2.50/67.5} = 2.2_2 \times 10^{-5}$$

5-12. Let α be the degree of dissociation in 0.20 $\underline{M}$ HA and α' in 0.50 $\underline{M}$ HA. Then,

$$K_a = \frac{\alpha^2 C}{1-\alpha} = \frac{(0.040)^2(0.20)}{1-0.040} = 3.33 \times 10^{-4} = \frac{\alpha'^2 \cdot 0.50}{1-\alpha'}, \text{ or } \alpha' = 0.0255 \text{ or } 2.55\%$$

5-13. (a) $$\alpha = \frac{[CN^-]}{C_{HCN}} = \frac{[CN^-]}{[HCN]+[CN^-]} = \frac{[CN^-]}{[H^+][CN^-]/K_a + [CN^-]} = \frac{K_a}{[H^+]+K_a} \qquad (1)$$

At very dilute HCN solutions ($C_{HCN} \rightarrow 0$), $[H^+] = 1.00 \times 10^{-7}$ $\underline{M}$. Substituting in Equation (1), we obtain

$$\alpha_{max} = \frac{4 \times 10^{-10}}{1.00 \times 10^{-7} + 4 \times 10^{-10}} = 0.004 \text{ or } 0.4\%$$

(b) Similarly,

$$\alpha_{max} = \frac{1.8 \times 10^{-5}}{1.00 \times 10^{-7} + 1.8 \times 10^{-5}} = 0.9945 \text{ or } 99.45\%$$

(c) $$\alpha_{max} = \frac{K_{NH_4^+}}{[H^+] + K_{NH_4^+}} = \frac{1.00 \times 10^{-14}/1.8 \times 10^{-5}}{1.00 \times 10^{-7} + (1.00 \times 10^{-14}/1.8 \times 10^{-5})} = 0.0055 \text{ or } 0.55\%$$

5-14. $$1.00 \times 10^{-5} = \frac{\alpha^2 C}{1-\alpha} = \frac{\alpha^2 \cdot 0.100}{1-\alpha}, \text{ from which } \alpha = 0.00995$$

Let V mL be the volume of the solution and C' the concentration of HA, when $\alpha' = 3\alpha = 3 \times 0.00995 = 0.02985$. We have

$$1.00 \times 10^{-5} = \frac{(0.02985)^2 C'}{1 - 0.02985}, \text{ or } C' = 0.01089 \ \underline{M}, \text{ and}$$

$$V = \frac{200 \text{ mL} \times 0.100 \text{ mmol/mL}}{0.01089 \text{ mmol/mL}} = 1837 \text{ mL}$$

5-15. Let α be the degree of dissociation of both acids and C the concentration of monochloroacetic acid. We have

$$1.8 \times 10^{-5} = \frac{\alpha^2 \, 0.0200}{1-\alpha}, \text{ and } 1.4 \times 10^{-3} = \frac{\alpha^2 C}{1-\alpha}$$

$$\text{or } \frac{1.8 \times 10^{-5}}{0.0200} = \frac{\alpha^2}{1-\alpha} = \frac{1.4 \times 10^{-3}}{C}, \text{ from which } C = 1.56 \ \underline{M}$$

5-16. $$K_a = 4.5 \times 10^{-4} = \frac{[H^+][NO_2^-]}{[HNO_2]} \simeq \frac{[H^+]^2}{1.00 - [H^+]}, \text{ or } [H^+] = 0.021 \ \underline{M} = [NO_2^-]$$

$\therefore$ $[HNO_2] = 1.00 - 0.021 = 0.979$ $\underline{M}$, and $\alpha = 0.021/1.00 = 0.021$ or 2.1% .

5-17. (a) See Example 5-3.

$\log K_a^0 = \log K_a + \log f_{H+} + \log f_{HCOO-} - \log f_{HCOOH}$, or since $f_{HCOOH} \simeq 1$,

$\log K_a^0 = \log K_a - A\sqrt{\mu} - A\sqrt{\mu}$

or $\log K_a = \log K_a^0 + 2A\sqrt{\mu}$ (1)

(b) $\log K_a^0 = \log K_a + \log f_{H+} + \log f_{HPO_4^{2-}} - \log f_{H_2PO_4^-} = \log K_a - A\sqrt{\mu} - 4A\sqrt{\mu} + A\sqrt{\mu}$

or $\log K_a = \log K_a^0 + 4A\sqrt{\mu}$ (2)

(c) Since $CH_3NH_3^+ \rightleftharpoons H^+ + CH_3NH_2$, we have

$\log K_a^0 = \log K_a + \log f_{H+} + \log f_{CH_3NH_2} - \log f_{CH_3NH_3^+}$, or since $f_{CH_3NH_2} \simeq 1$,

$\log K_a^0 = \log K_a - A\sqrt{\mu} + A\sqrt{\mu}$

or $\log K_a = \log K_a^0$ (3)

It can be seen from Equations (1), (2), and (3), that for the same change in μ, the largest change in K_a is observed for $H_2PO_4^-$ and the minimum (practically no change) for $CH_3NH_3^+$.

5-18. Before the addition of HCl, $[H^+] \simeq \sqrt{1.8 \times 10^{-5} \times 0.100} = 1.34 \times 10^{-3}$ M

∴ after the addition of HCl, $[H^+] = 2 \times 1.34 \times 10^{-3} = 2.68 \times 10^{-3}$ M,

$[CH_3COO^-]/[CH_3COOH] = 1.8 \times 10^{-5}/2.68 \times 10^{-3} = 6.72 \times 10^{-3}$, (1)

electroneutrality : $[Cl^-] + [CH_3COO^-] = [H^+] = 2.68 \times 10^{-3}$, (2)

mass balance : $[CH_3COO^-] + [CH_3COOH] = 0.100$ (3)

Combining Equations (1), (2), and (3), we have

$[CH_3COO^-] + [CH_3COO^-]/6.72 \times 10^{-3} = 0.100$, or $[CH_3COO^-] = 6.675 \times 10^{-4}$ M.

Substituting this value in Equation (2), we obtain

$[Cl^-] = 2.68 \times 10^{-3} - 6.675 \times 10^{-4} = 2.01 \times 10^{-3}$ M

∴ 2.01×10^{-3} mol HCl/L × 36.46 g/mol = 0.0733 g HCl should be added to one liter of 0.100 M CH_3COOH.

5-19. Let y mL be the required volume of water and C the analytical concentration of CH_3COOH in the final solution. We have

$$1.8 \times 10^{-5} \simeq \frac{[H^+]^2}{C - [H^+]} = \frac{(0.00100)^2}{C - 0.00100}, \text{ or } C = 0.05656 \text{ M}$$

∴ 200 mL × 0.100 mmol/mL = (200 + y) mL × 0.05656 mmol/mL, or y = 154 mL

5-20. Let V mL be the volume of the final solution and C the concentration of ammonia. We have

$$1.8 \times 10^{-5} \simeq \frac{[OH^-]^2}{C - [OH^-]} = \frac{(4.8 \times 10^{-5})^2}{C - 4.8 \times 10^{-5}}, \text{ or } C = 1.76 \times 10^{-4} \text{ M}$$

∴ 10.0 mL × 0.300 mmol/mL = V mL × 1.76×10^{-4} mmol/mL, or V = 17,046 mL ≡ 17.0 L

5-21. (a) $M_{HCl} = \frac{1.095 \text{ g soln}}{\text{mL}} \times \frac{20.0 \text{ g HCl}}{100 \text{ g soln}} \times \frac{1 \text{ mmol HCl}}{0.03646 \text{ g HCl}} = 6.00 \text{ mmol/mL}$

Initially, we have 5.00 mL HCl X 6.00 mmol/mL = 30.0 mmol HCl , and 40.0 mL NH_3 X 1.00 mmol/mL = 40.0 mmol NH_3. After reaction, we have 30.0 mmol NH_4^+ and 40.0 - 30.0 = 10.0 mmol NH_3

$\therefore$ $[OH^-] = 1.8 \times 10^{-5}(10.0/200)/(30.0/200) = 6.0 \times 10^{-6}$ M , $[H^+] = 1.00 \times 10^{-14}/6.0 \times 10^{-6} = 1.7 \times 10^{-9}$ M

(b) Initially, $M_{NH_3} = 14.8$ (see Solution 3-7b). After dilution, $M_{NH_3} = 14.8(25.0/1000) = 0.370$ M

$\therefore$ $[OH^-] \simeq \sqrt{1.8 \times 10^{-5} \times 0.370} = 2.58 \times 10^{-3}$ M, $[H^+] = 1.00 \times 10^{-14}/2.58 \times 10^{-3} = 3.9 \times 10^{-12}$ M

5-22. (a) $[H^+] = 10^{-1.40} = 4.0 \times 10^{-2}$ M

(b) $[OH^-] = 1.00 \times 10^{-14}/10^{-12.60} = 4.0 \times 10^{-2}$ M

5-23. Initially, $[OH^-]_1 \simeq \sqrt{1.8 \times 10^{-5} \times 0.100} = 1.34 \times 10^{-3}$ M,

$\therefore$ $[H^+]_1 = 1.00 \times 10^{-14}/1.34 \times 10^{-3} = 7.46 \times 10^{-12}$ M .

After addition of NH_4Cl , $[H^+]_2 = 100\,[H^+]_1 = 7.46 \times 10^{-10}$ M

$\therefore$ $K_{NH_4^+} = \frac{1.00 \times 10^{-14}}{1.8 \times 10^{-5}} = \frac{[H^+][NH_3]}{[NH_4^+]} = \frac{7.46 \times 10^{-10} \times 0.100}{[NH_4^+]}$, or $[NH_4^+] = 0.134$ M

$\therefore$ 0.134 mol NH_4Cl/L X 53.49 g/mol X 0.250 L = 1.79 g of NH_4Cl should be added to 250 mL of 0.100 M NH_3

5-24. $[OH^-] = 0.050 \text{ mol } Ba(OH)_2/L \times 2 \text{ mol } OH^-/\text{mol } Ba(OH)_2 = 0.100$ M

$\therefore$ $[H^+] = 1.00 \times 10^{-14}/0.100 = 1.00 \times 10^{-13}$ M, pH $= -\log(1.00 \times 10^{-13}) = 13.00$, pOH = 1.00

5-25. $K_{NH_4^+} = \frac{1.00 \times 10^{-14}}{1.8 \times 10^{-5}} = \frac{[H^+][NH_3]}{[NH_4^+]} \simeq \frac{[H^+]^2}{[NH_4^+]} = \frac{(10^{-4.45})^2}{[NH_4^+]}$, or $[NH_4^+] = 2.27$ M

$\therefore$ 2.27 mol NH_4Cl/L X 53.49 g/mol X 0.250 L = 30.3 g NH_4Cl are required .

5-26. Initially, $[H^+]_1 \simeq \sqrt{1.8 \times 10^{-5} \times 0.100} = 1.34 \times 10^{-3}$ M. After the addition of $CH_3COONa{\cdot}3H_2O$,

$[H^+]_2 = [H^+]_1/100 = 1.34 \times 10^{-5}$ M

$\therefore$ $1.8 \times 10^{-5} = \frac{[H^+][CH_3COO^-]}{[CH_3COOH]} = \frac{1.34 \times 10^{-5}\,[CH_3COO^-]}{0.100 - 1.34 \times 10^{-5}}$, or $[CH_3COO^-] = 0.134$ M

$\therefore$ 0.134 mol $CH_3COONa{\cdot}3H_2O$ / L X 136.00 g/mol X 0.200 L = 3.66 g of $CH_3COONa{\cdot}3H_2O$ should be added to 200 mL of 0.100 M CH_3COOH .

5-27. $K_w = 1.00 \times 10^{-14} = [H^+][OH^-] = [H^+][H^+]/10$, or $[H^+] = 10^{-6.50}$
$\therefore$ pH = $-\log 10^{-6.50} = 6.50$

5-28. $[H^+]_{initial} = 10^{-pH}$, $[H^+]_{final} = 10^{-(pH + 1.60)}$
$\therefore [H^+]_{final} / [H^+]_{initial} = 10^{-1.60} = 0.0251$, that is $[H^+]$ is reduced to 2.51 % of its initial value.

5-29. $$\alpha_1 = \frac{K_1 [H^+]}{[H^+]^2 + K_1[H^+] + K_1K_2} \qquad \text{[text, Equation (5-55)]} \qquad (1)$$

$$\alpha_2 = \frac{K_1 K_2}{[H^+]^2 + K_1[H^+] + K_1K_2} \qquad \text{[text, Equation (5-56)]} \qquad (2)$$

Electroneutrality: $[H^+] = [HC_2O_4^-] + 2[C_2O_4^{2-}] + [OH^-] \simeq [HC_2O_4^-] + 2[C_2O_4^{2-}] =$
$\alpha_1 C + 2\alpha_2 C$ (3)

Combining Equations (1), (2), and (3), we obtain

$$[H^+] = \frac{K_1 [H^+] C + 2 K_1 K_2 C}{[H^+]^2 + K_1[H^+] + K_1 K_2}$$

or $[H^+]^3 + K_1[H^+]^2 + (K_1 K_2 - K_1 C)[H^+] - 2 K_1 K_2 C = 0$ (4)

Substituting the data in Equation (4) ($C = 0.0100$), we obtain

$[H^+]^3 + 3.8 \times 10^{-2} [H^+]^2 - 3.781 \times 10^{-4} [H^+] - 3.8 \times 10^{-8} = 0$ (5)

Solving Equation (5) by the method of successive approximations, we have
$[H^+] = 8.27 \times 10^{-3}$ M $\therefore$ pH = $-\log(8.27 \times 10^{-3}) = 2.08$.

5-30. (a) $SO_3^{2-} + H_2O \rightleftharpoons HSO_3^- + OH^-$

$$K_h = \frac{[HSO_3^-][OH^-]}{[SO_3^{2-}]} \cdot \frac{[H^+]}{[H^+]} = \frac{K_w}{K_{a2}} = \frac{1.00 \times 10^{-14}}{5.6 \times 10^{-8}} \simeq \frac{[OH^-]^2}{0.225 - [OH^-]} ,$$

or $[OH^-] = 2.00 \times 10^{-4}$ M $= [HSO_3^-]$, $[SO_3^{2-}] = 0.225 - [HSO_3^-] \simeq 0.225$ M ,

$[H^+] = 1.00 \times 10^{-14}/2.00 \times 10^{-4} = 5.0 \times 10^{-11}$ M, pH = $-\log(5.0 \times 10^{-11}) = 10.30$,

$[Na^+] = 0.450$ M , $[H_2SO_3] = (5.0 \times 10^{-11})(2.00 \times 10^{-4})/1.3 \times 10^{-2} = 7.7 \times 10^{-13}$ M

(b) $NH_4^+ + CO_3^{2-} \rightleftharpoons NH_3 + HCO_3^-$

$$K_h = \frac{[NH_3][HCO_3^-]}{[NH_4^+][CO_3^{2-}]} \cdot \frac{[H^+][OH^-]}{[H^+][OH^-]} = \frac{K_w}{K_b K_{a_2}} = \frac{1.00 \times 10^{-14}}{(1.8 \times 10^{-5})(4.8 \times 10^{-11})} = 11.6 \qquad (1)$$

Let $y = [NH_3] \simeq [HCO_3^-]$, whereupon $[NH_4^+] = 0.1000 - y$, $[CO_3^{2-}] = 0.0500 - y$.
Substituting in Equation (1), we have

$$\frac{y^2}{(0.100 - y)(0.0500 - y)} = 11.6 \text{ , or } y = 0.0444$$

$\therefore$ $[NH_3] = [HCO_3^-] = 0.0444$ $\underline{M}$, $[NH_4^+] = 0.0556$ $\underline{M}$, $[CO_3^{2-}] = 0.0056$ $\underline{M}$,
$[H^+] = 4.8 \times 10^{-11} \times 0.0444/0.0056 = 3.8 \times 10^{-10}$ $\underline{M}$, pH = $-\log(3.8 \times 10^{-10}) = 4.42$,
$[OH^-] = 1.00 \times 10^{-14}/3.8 \times 10^{-10} = 2.63 \times 10^{-5}$ $\underline{M}$, $[H_2CO_3] =$
$3.8 \times 10^{-10} \times 0.0444/4.2 \times 10^{-7} = 4.0 \times 10^{-5}$ $\underline{M}$.

(c) See Example 5-28.

$$K_h = \frac{[Al(H_2O)_5(OH)^{2+}][H^+]}{[Al(H_2O)_6^{3+}]} \simeq \frac{[H^+]^2}{0.070 - [H^+]} = K_a = 1.12 \times 10^{-5} \text{ , or } [H^+] =$$

8.9×10^{-4} $\underline{M}$ $= [Al(H_2O)_5(OH)^{2+}]$, pH = $-\log(8.9 \times 10^{-4}) = 3.05$,
$[Al(H_2O)_6^{3+}] = 0.070 - 8.9 \times 10^{-4} = 0.069$ $\underline{M}$, $[OH^-] = 1.00 \times 10^{-14}/8.9 \times 10^{-4} =$
1.12×10^{-11} $\underline{M}$, $[NO_3^-] = 0.210$ $\underline{M}$

(d) $$K_{NH_4^+} = \frac{1.00 \times 10^{-14}}{1.8 \times 10^{-5}} = \frac{[H^+][NH_3]}{[NH_4^+]} \simeq \frac{[H^+]^2}{0.200 - [H^+]} \text{ , or } [H^+] = 1.05 \times 10^{-5} \underline{M} =$$

$[NH_3]$, pH = $-\log(1.05 \times 10^{-5}) = 4.98$, $[OH^-] = 1.00 \times 10^{-14}/1.05 \times 10^{-5} =$
9.5×10^{-10} $\underline{M}$, $[NH_4^+] = 0.200 - [NH_3] \simeq 0.200$ $\underline{M}$, $[NO_3^-] = 0.210$ $\underline{M}$

5-31. See Example 5-25.
After mixing and prior to neutralization reactions, the solution is 0.0500 $\underline{M}$ in NaOH, 0.0400 $\underline{M}$ in HCl, 0.0300 $\underline{M}$ in Na_2HPO_4, and 0.0300 $\underline{M}$ in NaH_2PO_4. NaOH neutralizes HCl, leaving an excess of 0.0100 $\underline{M}$ NaOH which reacts with 0.0100 $\underline{M}$ NaH_2PO_4, resulting in a solution 0.0400 $\underline{M}$ in Na_2HPO_4 and 0.0200 $\underline{M}$ in NaH_2PO_4.

$$\therefore \text{ pH} = pK_2 + \log\frac{[Na_2HPO_4]}{[NaH_2PO_4]} = 7.21 + \log\frac{0.0400}{0.0200} = 7.51 .$$

5-32. Initially, $[H^+] \simeq \sqrt{1.8 \times 10^{-5} \times 0.100} = 1.34 \times 10^{-3}$ $\underline{M}$ $\therefore$ $pH_{initial} = -\log(1.34 \times 10^{-3}) =$ 2.87 .

(a) After dilution, $[H^+] \simeq \sqrt{1.8 \times 10^{-5}(50 \times 0.100/1000)} = 3.0 \times 10^{-4}$ $\underline{M}$, pH = 3.52

$\therefore$ $\Delta pH = 3.52 - 2.87 = 0.65$

(b) 20.00 mL X 0.050 mmol/mL = 1.00 mmol CH_3COOH is neutralized, 1.00 mmol CH_3COO^- is formed, and (50 mL X 0.100 mmol/mL) - 1.00 = 4.00 mmol CH_3COOH remain in solution

$$\therefore \ pH = pK_a + \log \frac{[CH_3COO^-]}{[CH_3COOH]} = 4.74 + \log \frac{1.00/70}{4.00/70} = 4.14,$$

$\Delta pH = 4.14 - 2.87 = 1.27$

(c) 82 mg CH_3COONa / 82.03 mg/mmol = 1.00 mmol CH_3COONa

$$\therefore \ pH = 4.74 + \log \frac{1.00/50}{5.00/50} = 4.04, \quad \Delta pH = 4.04 - 2.87 = 1.17$$

Hence, the addition of NaOH results in the largest increase in pH .

5-33. 2.00 mmol of N_2H_4 consume 8.00 mmol of $NaHCO_3$

$$\therefore \ pH = pK_1 + \log \frac{[HCO_3^-]}{[H_2CO_3]} = 6.38 + \log \frac{(16.00 - 8.00)/50.00}{8.00/50.00} = 6.38$$

5-34. $[OH^-] \simeq \sqrt{C K_w/K_a}$ [text, Equation (5-100)] $\therefore$ $[H^+] = K_w/[OH^-] = K_w/\sqrt{C K_w/K_a} = \sqrt{K_a K_w/C}$, $pH = -\log \sqrt{K_a K_w/C} = (pK_a + pK_w + \log C)/2$

5-35. Let C be the molarity of H_2SO_4. We have

$$K_2 = \frac{[H^+][SO_4^{2-}]}{[HSO_4^-]} = \frac{0.010\,[SO_4^{2-}]}{[HSO_4^-]} = 1.2 \times 10^{-2} \qquad (1)$$

Electroneutrality : $[H^+] \simeq [HSO_4^-] + 2[SO_4^{2-}] = 0.0100$ ($[OH^-] = 1.00 \times 10^{-12}$ M , negligible) (2)

Solving the simultaneous Equations (1) and (2) gives $[HSO_4^-] = 0.00294$ M, $[SO_4^{2-}] = 0.00353$ M

$[H_2SO_4] = 0.010 \times 0.00294/1.0 \times 10^2 = 2.9 \times 10^{-7}$ M

$\therefore$ $C = [H_2SO_4] + [HSO_4^-] + [SO_4^{2-}] = 2.9 \times 10^{-7} + 0.00294 + 0.00353 = 0.0065$ M

5-36. pH = 2.00 , $[H^+] = 0.010$ M ; pH = 3.00 , $[H^+] = 0.0010$ M

$\therefore$ $[H^+]_{final} = (0.010 + 0.0010)/2 = 0.0055$ M , $pH = -\log(0.0055) = 2.26$

5-37. (a) Electroneutrality : $[OH^-] = [Na^+] + [H^+] = 1.00 \times 10^{-7} + [H^+]$, or $[H^+] = [OH^-] - 1.00 \times 10^{-7}$

$\therefore K_w = 1.00 \times 10^{-14} = [H^+][OH^-] = ([OH^-] - 1.00 \times 10^{-7})[OH^-]$, or

$[OH^-]^2 - 1.00 \times 10^{-7}[OH^-] - 1.00 \times 10^{-14} = 0$. Solving the quadratic equation, gives $[OH^-] = 1.62 \times 10^{-7}$ M. Hence, $[H^+] = 1.00 \times 10^{-14}/1.62 \times 10^{-7} = 6.2 \times 10^{-8}$ M ,

$pH = -\log(6.2 \times 10^{-8}) = 7.21$

(b) Similarly, we have $[OH^-]^2 - 1.00 \times 10^{-8}[OH^-] - 1.00 \times 10^{-14} = 0$, or $[OH^-] = 1.05 \times 10^{-7}$ $\underline{M}$.
Hence, $[H^+] = 1.00 \times 10^{-14}/1.05 \times 10^{-7} = 9.5 \times 10^{-8}$ $\underline{M}$, pH = $-\log(9.5 \times 10^{-8}) = 7.02$

(c) See Example (5-5).
Electroneutrality : $[H^+] = [Cl^-] + [OH^-] = 1.00 \times 10^{-8} + [OH^-]$, or $[OH^-] =$
$[H^+] - 1.00 \times 10^{-8}$ $\therefore$ $K_w = 1.00 \times 10^{-14} = [H^+]([H^+] - 1.00 \times 10^{-8})$, or
$[H^+]^2 - 1.00 \times 10^{-8}[H^+] - 1.00 \times 10^{-14} = 0$. Solving the quadratic equation gives
$[H^+] = 1.05 \times 10^{-7}$ $\underline{M}$. Hence, pH = $-\log(1.05 \times 10^{-7}) = 6.98$

5-38. (a) $[H^+] = 0.0500$ mmol/mL $(50.0/100.0) = 0.0250$ $\underline{M}$ $\therefore$ pH = $-\log 0.0250 = 1.60$

(b) $[H^+] = (50.0\text{ mL} \times 0.0500\text{ mmol/mL} - 50.0\text{ mL} \times 0.0400\text{ mmol/mL})/100.0\text{ mL} = 0.00500$ $\underline{M}$
$\therefore$ pH = $-\log(0.00500) = 2.30$

(c) We mix 50.0 mL X 0.0500 mmol H^+/mL = 2.50 mmol H^+, and
50.0 mL X 0.0250 mmol $Ba(OH)_2$/mL X 2 mmol OH^-/mmol $Ba(OH)_2$ = 2.50 mmol OH^-
$\therefore$ the resulting solution is neutral having a pH of 7.00

(d) As in (a), pH = 1.60

(e) 2.50 mmol HCl react with 50.0 mL X 0.0500 mmol NH_3/mL = 2.50 mmol NH_3,
forming 2.50 mmol NH_4Cl $\therefore$ $[NH_4^+] = 2.50$ mmol/100.0 mL = 0.0250 $\underline{M}$. Hence,
$[H^+] = \sqrt{C K_w/K_b}$ [text, Equation (5-105)] = $\sqrt{0.0250 \times 1.00 \times 10^{-14}/1.8 \times 10^{-5}} =$
$3.7_3 \times 10^{-6}$ $\underline{M}$, pH = $-\log(3.7_3 \times 10^{-6}) = 5.43$.

5-39. (a) $M_{NH_3} = (25.0\text{ mL} \times 0.0840\text{ mmol }NH_3/\text{mL})/45.0\text{ mL} = 0.0467$ mmol/mL
$\therefore$ $[OH^-] \simeq \sqrt{1.8 \times 10^{-5} \times 0.0467} = 9.17 \times 10^{-4}$ $\underline{M}$, $[H^+] = 1.00 \times 10^{-14}/9.17 \times 10^{-4} =$
1.09×10^{-11} $\underline{M}$, pH = $-\log(1.09 \times 10^{-11}) = 10.96$

(b) $M_{NH_3} = (25.0 \times 0.084 - 20.0 \times 0.0600)\text{mmol}/45.0\text{ mL} = 0.0200 \simeq [NH_3]$
$M_{NH_4Br} = (20.0\text{ mL} \times 0.0600\text{ mmol/mL})/45.0\text{ mL} = 0.0267 \simeq [NH_4^+]$
$\therefore$ $[OH^-] = 1.8 \times 10^{-5}(0.0200/0.0267) = 1.35 \times 10^{-5}$ $\underline{M}$, $[H^+] = 1.00 \times 10^{-14}/1.35 \times 10^{-5} =$
7.41×10^{-10} $\underline{M}$, pH = $-\log(7.41 \times 10^{-10}) = 9.13$

(c) $M_{NH_3} = 0.0840(25.0/45.0) = 0.0467 \simeq [NH_3]$, $M_{NH_4Cl} = 0.0600(20.0/45.0) = 0.0267 \simeq [NH_4^+]$
$\therefore$ $[OH^-] = 1.8 \times 10^{-5}(0.0467/0.0267) = 3.15 \times 10^{-5}$ $\underline{M}$, $[H^+] = 1.00 \times 10^{-14}/3.15 \times 10^{-5} =$
3.17×10^{-10} $\underline{M}$, pH = $-\log(3.17 \times 10^{-10}) = 9.50$

(d) We mix 25.0 mL X 0.0840 mmol NH_3/mL = 2.10 mmol NH_3,
and 20.0 mL X 0.1050 mmol CH_3COOH/mL = 2.10 mmol CH_3COOH
$\therefore$ $[CH_3COONH_4] = 2.10$ mmol/45.0 mL = 0.0467 $\underline{M}$

Since $K_{CH_3COOH} = K_{NH_3} = 1.8 \times 10^{-5}$, the resulting solution is neutral having a pH of 7.00 [See text, Equation (5-112)].

5-40. After mixing, $M_{NH_3} = (0.500 - 0.0500)/3 = 0.150\ \underline{M} \simeq [NH_3]$,
$[NH_4Cl] = (0.100 + 0.0500)/3 = 0.050\ \underline{M} \simeq [NH_4^+]$
$\therefore\ [OH^-] = 1.8 \times 10^{-5} \times 0.150/0.050 = 5.4 \times 10^{-5}\ \underline{M}$, $[H^+] = 1.00 \times 10^{-14}/5.4 \times 10^{-5} =$
$= 1.85 \times 10^{-10}\ \underline{M}$, $pH = -\log(1.85 \times 10^{-10}) = 9.73$

5-41. $pH = 1.20$, $\therefore\ [H^+] = 10^{-1.20} = 0.063\ \underline{M}$; $pH = 2.00$, $[H^+] = 0.010\ \underline{M}$;
$pH = 4.00$, $[H^+] = 0.00010\ \underline{M}$
$\therefore\ [H^+]_{final} = (0.063 + 0.010 + 0.00010)/3 = 0.0244\ \underline{M}$, $pH = -\log(0.0244) = 1.61$

5-42. See Example 5-9.

(a) $[H^+] = 10^{-7.16} = 6.9 \times 10^{-8}\ \underline{M}$.

$$\alpha_0 = \frac{[HIn]}{[HIn] + [In^-]} = \frac{[HIn]}{[HIn] + (K_a[HIn]/[H^+])} = \frac{[H^+]}{[H^+] + K_a} =$$

$$\frac{6.9 \times 10^{-8}}{6.9 \times 10^{-8} + 4.0 \times 10^{-8}} = 0.63$$

Hence, 63% of the indicator is present in the acid form HIn.

(b) $$\alpha_0 = \frac{[HIn]}{C} = \frac{6.9 \times 10^{-9}}{6.9 \times 10^{-9} + 4.0 \times 10^{-8}} = 0.147$$

Hence, 14.7% of the indicator is present in the HIn form.

(c) $$\alpha_0 = \frac{[HIn]}{C} = \frac{2.51 \times 10^{-10}}{2.51 \times 10^{-10} + 4.0 \times 10^{-8}} = 0.0062$$

Hence, 0.62% of the indicator is present in the HIn form.

5-43. (a) Let y mL be the volume of 1.00 $\underline{M}$ NaOH added. We have
$[CH_3COO^-] = 1.00\,y/(200 + y)\ \underline{M}$, $[CH_3COOH] = (200 \times 0.100 - 1.00\,y)/(200 + y)\ \underline{M}$

$$\therefore\ pH = pK_{In} + \log\frac{[In^-]}{[HIn]} = 4.9 + \log\frac{1}{10} = 3.9 = pK_{CH_3COOH} + \log\frac{[CH_3COO^-]}{[CH_3COOH]}$$

or $$3.9 = 4.74_5 + \log\frac{1.00\,y/(200 + y)}{(20.0 - 1.00\,y)/(200 + y)}$$, or $y = 2.50$ mL

(b) $$pH = 4.9 + \log\frac{10}{1} = 5.9 = 4.74_5 + \log\frac{1.00\,y/(200 + y)}{(20.0 - 1.00\,y)/(200 + y)}$$, or $y = 18.7$ mL

5-44. See Solution (5-42).

$[OH^-] \simeq \sqrt{C K_w / K_a}$ [text, Equation (5-100)] $= \sqrt{0.050 \times 1.00 \times 10^{-14}/1.8 \times 10^{-5}} = 5.27 \times 10^{-6}$ M

$\therefore$ $[H^+] = 1.00 \times 10^{-14}/5.27 \times 10^{-6} = 1.90 \times 10^{-9}$ M . We have

$$\alpha_1 = \frac{[In^-]}{[HIn] + [In^-]} = \frac{[In^-]}{([H^+][In^-]/K_{HIn}) + [In^-]} = \frac{K_{HIn}}{[H^+] + K_{HIn}} = \frac{3.16 \times 10^{-10}}{1.90 \times 10^{-9} + 3.16 \times 10^{-10}} =$$

0.143

Hence, 14.3% of the indicator is present in the alkaline form In^- .

5-45. $H_2C_2O_4 \rightleftharpoons H^+ + HC_2O_4^-$, $K_1 = [H^+][HC_2O_4^-]/[H_2C_2O_4]$ (1)

$HC_2O_4^- \rightleftharpoons H^+ + C_2O_4^{2-}$, $K_2 = [H^+][C_2O_4^{2-}]/[HC_2O_4^-]$ (2)

$C = [H_2C_2O_4] + [HC_2O_4^-] + [C_2O_4^{2-}]$ (3)

From Equations (1) and (2), we have

$[H_2C_2O_4] = [H^+][HC_2O_4^-]/K_1$ (1a)

$[C_2O_4^{2-}] = K_2 [HC_2O_4^-]/[H^+]$ (2a)

Combining Equations (3), (1a), and (2a), we have

$C = [H^+][HC_2O_4^-]/K_1 + [HC_2O_4^-] + K_2 [HC_2O_4^-]/[H^+]$ (4)

Solving Equation (4) for $[HC_2O_4^-]$, we have

$$[HC_2O_4^-] = \frac{K_1 [H^+] C}{[H^+]^2 + K_1[H^+] + K_1 K_2}$$

5-46. See Example (5-7). Since $[H_2SO_4]$ and $[OH^-]$ are negligible, we have

$K_2 = [H^+][SO_4^{2-}]/[HSO_4^-] = 1.2 \times 10^{-2}$ (1)

Mass balance : $0.0100 \simeq [HSO_4^-] + [SO_4^{2-}]$ (2)

Electroneutrality : $[H^+] \simeq [HSO_4^-] + 2[SO_4^{2-}]$ (3)

Combining Equations (2) and (3), we have $[HSO_4^-] = 0.0200 - [H^+]$,

and $[SO_4^{2-}] = [H^+] - 0.0100$ $\therefore$ Equation (1) becomes

$[H^+]([H^+] - 0.0100)/(0.0200 - [H^+]) = 1.2 \times 10^{-2}$, or $[H^+] = 0.0145$ M .

Hence, $[HSO_4^-] = 0.0200 - 0.0145 = 0.0055$ M , $[SO_4^{2-}] = 0.0145 - 0.0100 = 0.0045$ M ,

$[OH^-] = 1.00 \times 10^{-14}/0.0145 = 6.9 \times 10^{-13}$ M .

5-47. $B + H_2O \rightleftharpoons BH^+ + OH^-$, $K_1 = [BH^+][OH^-]/[B]$ (1)

$BH^+ + H_2O \rightleftharpoons BH_2^{2+} + OH^-$, $K_2 = [BH_2^{2+}][OH^-]/[BH^+]$ (2)

Mass balance : $C = [B] + [BH^+] + [BH_2^{2+}]$ (3)

Electroneutrality : $[OH^-] = [H^+] + [BH^+] + 2[BH_2^{2+}]$ (4)

$H_2O \rightleftharpoons H^+ + OH^-$, $K_w = [H^+][OH^-]$ (5)

Combining Equations (1), (2), and (3), we have

$$C = \frac{[BH^+][OH^-]}{K_1} + [BH^+] + \frac{K_2\,[BH^+]}{[OH^-]} = [BH^+]\left(\frac{[OH^-]^2 + K_1[OH^-] + K_1K_2}{K_1[OH^-]}\right) \quad (6)$$

Combining Equations (2), (4), and (5), we have

$$[OH^-] - [H^+] = \frac{[OH^-]^2 - K_w}{[OH^-]} = [BH^+] + \frac{2K_2\,[BH^+]}{[OH^-]} = [BH^+]\left(\frac{[OH^-] + 2K_2}{[OH^-]}\right) \quad (7)$$

Dividing Equations (6) and (7), we have

$$\frac{C[OH^-]}{[OH^-]^2 - K_w} = \frac{[OH^-]^2 + K_1[OH^-] + K_1K_2}{K_1([OH^-] + 2K_2)}$$, from which

$$[OH^-]^4 + K_1[OH^-]^3 + (K_1K_2 - K_w - CK_1)[OH^-]^2 - (K_1K_w + 2CK_1K_2)[OH^-] + K_1K_2K_w = 0$$

5-48. (a) $[H^+] = 10^{-1.4} = 0.04$ M $\therefore$ $[H_3AsO_4]/[H_2AsO_4^-] = [H^+]/K_1 = 0.04/6.0 \times 10^{-3} = 6.7$

Hence, H_3AsO_4 is the main species.

(b) $[H^+] = 1 \times 10^{-6}$ M $\therefore$ $[H_2AsO_4^-]/[HAsO_4^{2-}] = [H^+]/K_2 = 1 \times 10^{-6}/1 \times 10^{-7} = 10$

Hence, $H_2AsO_4^-$ is the main species.

(c) $[H^+] = 10^{-10.5} = 3 \times 10^{-11}$ M $\therefore$ $[HAsO_4^{2-}]/[AsO_4^{3-}] = [H^+]/K_3 = 3 \times 10^{-11}/3 \times 10^{-12} = 10$

Hence, $HAsO_4^{2-}$ is the main species.

(d) $[H^+] = 10^{-12.5} = 3 \times 10^{-13}$ M $\therefore$ $[AsO_4^{3-}]/[HAsO_4^{2-}] = K_3/[H^+] = 3 \times 10^{-12}/3 \times 10^{-13} = 10$

Hence, AsO_4^{3-} is the main species.

Note. The exact values of the various arsenic species can be calculated using the α-functions [text, Equations (5-57),...,(5-57n)].

5-49. (a)

pH	α_0	α_1	α_2
0	1.000	1.00×10^{-7}	1.00×10^{-21}
1	1.000	1.00×10^{-6}	1.00×10^{-19}
2	1.000	1.00×10^{-5}	1.00×10^{-17}
3	1.000	1.00×10^{-4}	1.00×10^{-15}
4	0.999	9.99×10^{-4}	9.99×10^{-14}
5	0.990	9.90×10^{-3}	9.90×10^{-12}
6	0.909	9.09×10^{-2}	9.09×10^{-10}
7	0.500	0.500	5.00×10^{-8}
8	9.09×10^{-2}	0.909	9.09×10^{-7}
9	9.90×10^{-3}	0.990	9.90×10^{-6}
10	9.99×10^{-4}	0.999	9.99×10^{-5}
11	9.99×10^{-5}	0.999	9.99×10^{-4}
12	9.90×10^{-6}	0.990	9.90×10^{-3}
13	9.09×10^{-7}	0.909	9.09×10^{-2}
14	5.00×10^{-8}	0.500	0.500

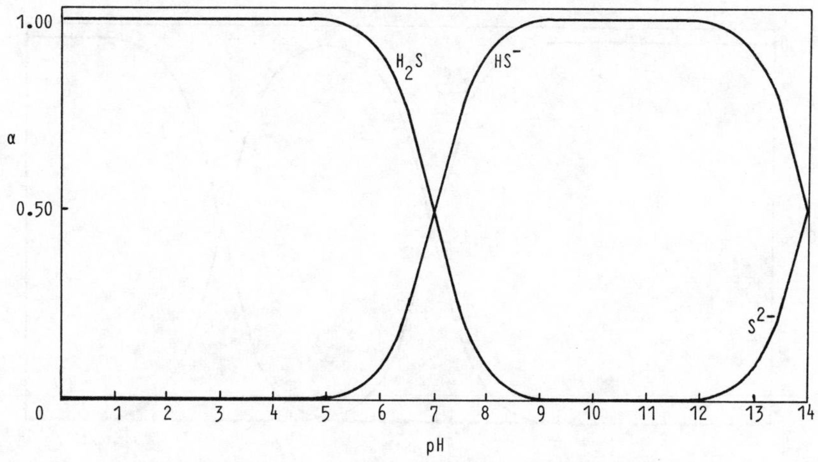

(b)

pH	α_0	α_1	α_2
0	1.000	4.20×10^{-7}	2.02×10^{-17}
1	1.000	4.20×10^{-6}	2.02×10^{-15}
2	1.000	4.20×10^{-5}	2.02×10^{-13}
3	1.000	4.20×10^{-4}	2.02×10^{-11}
4	0.996	4.18×10^{-3}	2.01×10^{-9}
5	0.960	4.03×10^{-2}	1.93×10^{-7}
6	0.704	0.296	1.42×10^{-5}
7	0.192	0.807	3.88×10^{-4}
8	2.31×10^{-2}	0.972	4.67×10^{-3}
9	2.27×10^{-3}	0.952	4.57×10^{-2}
10	1.69×10^{-4}	0.676	0.324
11	4.11×10^{-6}	0.172	0.828
12	4.86×10^{-8}	2.04×10^{-2}	0.980
13	4.95×10^{-10}	2.08×10^{-3}	0.998
14	4.96×10^{-12}	2.08×10^{-4}	1.000

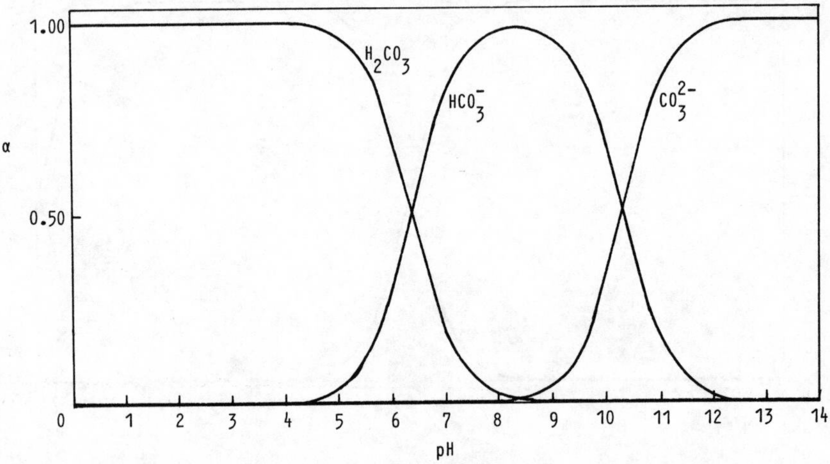

(c)

pH	α_0	α_1	α_2	α_3
0	0.994	5.96×10^{-3}	5.96×10^{-10}	1.79×10^{-21}
1	0.943	5.66×10^{-2}	5.66×10^{-8}	1.69×10^{-18}
2	0.625	0.375	3.75×10^{-6}	1.12×10^{-15}
3	0.143	0.857	8.57×10^{-5}	2.57×10^{-13}
4	1.64×10^{-2}	0.983	9.83×10^{-4}	2.95×10^{-11}
5	1.65×10^{-3}	0.988	9.88×10^{-3}	2.97×10^{-9}
6	1.51×10^{-4}	0.909	9.09×10^{-2}	2.73×10^{-7}
7	8.33×10^{-6}	0.500	0.500	1.50×10^{-5}
8	1.51×10^{-7}	9.09×10^{-2}	0.909	2.73×10^{-4}
9	1.65×10^{-9}	9.87×10^{-3}	0.987	2.96×10^{-3}
10	1.62×10^{-11}	9.70×10^{-4}	0.970	2.91×10^{-2}
11	1.28×10^{-13}	7.69×10^{-5}	0.769	0.231
12	4.17×10^{-16}	2.50×10^{-6}	0.250	0.750
13	5.38×10^{-19}	3.23×10^{-8}	3.23×10^{-2}	0.968
14	5.54×10^{-22}	3.32×10^{-10}	3.32×10^{-3}	0.997

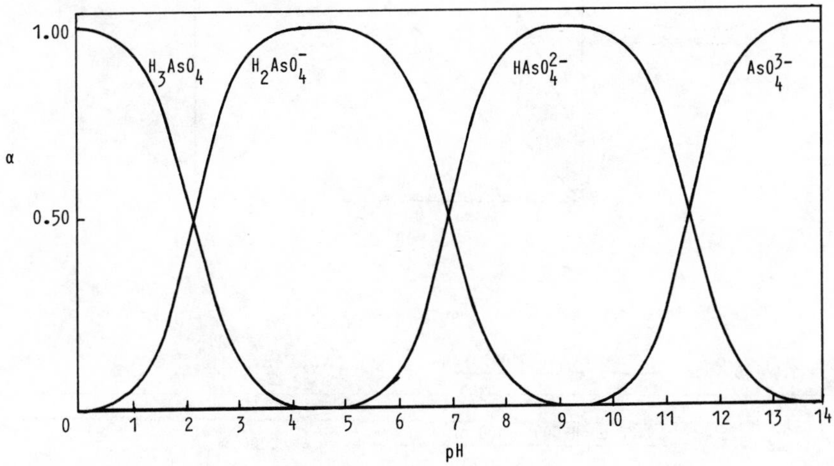

5-50. (a) $[H^+] + [H_2AsO_4^-] + 2[H_3AsO_4] = [OH^-] + [AsO_4^{3-}]$

(b) $[H^+] + [H_2PO_4^-] + 2[H_3PO_4] = [OH^-] + [PO_4^{3-}] + [NH_3]$

(c) $[H^+] + [H_3PO_4] = [OH^-] + [HPO_4^{2}] + 2[PO_4^{3-}] + [NH_3]$

(d) $[H^+] + [CH_3COOH] = [OH^-]$

(e) $[H^+] = [OH^-] + [H_2PO_4^-] + 2[HPO_4^-] + 3[PO_4^{3-}]$

(f) $[H^+] + [H_2CO_3] = [OH^-] + [CO_3^{2-}]$

(g) $[H^+] = [OH^-] + [NO_3^-]$

5-51.

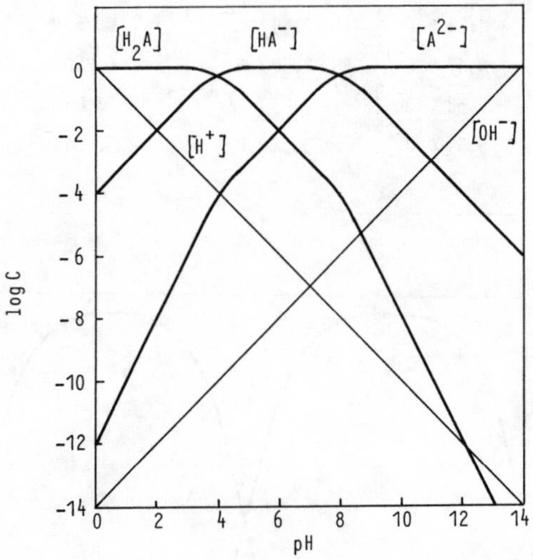

5-52. Let C be the total concentration of acetic acid, we have

$$1.8 \times 10^{-5} \simeq \frac{\alpha^2 C}{1-\alpha} = \frac{(0.0100)^2 C}{1 - 0.0100} \quad \text{or} \quad C = 0.178_2 \ \underline{M}$$

$$[CH_3COONa] = \frac{(0.82 \text{ g } CH_3COONa/100 \text{ mL})(1000 \text{ mL/L})}{82.03 \text{ g/mol}} = 0.100 \ \underline{M}$$

$$\therefore \ [H^+] = (1.8 \times 10^{-5})(0.178_2)/0.100 = 3.21 \times 10^{-5} \ \underline{M}$$

5-53. $[H^+] = 1.8 \times 10^{-5} \times \dfrac{(160 \times 0.30 - 20.0 \times 0.20)/180}{(20.0 \times 0.20)/180} = 2.0 \times 10^{-4}\ \underline{M}$

5-54. $M_{HCl} = 11.5_2$ (Solution 3-8c)

$K_a = 1.8 \times 10^{-5} = \dfrac{(1.80 \times 10^{-5})\,[CH_3COO^-]}{[CH_3COOH]}$, or $[CH_3COO^-]/[CH_3COOH] = 1.00$

Initially, we have 100 mL $CH_3COONa \times 1.00$ mmol/mL = 100 mmol CH_3COONa.
In order to have $[CH_3COO^-]/[CH_3COOH] = 1.00$, 50.0 mmol of HCl should be added, so that 50.0 mmol of CH_3COOH are produced ($HCl + CH_3COONa \rightleftharpoons CH_3COOH + NaCl$) and 50.0 mmol of CH_3COONa remain $\therefore$ 50.0 mmol HCl / (11.5_2 mmol/mL) = 4.34 mL HCl should be added.

5-55. pH = 9.00 [Example 5-11]; $C_{H_2A} = 0.3000$ g $H_2A/(150$ g/mol $\times$ 0.200 L) = 0.0100 $\underline{M}$.
We have $\alpha_2 = 0.100/2 = 0.050$ $\therefore$ $\alpha_1 = 1.00 - 0.100 - 0.050 = 0.85$. Hence, we have

$$0.100 = \frac{[H^+]^2}{[H^+]^2 + K_1[H^+] + K_1K_2} \qquad (1)$$

$$0.85 = \frac{K_1[H^+]}{[H^+]^2 + K_1[H^+] + K_1K_2} \qquad (2)$$

$$0.050 = \frac{K_1K_2}{[H^+]^2 + K_1[H^+] + K_1K_2} \qquad (3)$$

Dividing Equations (2) and (1), we have $K_1/[H^+] = 8.5$; hence, $K_1 = 8.5 \times 10^{-9}$.
Dividing Equations (1) and (3), we have $[H^+]^2 = 2K_1K_2$; hence,
$K_2 = (1.00 \times 10^{-9})^2/(2 \times 8.5 \times 10^{-9}) = 5.9 \times 10^{-11}$. Consequently, we have
$[H_2A] = 0.100 \times 0.0100 = 0.00100\ \underline{M}$, $[HA^-] = 0.85 \times 0.0100 = 0.0085\ \underline{M}$, and
$[A^{2-}] = 0.050 \times 0.0100 = 0.00050\ \underline{M}$.

5-56. $$4.85 = pK_a + \log\frac{[CH_3COO^-]}{[CH_3COOH]} = 4.74_5 + \log\frac{[CH_3COO^-]}{[CH_3COOH]} \qquad (1)$$

$$[CH_3COO^-] + [CH_3COOH] = 0.500 \qquad (2)$$

Solving the simultaneous Equations (1) and (2) gives $[CH_3COO^-] = 0.280\ \underline{M}$.

5-57. $pOH = pK_b + \log\dfrac{[NH_4^+]}{[NH_3]}$ or $14.00 - 8.96 = 4.74 + \log\left(\dfrac{100x + 40.0}{120 - 40.0}\right)$

or $x = 1.18\underline{M}$ $\therefore$ $pOH = 4.74 + \log(1.18/1.20) = 4.74$, $pH = 14.00 - 4.74 = 9.26$.

5-58. $pOH = 4.74 + \log([NH_4^+]/[NH_3]) = 4.74 + \log(0.05/99.95) = 1.44 \therefore pH = 14.00 - 1.44 = 12.56$

5-59. (a) In the initial solution, we have $[H^+] = 1.2 \times 10^{-2}(0.500 + [H^+])/(0.500 - [H^+]) = 0.0115$ $\underline{M}$; and $pH = -\log(0.0115) = 1.93_9$

When NaOH is added to the buffer, 20 mL X 0.100 mmol/mL = 2.00 mmol of Na_2SO_4 are formed ($NaHSO_4 + NaOH \rightleftharpoons Na_2SO_4 + H_2O$)

Let $[H^+] = y$, after the addition of NaOH, whereupon

$[SO_4^{2-}] = [(180 \times 0.500 + 2.00)/200] + y = 0.460 + y$,

$[HSO_4^-] = [(180 \times 0.500 - 2.00)/200] - y = 0.440 - y$, and

$1.2 \times 10^{-2} = y(0.460 + y)/(0.440 - y)$, or $y = 0.0109 = [H^+]$.

$\therefore$ $pH = -\log 0.0109 = 1.96_3$. Hence, the pH is increased by $1.96_3 - 1.93_9 = 0.024$ units

(b) When 20.0 mL X 0.100 mmol/mL = 2.00 mmol H_2SO_4 are added to the buffer, 2.00 mmol of Na_2SO_4 are consumed and 4.00 mmol of $NaHSO_4$ are formed ($Na_2SO_4 + H_2SO_4 \rightleftharpoons 2NaHSO_4$).

Let $[H^+] = z$, after the addition of H_2SO_4, whereupon

$[SO_4^{2-}] = [(180 \times 0.500 - 2.00)/200] + z = 0.440 + z$

$[HSO_4^-] = [(180 \times 0.500 + 4.00)/200] - z = 0.470 - z$, and

$1.2 \times 10^{-2} = z(0.440 + z)/(0.470 - z)$, or $z = 0.0121_5 = [H^+]$.

$\therefore$ $pH = -\log(0.0121_5) = 1.91_5$. Hence, the pH is decreased by $1.93_9 - 1.91_5 = 0.024$ units.

(c) Substituting the data in Equation (5-90), we have $\beta = 2.303\,(0.500)^2/(0.500+0.500) = 0.576$

5-60. (a) In the initial solution, we have $[OH^-] \simeq 1.8 \times 10^{-5}(0.170/0.187) = 1.64 \times 10^{-5}$ $\underline{M}$,

$[H^+] = 1.00 \times 10^{-14}/1.64 \times 10^{-5} = 6.1 \times 10^{-9}$ $\underline{M}$, $pH = -\log(6.9 \times 10^{-9}) = 9.21_4$.

When HCl is added to the buffer, 20 mL X 0.100 mmol/mL = 2.00 mmol of NH_4Cl are formed ($NH_3 + HCl \rightleftharpoons NH_4Cl$). Let $[OH^-] = y$, after the addition of HCl, whereupon

$[NH_3] = [(200 \times 0.170 - 2.00)/220] - y = 0.1455 - y$,

$[NH_4^+] = [(200 \times 0.187 + 2.00)/220] + y = 0.1791 + y$, and

$$[OH^-] = 1.8 \times 10^{-5} \times \frac{0.1455 - y}{0.1791 + y} \simeq 1.8 \times 10^{-5} \times \frac{0.1455}{0.1791} = 1.46_2 \times 10^{-5}\ \underline{M}$$

$\therefore$ $[H^+] = 1.00 \times 10^{-14}/1.46_2 \times 10^{-5} = 6.84 \times 10^{-10}$ $\underline{M}$, $pH = -\log(6.84 \times 10^{-10}) = 9.16_5$.

Hence, the pH is decreased by $9.21_4 - 9.165 = 0.049$ units.

(b) When NaOH is added to the buffer, 20.0 mL X 0.100 mmol/mL = 2.00 mmol of NH_3 are formed ($NH_4^+ + OH^- \rightleftharpoons NH_3 + H_2O$). Let $[OH^-] = z$, after the addition of NaOH, whereupon

$[NH_3] = [(200 \times 0.170 + 2.00)/220] + z = 0.1636 + z$,

$[NH_4^+] = [(200 \times 0.187 - 2.00)/220] - z = 0.1609 - z$, and

$$[OH^-] = 1.8 \times 10^{-5} \times \frac{0.1636 + z}{0.1609 - z} \simeq 1.8 \times 10^{-5} \times \frac{0.1636}{0.1609} = 1.83 \times 10^{-5}\ \underline{M}$$

$\therefore\ [H^+] = 1.00 \times 10^{-14}/1.83 \times 10^{-5} = 5.46 \times 10^{-10}\ \underline{M}$, pH = $-\log(5.46 \times 10^{-10}) = 9.26_2$.

Hence, the pH is increased by $9.26_2 - 9.21_4 = 0.048$ units.

5-61. (a) See Example 5-15.

In the initial solution, we have $[H^+] = 1.8 \times 10^{-5}(0.100/0.100) = 1.8 \times 10^{-5}\ \underline{M}$, and pH = 4.74_5.

After the addition of NaOH, $[CH_3COOH] \simeq 0.100 - 0.010 = 0.090$, $[CH_3COO^-] \simeq 0.100 + 0.010 = 0.110$ $\therefore$ $[H^+] \simeq 1.8 \times 10^{-5}(0.090/0.110) = 1.47 \times 10^{-5}\ \underline{M}$, pH = $-\log(1.47 \times 10^{-5}) = 4.83_2$. Hence, $[H^+]$ is decreased from $1.8 \times 10^{-5}\ \underline{M}$ to $1.47 \times 10^{-5}\ \underline{M}$, whereas pH is increased by $4.83_2 - 4.74_5 = 0.087$ units.

(b) After the addition of HCl, $[CH_3COOH] \simeq 0.100 + 0.010 = 0.110$, $[CH_3COO^-] \simeq 0.100 - 0.010 = 0.090$ $\therefore$ $[H^+] \simeq 1.8 \times 10^{-5}(0.110/0.090) = 2.20 \times 10^{-5}\ \underline{M}$, pH = $-\log(2.20 \times 10^{-5}) = 4.65_8$. Hence, $[H^+]$ is increased from $1.8 \times 10^{-5}\ \underline{M}$ to $2.20 \times 10^{-5}\ \underline{M}$, whereas pH is decreased by $4.74_5 - 4.65_8 = 0.087$ units.

5-62. Let y mL be the required volume of 0.200 $\underline{M}$ MH_3 ≡ 0.200 y mmol NH_3. We have

$$K_{NH_4^+} = \frac{1.00 \times 10^{-14}}{1.8 \times 10^{-5}} = \frac{[NH_3][H^+]}{[NH_4^+]} \simeq \frac{[0.200\,y/(200 + y)](1.00 \times 10^{-9})}{(200 \times 0.200)/(200 + y)}$$

or y = 111. Hence, 111 mL of 0.200 $\underline{M}$ NH_3 should be added.

5-63. We need (0.500 mol NH_4Cl/L)(53.49 g/mol) = 26.7_4 g NH_4Cl.

$[OH^-] = 1.00 \times 10^{-4}\ \underline{M}$ $\therefore$ $[NH_3] \simeq (0.500)(1.00 \times 10^{-4})/1.8 \times 10^{-5} = 2.78\ \underline{M}$.

Hence, we need (1000 mL)(2.78 mmol NH_3/mL)/(15.0 mmol/mL) = 185 mL 15 $\underline{M}$ NH_3.

5-64. $[NH_4^+]/[NH_3] = K_b/[OH^-] = 1.8 \times 10^{-5}/1.00 \times 10^{-5} = 1.8$ (1)

$[NH_4^+] + [NH_3] = 0.200$ (2)

Solving the simultaneous Equations (1) and (2) gives $[NH_3] = 0.0714\ \underline{M}$, $[NH_4^+] = 0.1286\ \underline{M}$

$\therefore$ we need (1000 mL X 0.200 mmol/mL)/(1.50 mmol NH_3/mL) = 133 mL 1.5 $\underline{M}$ NH_3,

and (0.1286 mmol/mL X 1000 mL)/(1.50 mmol HCl/mL) = 86 mL 1.5 $\underline{M}$ HCl.

Hence, 133 mL of 1.5 $\underline{M}$ NH_3, 86 mL of 1.5 $\underline{M}$ HCl, and 781 mL of water should be mixed to prepare one liter of buffer.

5-65. Suppose that y mL of CH_3COOH and consequently (400 − y) mL of CH_3COONa are required, whereupon we have

$[CH_3COO^-]/[CH_3COOH] = K_a/[H^+] = 1.8 \times 10^{-5}/1.00 \times 10^{-4} = 0.18$, or

$$\frac{0.500\,(400 - y)/400}{0.500\,y/400} = 0.18\ , \text{ or } y = 339$$

∴ 339 mL of CH_3COOH and 61 mL of CH_3COONa are required

5-66. $\alpha_0 = 8.2 \times 10^{-6}$, $\alpha_1 = 0.62$, $\alpha_2 = 0.38$, $\alpha_3 = 3.8 \times 10^{-6}$ [Example (5-23)].
From the very small values of α_0 and α_3 , it is concluded that the solution essentially contains only NaH_2PO_4 and Na_2HPO_4 .
∴ $[NaH_2PO_4] = [H_2PO_4^-] = 0.62 \times 0.100 = 0.062$ M , $[Na_2HPO_4] = [HPO_4^{2-}] = 0.38 \times 0.100 =$ 0.038 M , $[Na^+] = 0.062 + (2 \times 0.038) = 0.138$ M ,
$\mu = [0.138\,(1)^2 + 0.062\,(1)^2 + 0.038\,(2)^2]/2 = 0.176$.
In order to have $\mu = 0.500$, we should add 0.500 − 0.176 = 0.324 mol $NaClO_4$ per liter of buffer ≡ 0.324 mol $NaClO_4$/(0.00200 mol/mL) = 162 mL of 2 M $NaClO_4$. Hence ,
(0.138 mmol/mL X 1000 mL)/(0.50 mmol/mL) = 276 mL of 0.50 M NaOH ,
(0.100 mmol/mL X 1000 mL)/(0.50 mmol/mL) = 200 mL of 0.50 M H_3PO_4 , 162 mL of 2 M $NaClO_4$, and 1000 − (276 + 200 + 162) = 362 mL of H_2O should be mixed to prepare one liter of buffer.

5-67. $$\alpha_1 = \frac{[HA^-]}{0.100} = \frac{(1.1 \times 10^{-3})(1.00 \times 10^{-4})}{(1.00 \times 10^{-4})^2 + (1.1 \times 10^{-3})(1.00 \times 10^{-4}) + (1.1 \times 10^{-3})(6.9 \times 10^{-5})} = 0.562$$

$$\alpha_2 = \frac{[A^{2-}]}{0.100} = \frac{(1.1 \times 10^{-3})(6.9 \times 10^{-5})}{(1.00 \times 10^{-4})^2 + (1.1 \times 10^{-3})(1.00 \times 10^{-4}) + (1.1 \times 10^{-3})(6.9 \times 10^{-5})} = 0.387$$

Initially, the solution contains (250 mL)(0.100 mmol/mL) = 25.0 mmol of tartaric acid . The buffer contains 25.0 X 0.562 = 14.05 mmol of NaHA , and 25.0 X 0.387 = 9.675 mmol of Na_2A , and for their preparation 14.05 + (2 X 9.675) = 33.4 mmol of NaOH were added ≡ (33.4 mmol)(0.0400 g NaOH/mmol) = 1.34 g of NaOH .

5-68. Let y mL be the required volume of NaOH. We have

$$HCO_3^- + OH^- \rightleftharpoons CO_3^{2-} + H_2O$$

$$\therefore \frac{[HCO_3^-]}{[CO_3^{2-}]} = \frac{2.00}{1.00} = \frac{(60.0 \times 0.100 - 1.00\,y)/(60.0 + y)}{1.00\,y/(60.0 + y)}\ , \text{ or } y = 2.00 \text{ mL of 1 M NaOH}$$

$$pH = pK_2 + \log\frac{[CO_3^{2-}]}{[HCO_3^-]} = 10.32 + \log(1.00/2.00) = 10.02$$

5-69. $5.04 = 4.74 + \log \frac{[CH_3COO^-]}{[CH_3COOH]}$ or $\frac{[CH_3COO^-]}{[CH_3COOH]} = 2.00$

The solution contains initially (50.00 mL)(0.240 mmol HCl/mL) = 12.0 mmol of HCl

∴ 12.0 mmol of CH_3COONa are required for the reaction $CH_3COO^- + H^+ \rightleftharpoons CH_3COOH$, and an additional 24.0 mmol to make the ratio $[CH_3COO^-]/[CH_3COOH]$ equal to 2.00 . Hence, a total of (12.0 + 24.0) mmol X (0.08203 g CH_3COONa/mmol) = 2.95 g of CH_3COONa is required.

5-70. Let y mL be the required volume of NaOH. We have

$$\frac{[CH_3COO^-]}{[CH_3COOH]} = \frac{1.8 \times 10^{-5}}{1.00 \times 10^{-5}} = 1.8 = \frac{0.100\,y/(25.0 + y)}{(25.0 \times 0.100 - 0.100\,y)/(25.0 + y)}$$

or y = 16.1 mL of 0.100 M NaOH .

5-71. Let y mL be the required volume of NaOH. $[H^+] = 10^{-3.70} = 2.00 \times 10^{-4}$ M . We have

$$1.00 \times 10^{-4} = \frac{(2.00 \times 10^{-4})\,[1.00\,y/(100 + y)]}{(100 \times 1.00 - 1.00\,y)/(100 + y)}$$

or y = 33.3 mL of 1.00 M NaOH.

5-72. $[OH^-] = 1.00 \times 10^{-4}$ M , $[NH_3]$ = (21.4 mg/mL)/(17.03 mg/mmol) = 1.25_7 M.

$$\therefore\ 1.8 \times 10^{-5} = \frac{[NH_4^+]\,(1.00 \times 10^{-4})}{1.25_7}$$

or $[NH_4^+]$ = 0.226 M ≡ (0.226 mol NH_4Cl/L)(53.49 g/mol) = 12.1 g NH_4Cl/L .

5-73. We have 204 mg KH_2PO_4/(136.09 mg/mmol) = 1.50 mmol KH_2PO_4, and 5.00 mL X 0.100 mmol NaOH/mL = 0.500 mmol NaOH, which react ($KH_2PO_4 + NaOH \rightleftharpoons KNaHPO_4 + H_2O$) forming 0.500 mmol HPO_4^{2-} ∴ the solution contains 0.500 mmol HPO_4^{2-} and 1.50 - 0.500 = 1.00 mmol $H_2PO_4^-$. Hence,

$$pH = pK_2 + \log \frac{[HPO_4^{2-}]}{[H_2PO_4^-]} = 7.21 + \log \frac{(0.500/200)}{(1.00/200)} = 6.91$$

5-74. Initially, pH = 4.74 + log (1.00/1.00) = 4.74 ∴ after the addition of NaOH, we have

$$pH = 5.74 = 4.74 + \log \frac{[CH_3COO^-]}{[CH_3COOH]}$$

or $[CH_3COO^-]/[CH_3COOH] = 10.00$ (1)

$[CH_3COO^-] + [CH_3COOH] = 2.000$ (2)

Solving the simultaneous Equations (1) and (2) gives $[CH_3COO^-] = 1.818$. Hence,

$1.818 - 1.000 = 0.818$ mol of NaOH should be added to one liter of buffer X, i.e.,

0.818 mol NaOH/L X 40.00 g/mol X 0.500 L = 16.36 g NaOH/500 mL buffer X.

5-75. We have 200 mL NaOH X 0.250 mmol/mL = 50.0 mmol NaOH, and 10.70 g NH_4Cl/(0.05349 g/mmol) = 200.0 mmol NH_4Cl. They react, $NaOH + NH_4Cl \rightleftharpoons NaCl + NH_3 + H_2O$, forming 50.0 mmol of NH_3. The resulting buffer contains 50.0 mmol of NH_3 and 150.0 mmol of NH_4Cl

$$\therefore \quad pH = pK_{NH_4^+} + \log \frac{[NH_3]}{[NH_4^+]} = 9.26 + \log \frac{50.0/200}{150.0/200} = 8.78$$

5-76. Let $y = [CH_3COOH]$ in the buffer. We have

$1.8 \times 10^{-5} = 9.0 \times 10^{-6}\, [CH_3COO^-]/y$ or $[CH_3COO^-] = 2y$

When HCl is added to the buffer, the following reaction takes place

$$\begin{array}{lll} CH_3COO^- & + \; H^+ \rightleftharpoons & CH_3COOH \\ 0.0100\text{ mmol} & 0.0100\text{ mmol} & 0.0100\text{ mmol} \end{array}$$

$\therefore$ after the addition of HCl, we have $[CH_3COOH] = y + 0.010 - 1.00 \times 10^{-5} \simeq y + 0.010$,

$[CH_3COO^-] = 2y - 0.010 + 1.00 \times 10^{-5} \simeq 2y - 0.01$, and

$$[H^+] = 1.00 \times 10^{-5} = 1.8 \times 10^{-5} \times \frac{y + 0.010}{2y - 0.010}$$

or $y = 0.140$. Hence, $[CH_3COOH] = 0.140$ $\underline{M}$, $[CH_3COO^-] = 0.280$ $\underline{M}$.

5-77. We have 200 mL HCl X 0.200 mmol/mL = 40.0 mmol HCl, and 4.92 g CH_3COONa/(0.08203 g/mmol) = 60.0 mmol CH_3COONa. They react, $HCl + CH_3COONa \rightleftharpoons CH_3COOH + NaCl$, forming 40.0 mmol of CH_3COOH. The resulting buffer contains 40.0 mmol of CH_3COOH and 20.00 mmol of CH_3COONa.

$$\therefore \quad pH = 4.74 + \log \frac{20.0/200}{40.0/200} = 4.44 .$$

5-78. We have 200 mL NaOH X 1.00 mmol/mL = 200 mmol NaOH, and 300 mL CH_3COOH X 2.00 mmol/mL = 600 mmol CH_3COOH. They react, $NaOH + CH_3COOH \rightleftharpoons CH_3COONa + H_2O$, forming 200 mmol of CH_3COONa. The resulting buffer contains 200 mmol of CH_3COONa and 400 mmol of CH_3COOH.

$$\therefore \quad pH = 4.74 + \log \frac{200/500}{400/500} = 4.44 .$$

5-79. Let y mL be the required volume of 2.00 $\underline{M}$ HCl ≡ 2.00 y mmol HCl. We have

$$K_{NH_4^+} = \frac{1.00 \times 10^{-14}}{1.8 \times 10^{-5}} = \frac{[NH_3][H^+]}{[NH_4^+]} = \frac{[(1000 \times 0.100 - 2.00\,y)/(1000 + y)]\,(1.00 \times 10^{-9})}{2.00\,y/(1000 + y)}$$

or $y = 32.1$. Hence, 32.1 mL of 2.00 $\underline{M}$ HCl should be added.

5-80. $[OH^-] = 10^{-4.70} = 2.00 \times 10^{-5}$ $\underline{M}$, $[NH_4^+] = (1.8 \times 10^{-5})(0.600)/(2.0 \times 10^{-5}) = 0.540 \simeq C_{NH_4Cl}$

$\therefore$ (0.540 mol NH_4Cl/L)(53.49 g/mol)(0.200 L) = 5.78 g of NH_4Cl should be added.

5-81. Let y mL be the required volume of 1.00 $\underline{M}$ HCl ≡ 1.00 y mmol HCl. We have

$[OH^-] = 10^{-4.70} = 2.00 \times 10^{-5}$ $\underline{M}$, and

$$\frac{[NH_4^+]}{[NH_3]} = \frac{1.00\,y/(200 + y)}{(200 \times 0.600 - 1.00\,y)/(200 + y)} = \frac{K_b}{[OH^-]} = \frac{1.8 \times 10^{-5}}{2.00 \times 10^{-5}}$$

or y = 56.8. Hence, 56.8 mL of 1.00 $\underline{M}$ HCl should be added.

5-82. We have $a_{H^+} = 1.00 \times 10^{-5}$ $\underline{M}$, $-\log f_{CH_3COO^-} = [0.51\,(1)^2 \sqrt{0.100}\,]/(1 + \sqrt{0.100}) = 0.1225$

or $f_{CH_3COO^-} = 0.754$, and $f_{CH_3COOH} \simeq 1$. Substituting these values in the relation

$$K_a^o = 1.8 \times 10^{-5} = \frac{a_{H^+}\, f_{CH_3COO^-}\, [CH_3COO^-]}{f_{CH_3COOH}\, [CH_3COOH]} \text{, we have}$$

$$1.8 \times 10^{-5} = \frac{1.00 \times 10^{-5} \times 0.754\, [CH_3COO^-]}{[CH_3COOH]}$$

from which $[CH_3COO^-]/[CH_3COOH] = 2.387$ $\therefore$ $[CH_3COO^-] \simeq \mu = 0.100$ $\underline{M}$,

$[CH_3COOH] = 0.0419$ $\underline{M}$. Hence, the buffer contains in one liter 0.100 mol CH_3COONa/L X 82.03 g/mol = 8.2 g of CH_3COONa , and 0.0419 mol CH_3COOH/L X 60.05 g/mol = 2.52 g of CH_3COOH.

5-83. We have $a_{H^+} = 10^{-1.83} = 1.48 \times 10^{-2}$ $\underline{M}$, $f_{H^+} = 0.754$ [Solution 5-82].

$\therefore$ $[H^+] = 1.48 \times 10^{-2}/0.754 = 1.96 \times 10^{-2}$ $\underline{M}$ = [HCl] . Hence, we should add 0.100 - 0.0196 = 0.080_4 mol NaCl/L ≡ (0.080_4 mmol NaCl/mL)(0.05844 g/mmol)(100 mL) = 0.470 g NaCl/100 mL

5-84. Let y g be the weight of NaOH. Initially, we have

$$5.04 = pK_a + \log \frac{0.100}{0.100}$$

After the addition of NaOH, we have

$$5.10 = pK_a + \log \frac{0.100 + (y/40.00)}{0.100 - (y/40.00)}$$

Combining Equations (1) and (2), we have

$$0.06 = \log \frac{0.100 + (y/40.00)}{0.100 - (y/40.00)}$$

or y = 0.276 . Hence, 0.276 g of NaOH should be added .

5-85. Suppose that y mL of B and consequently (1000 - y) mL of HCl are mixed, whereupon (1000 - y) mL X 0.0500 mmol/mL = (50.0 - 0.0500 y) mmol of BH^+ are formed. The resulting buffer has $[OH^-] = 1.00 \times 10^{-5}$ M, and contains 0.100 y - (50.0 - 0.0500 y) = (0.150 y - 50.0) mmol of B and (50.0 - 0.0500 y) mmol of BH^+. We have

$$5.0 \times 10^{-5} = \frac{(50.0 - 0.0500\,y)(1.00 \times 10^{-5})}{0.150\,y - 50.0}$$

or y = 375. Hence, 375 mL of B should be mixed with 625 mL of HCl.

5-86. (a) $NH_3^+CH_2COOH \rightleftharpoons NH_3^+CH_2COO^- + H^+$

$$K_1 = \frac{[H^+][NH_3^+CH_2COO^-]}{[NH_3^+CH_2COOH]} = [H^+] \quad \therefore \quad pH = pK_1 = 2.35$$

(b) $NH_3^+CH_2COO^- \rightleftharpoons NH_2CH_2COO^- + H^+$

$$K_2 = \frac{[H^+][NH_2CH_2COO^-]}{[NH_3^+CH_2COO^-]} = [H^+] \quad \therefore \quad pH = pK_2 = 9.78$$

5-87. We have $[H^+] = 10^{-1.62} = 2.4 \times 10^{-2}$ M, and

$$[SO_4^{2-}] / [HSO_4^-] = K_2 / [H^+] = 1.2 \times 10^{-2} / 2.4 \times 10^{-2} = 0.50 \quad (1)$$

$$[SO_4^{2-}] + [HSO_4^-] \simeq 1.00 \quad ([H_2SO_4] \text{ is negligible}) \quad (2)$$

Solving the simultaneous Equations (1) and (2) gives $[HSO_4^-] = 0.667$ M, and $[SO_4^{2-}] = 0.333$ M. Hence, we need

(0.667 mol $NaHSO_4$/L)(120.06 g/mol)(0.500 L) = 40.0 g of $NaHSO_4$, and

(0.333 mol Na_2SO_4/L)(142.04 g/mol)(0.500 L) = 23.6 g of Na_2SO_4.

5-88. We have $[H^+] = 10^{-4.43} = 3.72 \times 10^{-5}$ M, $C_{H_2C_2O_4} = 0.9004$ g $H_2C_2O_4$/(90.04 g/mol X 0.100 L) = 0.100 M

$$\therefore \quad \alpha_1 = \frac{[HC_2O_4^-]}{0.100} = \frac{(3.8 \times 10^{-2})(3.72 \times 10^{-5})}{(3.72 \times 10^{-5})^2 + (3.8 \times 10^{-2})(3.72 \times 10^{-5}) + (3.8 \times 10^{-2})(5.0 \times 10^{-5})} = 0.428$$

$$\alpha_2 = \frac{(3.8 \times 10^{-2})(5.0 \times 10^{-5})}{(3.72 \times 10^{-5})^2 + (3.8 \times 10^{-2})(3.72 \times 10^{-5}) + (3.8 \times 10^{-2})(5.0 \times 10^{-5})} = 0.572$$

Initially, the solution contains (100 mL)(0.100 mmol/mL) = 10.0 mmol of oxalic acid. The buffer contains 10.0 X 0.428 = 4.28 mmol of $NaHC_2O_4$, and 10.0 X 0.572 = 5.72 mmol of $Na_2C_2O_4$, and for their preparation 4.28 + (2 X 5.72) = 15.7 mmol of NaOH were added ≡ 15.7 mL of 1.00 M NaOH.

5-89. We have

$$[CH_3COO^-]_1/[CH_3COOH]_1 = 1.8 \times 10^{-5}/1.00 \times 10^{-4} = 0.18 \quad (1)$$

$$[CH_3COO^-]_1 + [CH_3COOH]_1 = 0.100 \quad (2)$$

$$[CH_3COO^-]_2/[CH_3COOH]_2 = 1.8 \times 10^{-5}/1.00 \times 10^{-5} = 1.8 \quad (3)$$

$$[CH_3COO^-]_2 + [CH_3COOH]_2 = 0.100 \quad (4)$$

Solving the simultaneous Equations (1) and (2) gives $[CH_3COOH]_1 = 0.0847\ \underline{M}$, $[CH_3COO^-]_1 = 0.0153\ \underline{M}$. Similarly, from Equations (3) and (4) we obtain $[CH_3COOH]_2 = 0.0357\ \underline{M}$ and $[CH_3COO^-]_2 = 0.0643\ \underline{M}$ $\therefore$ $[CH_3COOH]_{final} = (0.0847 + 0.0357)/2 = 0.0602\ \underline{M}$, $[CH_3COO^-]_{final} = (0.0153 + 0.0643)/2 = 0.0398\ \underline{M}$, and $pH_{final} = 4.74 + \log(0.0398/0.0602) = 4.56$.

5-90. For the buffer of pH 10.00, we have $[OH^-] = 1.00 \times 10^{-4}\ \underline{M}$, and

$$[NH_4^+]_1/[NH_3]_1 = 1.8 \times 10^{-5}/1.00 \times 10^{-4} = 0.18 \quad (1)$$

$$[NH_4^+]_1 + [NH_3]_1 = 0.200 \quad (2)$$

Solving the simultaneous Equations (1) and (2) gives $[NH_3]_1 = 0.1695\ \underline{M}$, $[NH_4^+]_1 = 0.0305\ \underline{M}$.

For the buffer of pH 9.00, we have $[OH^-] = 1.00 \times 10^{-5}\ \underline{M}$, and

$$[NH_4^+]_2/[NH_3]_2 = 1.8 \times 10^{-5}/1.00 \times 10^{-5} = 1.8 \quad (3)$$

$$[NH_4^+]_2 + [NH_3]_2 = 0.100 \quad (4)$$

Solving the simultaneous Equations (3) and (4) gives $[NH_3]_2 = 0.0357\ \underline{M}$, $[NH_4^+]_2 = 0.0643\ \underline{M}$.

For the buffer of pH 9.50, we have $[OH^-] = 10^{-4.50} = 3.16 \times 10^{-5}\ \underline{M}$, and $[NH_4^+]/[NH_3] = 1.8 \times 10^{-5}/3.16 \times 10^{-5} = 0.570$. Let y mL be the volume of buffer of pH 10.00, whereupon

$$\frac{[NH_4^+]}{[NH_3]} = \frac{(100 \times 0.0643 + 0.0305\,y)/(100 + y)}{(100 \times 0.0357 + 0.1695\,y)/(100 + y)} = 0.570$$

or $y = 66.5$. Hence, 66.5 mL of buffer having pH 10.00 are required.

5-91. Initially, we have

$$5.00 = 5.30 + \log \frac{[X^-]_{init}}{[HX]_{init}} \quad \text{or} \quad [HX]_{init}/[X^-]_{init} = 2.00$$

Let $[X^-]_{init} \simeq [NaX]_{init} = y$, whereupon $[HX]_{init} = 2y$. After the addition of 10 mmol HCl/100 mL ≡ 0.100 mol HCl/L , $[X^-] = y - 0.100$, $[HX] = 2y + 0.100$, pH = 4.80

$$\therefore\ 4.80 = 5.30 + \log \frac{y - 0.100}{2y + 0.100}$$

or y = 0.358 . Hence, the initial concentration of NaX and HX should be 0.358 M and 0.716 M , respectively.

5-92. Suppose that y mL of HA and consequently (100 - y) mL of NaOH are mixed, whereupon (100 - y) mL X 0.0500 mmol/mL = (5.00 - 0.0500 y) mmol of A^- are formed. The resulting buffer has $[H^+] = 1.00 \times 10^{-5}$ M , and contains 0.100 y - (5.00 - 0.0500 y) = (0.150 y - 5.00) mmol of HA and (5.00 - 0.0500 y) mmol of A^-. We have

$$5.0 \times 10^{-5} = \frac{(5.00 - 0.0500\,y)(1.00 \times 10^{-5})}{0.150\,y - 5.00}$$

or y = 37.5 . Hence, 37.5 mL of HA should be mixed with 62.5 mL of NaOH .

5-93. (a) Let y g be the amount of $NaHCO_3$. We have y g $NaHCO_3$/(0.08401 g/mmol) = 11.90 y mmol $NaHCO_3$ and 3.18 g Na_2CO_3/(0.1059 g/mmol) = 30.0 mmol Na_2CO_3

$$\therefore\ pH = pK_2 + \log \frac{[CO_3^{2-}]}{[HCO_3^-]} = 10.68 = 10.32 + \log \frac{30.0/500}{11.90\,y/500} \quad \text{or} \quad y = 1.100\ g$$

(b) The solution contains 1.100 g $NaHCO_3$/(0.08401 g/mmol) = 13.09 mmol $NaHCO_3$ and 30.0 mmol Na_2CO_3. After the addition of 1.00 mL of 1.00 M HCl , which reacts with CO_3^{2-} ($CO_3^{2-} + H^+ \rightleftharpoons HCO_3^-$) , $[HCO_3^-]$ = 14.09 mmol/501 mL = 0.0281 M , $[CO_3^{2-}]$ = 29.0 mmol/501 mL = 0.0579 M ∴ pH = 10.32 + log (0.0579/0.0281) = 10.63 .

(c) The solution contains 2.52 g $NaHCO_3$/(0.08401 g/mmol) = 30.00 mmol $NaHCO_3$. Let y mL be the volume of NaOH , which reacts with HCO_3^- ($HCO_3^- + OH^- \rightleftharpoons CO_3^{2-} + H_2O$). We have

$$10.20 = 10.32 + \log \frac{(30.00 - y)/500}{y/500} \quad \text{or} \quad y = 17.0\ mL\ .$$

5-94. (a) Substituting the data in Equation (5-90), we have

$$\beta = 2.303 \times \frac{0.010 \times 0.10}{0.010 + 0.10} = 0.021$$

(b) $\beta = 2.303 \times \dfrac{0.010 \times 0.0040}{0.010 + 0.0040} = 0.0066$

(c) $\beta = 2.303 \times \dfrac{0.010 \times 0.0010}{0.010 + 0.0010} = 0.0021$

It can be seen that the buffer capacity increases with increasing concentrations of the buffer components. More exact values of buffer capacity can be found using Equation (5-89).

5-95. $[OH^-] \simeq 10^{-(14.00-8.34)} = 2.19 \times 10^{-6}$ $\underline{M}$ $\therefore$ $\alpha = 2.19 \times 10^{-6}/0.100 = 2.19 \times 10^{-5}$ or 2.19×10^{-3} %

$K_h = K_w/K_a \simeq \alpha^2 C$ $\therefore$ $K_a = (1.00 \times 10^{-14})/(2.19 \times 10^{-5})^2 (0.100) = 2.09 \times 10^{-4}$

5-96. See Example 5-28.

$$K_h \simeq \frac{[H^+]^2}{0.100 - [H^+]} = 1.12 \times 10^{-5} \text{ or } [H^+] = 1.05 \times 10^{-3}\ \underline{M}. \text{ Hence,}$$

$pH = -\log(1.05 \times 10^{-3}) = 2.98$, $\alpha = 1.05 \times 10^{-3}/0.100 = 0.0105$ or 1.05%.

5-97. See Example 5-29.

Solving Equation (5-109) by the method of successive approximations we find $[H^+] = 1.21 \times 10^{-9}$ $\underline{M}$. Hence, $pH = -\log(1.21 \times 10^{-9}) = 8.92$. Using Equations (5-113) and (5-114), we have

$$\alpha_{NH_4^+} = \frac{5.6 \times 10^{-10}}{5.6 \times 10^{-10} + 1.21 \times 10^{-9}} = 0.32 \text{ or } 32\%$$

$$\alpha_{CN^-} = \frac{1.21 \times 10^{-9}}{4 \times 10^{-10} + 1.21 \times 10^{-9}} = 0.75 \text{ or } 75\%$$

5-98. For the hydrolysis of the S^{2-} and SH^- ions, we have

$$S^{2-} + H_2O \rightleftharpoons HS^- + OH^-, \quad K_{h_1} = \frac{[HS^-][OH^-]}{[S^{2-}]} = \frac{K_w}{K_2} = \frac{1.00 \times 10^{-14}}{1.0 \times 10^{-14}} = 1.0 \quad (1)$$

$$HS^- + H_2O \rightleftharpoons H_2S + OH^-, \quad K_{h_2} = \frac{[H_2S][OH^-]}{[HS^-]} = \frac{K_w}{K_1} = \frac{1.00 \times 10^{-14}}{1.0 \times 10^{-7}} = 1.0 \times 10^{-7} \quad (2)$$

Since $K_{h_2} \ll K_{h_1}$, the hydrolysis of the HS^- is considered negligible. Let $[HS^-] = [OH^-] = y$. From Equation (1) we have $y^2/(0.100 - y) = 1.0$ or $y = 0.092$. Hence, $[HS^-] = [OH^-] = 0.092$ $\underline{M}$, $\alpha = 0.092/0.100 = 0.92$ or 92%, $[S^{2-}] = 0.100 - 0.092 = 0.008$ $\underline{M}$, $[H^+] = 1.00 \times 10^{-14}/0.092 = 1.09 \times 10^{-13}$ $\underline{M}$, $pH = -\log(1.09 \times 10^{-13}) = 12.96$, $[Na^+] = 0.200$ $\underline{M}$, $[H_2S] = [H^+][HS^-]/K_1 = (1.09 \times 10^{-13})(0.092)/(1.0 \times 10^{-7}) = 1.0 \times 10^{-7}$ $\underline{M}$.

5-99. (a) Let $H_2Glu \equiv$ Glutamic acid. We have

$$[H^+] = \sqrt{\frac{K_1 K_2 [H_2Glu] + K_1 K_w}{K_1 + [H_2Glu]}} = \sqrt{\frac{10^{-2.23} \times 10^{-4.42} \times 0.100 + 10^{-2.23} \times 10^{-14.00}}{10^{-2.23} + 0.100}} =$$

4.60×10^{-4} $\underline{M}$ $\therefore$ $pH = -\log(4.60 \times 10^{-4}) = 3.34$

(b) $pH = (pK_1 + pK_2)/2 = (2.23 + 4.42)/2 = 3.32$.

CHAPTER 6

6-1. $S_{Ag_2CrO_4} = \frac{(0.00259\ g/100\ mL)(1000\ mL/L)}{331.77\ g/mol} = 7.8 \times 10^{-5}\ \underline{M}$

$\therefore [CrO_4^{2-}] = 7.8 \times 10^{-5}\ \underline{M}$, $[Ag^+] = 2 \times 7.8 \times 10^{-5} = 1.56 \times 10^{-4}\ \underline{M}$,

$K_{sp(Ag_2CrO_4)} = (1.56 \times 10^{-4})^2(7.8 \times 10^{-5}) = 1.9 \times 10^{-12}$

6-2. Subtracting Equation (3) from Equation (4), we obtain

$$PbS + 2\,I^- \rightleftharpoons PbI_2 + S^{2-},\quad K_5 = \frac{[S^{2-}]}{[I^-]^2} \cdot \frac{[Pb^{2+}]}{[Pb^{2+}]} = \frac{K_{sp(PbS)}}{K_{sp(PbI_2)}} = \frac{8 \times 10^{-28}}{8.3 \times 10^{-9}} \qquad (5)$$

Similarly, for Reaction (2) we have

$$K_2 = \frac{[SO_4^{2-}]}{[I^-]^2} = \frac{K_{sp(PbSO4)}}{K_{sp(PbI_2)}} = \frac{1.3 \times 10^{-8}}{K_{sp(PbI_2)}} = 1.57$$

$\therefore K_{sp(PbI_2)} = 1.3 \times 10^{-8}/1.57 = 8.3 \times 10^{-9}$. Substituting this value in Equation (5), we obtain

$$\frac{K_{sp(PbS)}}{8.3 \times 10^{-9}} = \frac{8 \times 10^{-28}}{8.3 \times 10^{-9}} \qquad \therefore K_{sp(PbS)} = 8 \times 10^{-28}$$

6-3. $SrSO_4 \rightleftharpoons Sr^{2+} + SO_4^{2-}$

$\qquad\qquad y \qquad 0.0010 + y$

Let y be the molar solubility of $SrSO_4$. Then,

$y = 0.042\ g\ SrSO_4/(183.70\ g/mol) = 2.29 \times 10^{-4}\ \underline{M}$

$\therefore K_{sp(SrSO_4)} = [Sr^{2+}][SO_4^{2-}] = (2.29 \times 10^{-4})(1.0 \times 10^{-3} + 2.29 \times 10^{-4}) = 2.8 \times 10^{-7}$

6-4. Initially, $[NH_4Cl] = 0.75\ g\ NH_4Cl/(53.50\ g\ NH_4Cl/mol)(0.025\ L) = 0.561\ \underline{M}$.

After mixing, $[NH_4^+] = 0.280\ \underline{M}$, $[NH_3] = 0.050\ \underline{M}$, $[M^{2+}] = 0.0050\ \underline{M}$.

$\therefore [OH^-] = (1.8 \times 10^{-5})(0.050)/0.280 = 3.21 \times 10^{-6}\ \underline{M}$, $K_{sp[M(OH)_2]} = (5.0 \times 10^{-3})(3.21 \times 10^{-6})^2$ $= 5.2 \times 10^{-14}$.

6-5. (a) $Ag_2S \rightleftharpoons 2\,Ag^+ + S^{2-}$

$\qquad\quad S \qquad 2\,S \qquad S$

$\therefore K_{sp(Ag_2S)} = [Ag^+]^2[S^{2-}] = (2\,S)^2\,S = 4\,S^3$

(b) Similarly, $K_{sp(PbCl_2)} = 4\,S^3$, (c) $K_{sp(PbSO_4)} = S^2$, (d) $K_{sp(PbClF)} = S^3$,

(e) $K_{sp[Ca_3(PO_4)_2]} = 108\,S^5$

6-6. (a) $MX_2 \rightleftharpoons M^{2+} + 2X^-$

$S \quad S \quad 2S$

$K_{sp(MX_2)} = S(2S)^2 = 4S^3 \quad \therefore \quad S = \sqrt[3]{K_{sp(MX_2)}/4}$

(b) $MX_4 \rightleftharpoons M^{4+} + 4X^-$

$S \quad S \quad 4S$

$K_{sp(MX_4)} = S(4S)^4 = 256\,S^5 \quad \therefore \quad S = \sqrt[5]{K_{sp(MX_4)}/256}$

(c) $MY \rightleftharpoons M^{2+} + Y^{2-}$

$S \quad S \quad S$

$K_{sp(MY)} = S^2 \quad \therefore \quad S = \sqrt{K_{sp(MY)}}$

(d) $M_2Y_3 \rightleftharpoons 2M^{3+} + 3Y^{2-}$

$S \quad 2S \quad 3S$

$K_{sp(M_2Y_3)} = (2S)^2(3S)^3 = 108\,S^5 \quad \therefore \quad S = \sqrt[5]{K_{sp(M_2Y_3)}/108}$

(e) $M_3Z_2 \rightleftharpoons 3M^{2+} + 2Z^{3-}$

$S \quad 3S \quad 2S$

$K_{sp(M_3Z_2)} = (3S)^3(2S)^2 = 108\,S^5 \quad \therefore \quad S = \sqrt[5]{K_{sp(M_3Z_2)}/108}$

6-7. Since the molar solubility S_{BaSO_4} in 1.00 M HNO_3 is very small, essentially we have $[H^+] = 1.00$ M. We have

$$\alpha_2 = \frac{[SO_4^{2-}]}{S_{BaSO_4}} = \frac{K_1K_2}{[H^+]^2 + K_1[H^+] + K_1K_2} = \frac{(1.0 \times 10^2)(1.2 \times 10^{-2})}{(1.00)^2 + (1.0 \times 10^2)(1.00) + (1.0 \times 10^2)(1.2 \times 10^{-2})} =$$

$0.0117 = \frac{[SO_4^{2-}]}{[Ba^{2+}]}$, from which $[SO_4^{2-}] = 0.0117\,[Ba^{2+}]$. Hence,

$K_{sp(BaSO_4)} = 1.5 \times 10^{-9} = [Ba^{2+}][SO_4^{2-}] = 0.0117[Ba^{2+}]^2$

$\therefore \quad [Ba^{2+}] = S_{BaSO_4} = \sqrt{1.5 \times 10^{-9}/0.0117} = 3.6 \times 10^{-4}$ mol/L .

6-8. Let S be the molar solubility of $PbCl_2$. Then, $[Pb^{2+}] = S$, $[Cl^-] = 2S$.

$\therefore \quad K_{sp(PbCl_2)} = 1.6 \times 10^{-5} = [Pb^{2+}][Cl^-]^2 = S(2S)^2 = 4S^3$

$S = 0.0252$ mol/L $\equiv$ (0.0252 mol/L)(278.10×10^3 mg/mol)(0.500 L) = 3.5×10^3 mg $PbCl_2$/500 mL .

6-9. Molar solubility $S_{AgBr} = \sqrt{K_{sp(AgBr)}} = \sqrt{5 \times 10^{-13}} = 7.07 \times 10^{-7}$ mol/L

$\therefore$ solubility, g AgBr/100 mL = (7.07×10^{-7} mol AgBr/L)(187.77 g/mol) [100 mL/(1000 mL/L)] = 1.33×10^{-5}

Similarly,

solubility, g $Ag_2C_2O_4$/100 mL = $(\sqrt[3]{(1 \times 10^{-11})/4}$ mol $Ag_2C_2O_4$/L)(303.76 g/mol)(0.100 L)=0.0041

$$Ca_3(PO_4)_2 \rightleftharpoons 3\,Ca^{2+} + 2\,PO_4^{3-}$$
$$S \qquad 3\,S \qquad 2\,S$$

$$\therefore\ K_{sp}\left[Ca_3(PO_4)_2\right] = (3\,S)^3(2\,S)^2 = 108\,S^5 = 108\left[\frac{[1.22 \times 10^{-4}\ g\ Ca_3(PO_4)_2/100\ mL](1000\ mL/L)}{310.18\ g\ Ca_3(PO_4)_2/mol}\right]^5$$
$= 1.02 \times 10^{-25}$

Similarly,

$$K_{sp(PbBr_2)} = 4\,S^3 = 4\left[\frac{(0.384\ g\ PbBr_2/100\ mL)(1000\ mL/L)}{367.00\ g\ PbBr_2/mol}\right]^3 = 4.58 \times 10^{-6}$$

Solubility, g $MgNH_4PO_4$/100 mL = $(\sqrt[3]{2.0 \times 10^{-13}}$ mol $MgNH_4PO_4$/L)(137.31 g/mol)(0.100 L) = 8.0×10^{-4}

6-10. $$\frac{(0.250\ g\ PbS/100\ mL)(1000\ mL/L)}{239.25\ g\ PbS/moL} = 0.1045\ mol\ PbS/L\ \text{was formed}$$

$$\therefore\ S_{PbBr_2} = 0.1045\ mol/L\ ,\quad K_{sp(PbBr_2)} = 4\,S^3_{PbBr_2} = 4\,(0.1045)^3 = 4.60 \times 10^{-6}$$

6-11. $$ZnS + 2\,H^+ \rightleftharpoons Zn^{2+} + H_2S$$
$$1.00 - 2\,y \qquad y \qquad y$$

Let y be the molar solubility of ZnS. Then,

$$\left[S^{2-}\right] = \frac{K_{sp(ZnS)}}{\left[Zn^{2+}\right]} = \frac{1.6 \times 10^{-23}}{y} = \frac{K_1K_2\left[H_2S\right]}{\left[H^+\right]^2} = \frac{(1.0 \times 10^{-7})(1.0 \times 10^{-14})\,y}{(1.00 - 2\,y)^2}$$

or $$\frac{1.6 \times 10^{-23}}{1.0 \times 10^{-21}} = \frac{y^2}{(1 - 2\,y)^2}$$

$y = 0.101$ mol/L $\equiv$ (0.101 mol/L)(97.43 g ZnS/mol) = 9.8 g ZnS/L

6-12 (a) $$CH_3COOAg \rightleftharpoons CH_3COO^- + Ag^+$$
$$S \qquad \alpha_1 S \qquad S$$

$$K_{sp} = \left[CH_3COO^-\right]\left[Ag^+\right] = \alpha_1 S \cdot S = \alpha_1 S^2$$

$$\therefore\ S = \sqrt{\frac{K_{sp}}{\alpha_1}} = \sqrt{\frac{K_{sp}}{K_a/([H^+] + K_a)}} = \sqrt{K_{sp}\left(\frac{[H^+] + K_a}{K_a}\right)}$$

(b) $$Ag_2CO_3 \rightleftharpoons 2\,Ag^+ + CO_3^{2-}$$
$$S \qquad 2\,S \qquad \alpha_2 S$$

$$K_{sp} = \left[Ag^+\right]^2\left[CO_3^{2-}\right] = (2\,S)^2(\alpha_2 S) = 4\,\alpha_2 S^3$$

$$\therefore\ S = \sqrt[3]{\frac{K_{sp}}{4\alpha_2}} = \sqrt[3]{\frac{K_{sp}}{4}\left(\frac{[H^+]^2 + K_1[H^+] + K_1K_2}{K_1K_2}\right)}$$

(c) $Ag_3PO_4 \rightleftharpoons 3\,Ag^+ + PO_4^{3-}$

$\quad S \qquad 3\,S \qquad \alpha_3\,S$

$$K_{sp} = [Ag^+]^3[PO_4^{3-}] = (3\,S)^3(\alpha_3\,S) = 27\,\alpha_3\,S^4$$

$$\therefore\ S = \sqrt[4]{\frac{K_{sp}}{27\alpha_3}} = \sqrt[4]{\frac{K_{sp}}{27}\left(\frac{[H^+]^3 + K_1[H^+]^2 + K_1K_2[H^+] + K_1K_2K_3}{K_1K_2K_3}\right)}$$

(d) $CaF_2 \rightleftharpoons Ca^{2+} + 2\,F^-$ (disregard the formation of H_2F_2)

$\quad S \qquad S \qquad 2\,\alpha_1\,S$

$$K_{sp} = [Ca^{2+}][F^-]^2 = S\cdot(2\alpha_1\,S)^2 = 4\alpha_1^2\,S^3$$

$$\therefore\ S = \sqrt[3]{\frac{K_{sp}}{4\alpha_1^2}} = \sqrt[3]{\frac{K_{sp}}{4}\left(\frac{[H^+] + K_a}{K_a}\right)^2}$$

(e) $BiPO_4 \rightleftharpoons Bi^{3+} + PO_4^{3-}$

$\quad S \qquad S \qquad \alpha_3\,S$

$$K_{sp} = [Bi^{3+}][PO_4^{3-}] = S\cdot\alpha_3\,S = \alpha_3\,S^2$$

$$\therefore\ S = \sqrt{\frac{K_{sp}}{\alpha_3}} = \sqrt{K_{sp}\left(\frac{[H^+]^3 + K_1[H^+]^2 + K_1K_2[H^+] + K_1K_2K_3}{K_1K_2K_3}\right)}$$

6-13. 100 ppm $CaF_2 \equiv [(100\text{ mg }CaF_2/\text{L})/(78.08\text{ mg }CaF_2/\text{mmol})](10^{-3}\text{ mol/mmol}) = 1.28\times10^{-3}$ $\underline{M}$.
Solving for $[H^+]$ the Equation derived in Problem 6-12 d, we have

$$S^3 = \frac{K_{sp}}{4}\left(1 + \frac{[H^+]}{K_a}\right)^2$$

$$[H^+] = \left(\sqrt{4\,S^3/K_{sp}} - 1\right)K_a = \left[\sqrt{4\,(1.28\times10^{-3})^3/(1.7\times10^{-10})} - 1\right](6.9\times10^{-4}) = 4.16\times10^{-3}\ \underline{M}$$

$$\therefore\ pH = -\log(4.16\times10^{-3}) = 2.3_8$$

6-14. See Problem 6-12.

$$\frac{[H^+]^2}{0.25 - [H^+]} = 1.8\times10^{-5}$$

$$[H^+] = 2.12\times10^{-3}\ \underline{M}$$

$$K_{sp} = [M^{2+}][C_2O_4^{2-}] = S\cdot\alpha_2\,S = \alpha_2\,S^2 \qquad (M = Ca,\ Sr,\ Ba)$$

$$\therefore\ S = \sqrt{\frac{K_{sp}}{\alpha_2}} = \sqrt{K_{sp}\left(\frac{[H^+]^2 + K_1[H^+] + K_1K_2}{K_1K_2}\right)} =$$

$$\sqrt{K_{sp}\left[\frac{(2.12 \times 10^{-3})^2 + (3.8 \times 10^{-2})(2.12 \times 10^{-3}) + (3.8 \times 10^{-2})(5.0 \times 10^{-5})}{(3.8 \times 10^{-2})(5.0 \times 10^{-5})}\right]} = \sqrt{45.77 K_{sp}} \quad (1)$$

Substituting the appropriate values of K_{sp} in Equation (1) we obtain

$S_{CaC_2O_4} = \sqrt{45.77 \times 1.3 \times 10^{-9}} = 2.44 \times 10^{-4}$ $\underline{M} \equiv (2.44 \times 10^{-4}$ mmol/mL)(128.10 mg CaC_2O_4/mmol) X (100 mL) = 3.1 mg CaC_2O_4/100 mL

$S_{SrC_2O_4} = \sqrt{45.77 \times 5.6 \times 10^{-8}} = 1.60 \times 10^{-3}$ $\underline{M} \equiv (1.60 \times 10^{-3}$ mmol/mL)(175.64 mg SrC_2O_4/mmol) X (100 mL) = 28.1 mg SrC_2O_4/100 mL

$S_{BaC_2O_4} = \sqrt{45.77 \times 1.5 \times 10^{-8}} = 8.29 \times 10^{-4}$ $\underline{M} \equiv (8.29 \times 10^{-4}$ mmol/mL)(225.36 mg BaC_2O_4/mmol) X (100 mL) = 18.7 mg BaC_2O_4/100 mL

6-15. (a) Mol. weight of $X(OH)_3 = 52.0 + 3 \times 17.01 = 103.0$. Let S be the molar solubility of $X(OH)_3$. Then,

$$S = \frac{0.13\ \mu g / 100\ mL}{103.0 \times 10^3\ \mu g/mmol} = 1.26 \times 10^{-8}\ \underline{M}$$

$$K_{sp[X(OH)_3]} = [X^{3+}][OH^-]^3 = S(3S)^3 = 27S^4 = 27(1.26 \times 10^{-8})^4 = 7 \times 10^{-31}$$

At pH 6.50, $[OH^-] = 10^{-7.50} = 3.16 \times 10^{-8}$ $\underline{M}$

$$\therefore \quad [X^{3+}][OH^-]^3 = (0.0100)(3.16 \times 10^{-8})^3 = 3.16 \times 10^{-26} > 7 \times 10^{-31} = K_{sp[X(OH)_3]}$$

Hence, a precipitate will be formed.

(b) Cr

6-16.
$$\begin{array}{ccccccc} S^{2-} & + & H_2O & \rightleftharpoons & HS^- & + & OH^- \\ 0.100-y & & & & y & & y \end{array}$$

$$K_h = \frac{[HS^-][OH^-]}{[S^{2-}]} \cdot \frac{[H^+]}{[H^+]} = \frac{K_w}{K_{a2}} = \frac{1.00 \times 10^{-14}}{1.0 \times 10^{-14}} = 1 = \frac{y^2}{0.100 - y}$$

$y = 0.092$ $\therefore$ $[OH^-] = 0.092$ $\underline{M}$, $[S^{2-}] = 0.100 - 0.092 = 0.008$ $\underline{M}$ (neglect the hydrolysis of HS^- because it is negligible in comparison with the hydrolysis of S^{2-}).

We calculate the $[Mn^{2+}]$ at which MnS and $Mn(OH)_2$ start to precipitate. Since $[S^{2-}] = 0.008$ $\underline{M}$, $[Mn^{2+}] = 8 \times 10^{-14}/0.008 = 1 \times 10^{-11}$ $\underline{M}$, whereas since $[OH^-] = 0.092$ $\underline{M}$, $[Mn^{2+}] = 2 \times 10^{-13}/(0.092)^2 = 2.4 \times 10^{-11}$ $\underline{M}$. A smaller concentration of Mn^{2+} ions is required for MnS to start to precipitate than for $Mn(OH)_2$ $\therefore$ MnS will be precipitated first.

6-17. Since $K_{sp(ZnS)}$ is very small (1.6×10^{-23}), zinc is precipitated quantitatively, according to the reaction

$$\underset{0.010}{Zn^{2+}} + H_2S \rightleftharpoons ZnS + \underset{0.020}{2\,H^+}$$

Hence, at equilibrium, $[CH_3COOH] = 0.10 + 0.020 = 0.12\ \underline{M}$, $[CH_3COO^-] = 0.62 - 0.020 = 0.60\ \underline{M}$ $\therefore$ $[H^+] = (1.8 \times 10^{-5})(0.12)/0.60 = 3.6 \times 10^{-6}\ \underline{M}$,

$$\alpha_2 = \frac{[S^{2-}]}{C_{H_2S}} = \frac{[S^{2-}]}{0.10} = \frac{(1.0 \times 10^{-7})(1.0 \times 10^{-14})}{(3.6 \times 10^{-6})^2 + (1.0 \times 10^{-7})(3.6 \times 10^{-6}) + (1.0 \times 10^{-7})(1.0 \times 10^{-14})} =$$

7.5×10^{-11}

$\therefore$ $[S^{2-}] = 7.5 \times 10^{-12}\ \underline{M}$, and $[Zn^{2+}] = 1.6 \times 10^{-23}/7.5 \times 10^{-12} = 2.13 \times 10^{-12}\ \underline{M}$

Hence,

$$\frac{2.13 \times 10^{-12}}{0.010} \times 100 = 2.1 \times 10^{-8}\ \%\ \text{of zinc is not precipitated.}$$

6-18.

$$\underset{S}{M(OH)_2} \rightleftharpoons \underset{S}{M^{2+}} + \underset{2S}{2\,OH^-}$$

$$S = \frac{0.00242\ g/L}{242\ g/mol} = 1.00 \times 10^{-5}\ mol/L$$

$\therefore$ $K_{sp\,[M(OH)_2]} = [M^{2+}][OH^-]^2 = S(2S)^2 = 4S^3 = 4(1.00 \times 10^{-5})^3 = 4.00 \times 10^{-15}$

At pH 8.80, $[OH^-] = 10^{-5.20} = 6.31 \times 10^{-6}\ \underline{M}$ $\therefore$ $[M^{2+}] = (4.00 \times 10^{-15})/(6.31 \times 10^{-6})^2 = 1.00 \times 10^{-4}\ \underline{M}$

Hence,

$$\frac{1.00 \times 10^{-4}}{0.100} \times 100 = 0.100\ \%\ \text{of}\ M^{2+}\ \text{is not precipitated}$$

6-19. See Example 6-8.

Setting $[SO_4^{2-}] = 2[Sr^{2+}]$ in the $K_{sp(SrSO_4)}$ expression, we have $[Sr^{2+}](2[Sr^{2+}]) = 2[Sr^{2+}]^2 = 2.8 \times 10^{-7}$, or $[Sr^{2+}] = \sqrt{2.8 \times 10^{-7}/2} = 3.74 \times 10^{-4}\ \underline{M}$. We consider $[H^+] = [OH^-]$, whereupon for $[SO_4^{2-}] = 2[Sr^{2+}]$ and $[Sr^{2+}] = 3.74 \times 10^{-4}\ \underline{M}$ the electroneutrality principle becomes

$2[SO_4^{2-}] = 2[Sr^{2+}] + [K^+] = 2(2[Sr^{2+}]) = 4[Sr^{2+}]$

or $[K^+] = 2[Sr^{2+}] = 2 \times 3.74 \times 10^{-4} = 7.48 \times 10^{-4}\ \underline{M} \equiv (7.48 \times 10^{-4}/2)\ \underline{M}\ K_2SO_4$

Hence, we should add $(7.48 \times 10^{-4}/2\ mol/L)(174.27\ g\ K_2SO_4/mol) = 0.0652\ g\ K_2SO_4/L$

6-20. When $Mg(OH)_2$ is dissolved, $[Mg^{2+}] = (20.0 \times 0.050)/70.0 = 0.0143\ \underline{M}$

$\therefore$ $[OH^-] = \sqrt{8.9 \times 10^{-12}/0.0143} = 2.49 \times 10^{-5}\ \underline{M}$

$[NH_3] = C_{NaOH} = (50.0 \times 0.50)/70.0 = 0.357$ M $(NH_4Cl + NaOH \rightleftharpoons NH_3 + NaCl + H_2O)$

$\therefore [NH_4^+] = \dfrac{1.8 \times 10^{-5} \times 0.357}{2.49 \times 10^{-5}} = 0.258$ M, $C_{NH_4Cl} = [NH_3] + [NH_4^+] = 0.357 + 0.258 = 0.615$ M

Hence,

(0.615 mol/L)(53.49 g NH_4Cl/mol)(0.070 L) = 2.30 g NH_4Cl should be added.

6-21. $$ZnCl_2 + H_2S \rightleftharpoons ZnS + 2\,HCl \qquad (1)$$

At equilibrium, let $[Zn^{2+}] = y$. Hence, (0.100 − y) mol Zn^{2+} have been precipitated, and 2 (0.100 − y) = (0.200 − 2 y) mol H^+ have been produced, according to Reaction (1)

$$[H^+]^2 [S^{2-}] = (1.0 \times 10^{-7})(1.0 \times 10^{-14})(0.10) = 1.0 \times 10^{-22} \qquad (2)$$

$$[Zn^{2+}][S^{2-}] = 1.6 \times 10^{-23} \qquad (3)$$

Dividing Equations (2) and (3), we obtain

$$\frac{[H^+]^2}{[Zn^{2+}]} = 6.25 = \frac{(0.200 - 2\,y)^2}{y}$$

$y = [Zn^{2+}] = 0.0057$ M

$\therefore$ (0.0057)/0.100) 100 = 5.7% of zinc is left in the solution.

6-22. (a) Let y be the molar solubility of Ag_2CrO_4. Then, $[Ag^+] = 2\,y$,

$[CrO_4^{2-}] = y + 0.100 \quad \therefore (2\,y)^2 (y + 0.100) = 1.9 \times 10^{-12} \simeq 0.400\,y^2$

$y = 2.2 \times 10^{-6}$ mol/L. Note, that 2.2×10^{-6} is negligible with respect to 0.100 .

(b) Let z be the molar solubility of Ag_2CrO_4. Then, $[Ag^+] = 0.100 + 2\,z$,

$[CrO_4^{2-}] = z$. Hence, $(0.100 + 2\,z)^2 z = 1.9 \times 10^{-12} \simeq (0.100)^2 z$

$z = 1.9 \times 10^{-10}$ mol/L.

6-23. See Example 6-7.

After mixing, we have

$$[Ag^+] = \frac{8.0\ g}{(169.87\ g/mol)(0.200\ L)} = 0.235\ \underline{M}$$

$$[C_2O_4^{2-}] = \frac{12.0\ g}{(134.00\ g/mol)(0.200\ L)} = 0.448\ \underline{M}$$

Hence, there is an excess of [0.448 − (0.235/2)] = 0.330 M $Na_2C_2O_4$. Let y be the molar solubility of $Ag_2C_2O_4$. Then, $[Ag^+] = 2\,y$, $[C_2O_4^{2-}] = y + 0.330$ $\therefore K_{sp(Ag_2C_2O_4)} = 1 \times 10^{-11} = (2\,y)^2(0.330 + y) \simeq (2\,y)^2(0.330)$, from which $y = 2.75 \times 10^{-6}$. Hence,

$[Ag^+] = 2\,y = 5.5 \times 10^{-6}$ M,

$[C_2O_4^{2-}] = 0.330 + 2.75 \times 10^{-6} \simeq 0.330$ M,

$[Na^+] = 2 \times 0.448 = 0.896$ M,

$[NO_3^-] = 0.235$ M.

6-24. (a) See Example 6-7 . We mix

$25.0\ mL \times 0.050\ mmol/mL = 1.25\ mmol\ K_2CrO_4$

$25.0\ mL \times 0.120\ mmol/mL = 3.00\ mmol\ AgNO_3$

Hence, 2.50 mmol of Ag^+ will react with 1.25 mmol of CrO_4^{2-}, leaving an excess of 0.50 mmol of $AgNO_3$ $\therefore$ $[Ag^+] = 0.50/50.0 = 0.0100\ \underline{M}$. Let y be the molar solubility of Ag_2CrO_4. Then, $[Ag^+] = 2y + 0.0100$, $[CrO_4^{2-}] = y$ $\therefore$ $K_{sp(Ag_2CrO_4)} = 1.9 \times 10^{-12} = (2y + 0.0100)^2 y \simeq (0.0100)^2 y$, from which $y = 1.9 \times 10^{-8}\ \underline{M}$.

(b) $[Ag^+] = 0.0100 + 2(1.9 \times 10^{-8}) \simeq 0.0100\ \underline{M}$,

$[CrO_4^{2-}] = 1.9 \times 10^{-8}\ \underline{M}$,

$[K^+] = (2 \times 1.25)/50.0 = 0.050\ \underline{M}$

$[NO_3^-] = 3.00/50.0 = 0.060\ \underline{M}$.

6-25. $25.0\ mL \times 0.040\ mmol/mL = 1.00\ mmol\ MgCl_2 \equiv 2.00\ mmol\ Cl^-$

$25.0\ mL \times 0.050\ mmol/mL = 1.25\ mmol\ AgNO_3$

At equilibrium, there will be an excess of 0.75 mmol Cl^- $\therefore$

$[Cl^-] = 0.75\ mmol/50.0\ mL = 0.0150\ \underline{M}$

$[Ag^+] = 1.8 \times 10^{-10}/0.0150 = 1.2 \times 10^{-8}\ \underline{M}$

$[Mg^{2+}] = 1.00\ mmol/50.0\ mL = 0.020\ \underline{M}$

$[NO_3^-] = 1.25\ mmol/50.0\ mL = 0.025\ \underline{M}$

6-26. After mixing and before precipitation occurs, we have

$[Mg^{2+}] = (50\ mL \times 0.060\ mmol/mL)/75\ mL = 0.040\ \underline{M}$

$[OH^-] = (25\ mL \times 0.090\ mmol/mL)/75\ mL = 0.030\ \underline{M}$

At equilibrium, there will be an excess of 0.025 $\underline{M}$ Mg^{2+}. Let y be the molar solubility of $Mg(OH)_2$. Then,

$(y + 0.025)(2y)^2 = 8.9 \times 10^{-12}$, from which $y = 9.4_3 \times 10^{-6}\ \underline{M}$ $\therefore$

$[Mg^{2+}] = 9.4_3 \times 10^{-6} + 0.025 \simeq 0.025\ \underline{M}$

$[OH^-] = 2 \times 9.4_3 \times 10^{-6} = 1.89 \times 10^{-5}\ \underline{M}$

$[H^+] = 1.00 \times 10^{-14}/1.89 \times 10^{-5} = 5.3 \times 10^{-10}\ \underline{M}$

$[NO_3^-] = (50\ mL \times 0.060\ mmol\ MgCl_2/mL \times 2\ mmol\ Cl^-/mmol\ MgCl_2)/75\ mL = 0.080\ \underline{M}$

$[Na^+] = (25\ mL \times 0.090\ mmol/mL)/75\ mL = 0.030\ \underline{M}$

6-27. Let S be the molar solubility of $BaSO_4$.

$\log K_{sp}^0 = \log K_{sp} + \log f_{Ba^{2+}} + \log f_{SO_4^{2-}} = \log K_{sp} - 4A\sqrt{\mu} - 4A\sqrt{\mu}$, or

$\log K_{sp} = \log S^2 = \log K_{sp}^0 + 8A\sqrt{\mu} = \log(1.5 \times 10^{-9}) + 8 \times 0.51\sqrt{0.100 + 4S}$, or

$$\log S^2 = -8.824 + 4.08\sqrt{0.100 + 4S} \qquad (1)$$

we solve Equation (1) by the method of successive approximations, starting with $S = \sqrt{1.5 \times 10^{-9}} = 3.873 \times 10^{-5}$ at the right side of the equation. In the third cycle we find $S = 1.72 \times 10^{-4}$ mol/L .

6-28. Proceeding as in Solution 6-12 a , we obtain

$$S = \sqrt{K_{sp}\left(\frac{[H^+] + K_a}{K_a}\right)} = \sqrt{1.6 \times 10^{-14}\left(\frac{1.0 \times 10^{-7} + 4 \times 10^{-10}}{4 \times 10^{-10}}\right)} = 2.0 \times 10^{-6} \text{ mol/L}$$

6-29. (a) $ZnC_2O_4 \rightleftharpoons Zn^{2+} + C_2O_4^{2-}$

$\quad S \qquad S \qquad \alpha_2 S$

$$K_{sp} = [Zn^{2+}][C_2O_4^{2-}] = S \cdot \alpha_2 S = \alpha_2 S^2$$

$$\therefore S = \sqrt{\frac{K_{sp}}{\alpha_2}} = \sqrt{K_{sp}\left(\frac{[H^+]^2 + K_1[H^+] + K_1K_2}{K_1K_2}\right)} \qquad (1)$$

Substituting the data in Equation (1), we obtain

$$S = \sqrt{\frac{1.5 \times 10^{-9}\left[(1.0 \times 10^{-4})^2 + (3.8 \times 10^{-2})(1.0 \times 10^{-4}) + (3.8 \times 10^{-2})(5.0 \times 10^{-5})\right]}{(3.8 \times 10^{-2})(5.0 \times 10^{-5})}} =$$

6.7×10^{-5} mol/L

(b) Similarly ,

$$S = \sqrt{\frac{1.5 \times 10^{-9}\left[(1.0 \times 10^{-5})^2 + (3.8 \times 10^{-2})(1.0 \times 10^{-5}) + (3.8 \times 10^{-2})(5.0 \times 10^{-5})\right]}{(3.8 \times 10^{-2})(5.0 \times 10^{-5})}} =$$

4.2×10^{-5} mol/L

(c) Similarly ,

$$S = \sqrt{\frac{1.5 \times 10^{-9}\left[(1.0 \times 10^{-7})^2 + (3.8 \times 10^{-2})(1.0 \times 10^{-7}) + (3.8 \times 10^{-2})(5.0 \times 10^{-5})\right]}{(3.8 \times 10^{-2})(5.0 \times 10^{-5})}} =$$

3.9×10^{-5} mol/L

Conclusion : The solubility of ZnC_2O_4 decreases with increasing pH .

6-30. See Problem 6- 12d.

$$S = \sqrt[3]{\frac{1.7 \times 10^{-10}}{4}\left(\frac{1.0 \times 10^{-4} + 6.9 \times 10^{-4}}{6.9 \times 10^{-4}}\right)^2} = 3.8 \times 10^{-4} \text{ mol/L}$$

6-31. See Problem 6-29 b.

$(4.2 \times 10^{-5}\ \text{mol/L})(153.39 \times 10^{3}\ \text{mg } ZnC_2O_4/\text{mol})(0.100\ \text{L}) = 0.644\ \text{mg } ZnC_2O_4/100\ \text{mL}$

6-32.

$$\frac{[H^+][F^-]}{[HF]} = K_a = 6.9 \times 10^{-4} \qquad (1)$$

$$[Ca^{2+}][F^-]^2 = K_{sp} = 1.7 \times 10^{-10} \qquad (2)$$

mass balance : $2[Ca^{2+}] = [F^-] + [HF]$ (3)

electroneutrality : $2[Ca^{2+}] + [H^+] = [Cl^-] + [F^-] + [OH^-] = C_{HCl} + [F^-] + [OH^-]$ (4)

$$[H^+][OH^-] = K_w = 1.00 \times 10^{-14} \qquad (5)$$

Combining Equations (1), (2) and (3),

$$\frac{2K_{sp}}{[F^-]^2} = [F^-] + \frac{[H^+][F^-]}{K_a} \qquad (6)$$

Combining Equations (2), (4) and (5),

$$\frac{2K_{sp}}{[F^-]^2} + [H^+] = C_{HCl} + [F^-] + \frac{K_w}{[H^+]} \qquad (7)$$

From Equation (6),

$$[H^+] = \frac{2K_{sp}K_a}{[F^-]^3} - K_a \qquad (6\,a)$$

Combining Equations (6 a) and (7),

$$\frac{2K_{sp}}{[F^-]^2} + \frac{2K_{sp}K_a}{[F^-]^3} - K_a = C_{HCl} + [F^-] + \frac{K_w}{\dfrac{2K_{sp}K_a}{[F^-]^3} - K_a} \qquad (8)$$

Solving Equation (8) by the method of successive approximations, we find $[F^-] = 5.03 \times 10^{-4}$ M. Substituting this value in Equation (2), we obtain $[Ca^{2+}] = S_{CaF_2} = 6.7 \times 10^{-4}$ M.

6-33. Proceeding as in Solution 6-29 a, we obtain

$$S = \sqrt{\frac{8.0 \times 10^{-28}\left[(1.0 \times 10^{-4})^2 + (1.0 \times 10^{-7})(1.0 \times 10^{-4}) + (1.0 \times 10^{-7})(1.0 \times 10^{-14})\right]}{(1.0 \times 10^{-7})(1.0 \times 10^{-14})}} =$$

8.9×10^{-8} mol/L

6-34. Since the solubility of PbS is extremely small, $[OH^-] \simeq 1 \times 10^{-7}$ M. Proceeding as in Solutions 6-29 a and 6-33, we obtain

$$S = \sqrt{\frac{8.0 \times 10^{-28}\left[(1.0 \times 10^{-7})^2 + (1.0 \times 10^{-7})(1.0 \times 10^{-7}) + (1.0 \times 10^{-7})(1.0 \times 10^{-14})\right]}{(1.0 \times 10^{-7})(1.0 \times 10^{-14})}} =$$

1.3×10^{-10} mol/L

6-35. Let S be the molar solubility of $CoCO_3$. Since $CoCO_3$ is fairly soluble, we assume that $[OH^-]$ from water can be neglected, as very small in comparison to $[OH^-]$ from the reaction

$$\underset{S}{CoCO_3} + H_2O \rightleftharpoons \underset{S}{Co^{2+}} + \underset{S}{HCO_3^-} + \underset{S}{OH^-} \qquad (1)$$

Equilibrium constant for Reaction (1) is equal to

$$K = [Co^{2+}][HCO_3^-][OH^-] = [Co^{2+}][HCO_3^-][OH^-]\frac{[CO_3^{2-}][H^+]}{[CO_3^{2-}][H^+]} = \frac{K_{sp}K_w}{K_2} =$$

$$\frac{(8 \times 10^{-13})(1.00 \times 10^{-14})}{4.8 \times 10^{-11}} = 1.67 \times 10^{-16} = S^3 \text{ or } S = \sqrt[3]{1.67 \times 10^{-16}} = 5.5 \times 10^{-6} \text{ mol/L}$$

$$\therefore (5.5 \times 10^{-6}\text{ mol/L})(118.94 \times 10^3 \text{ mg } CoCO_3/\text{mol})(0.100\text{ L}) = 0.065 \text{ mg } CoCO_3/100 \text{ mL}$$

6-36. (a) Proceeding as in Solution 6-35, we obtain

$$S = \sqrt[3]{\frac{K_{sp}K_w}{K_2}} = \sqrt[3]{\frac{(1.6 \times 10^{-9})(1.00 \times 10^{-14})}{4.8 \times 10^{-11}}} = 6.9 \times 10^{-5} \text{ mol/L}$$

(b) Proceeding as in Solution 6-35, we obtain

$$S = \sqrt[3]{\frac{K_{sp}K_w}{K_2}} = \sqrt[3]{\frac{(2 \times 10^{-14})(1.00 \times 10^{-14})}{3.2 \times 10^{-7}}} = 9 \times 10^{-8} \text{ mol/L}$$

(c)

$$\underset{S}{Ag_2CO_3} + H_2O \rightleftharpoons \underset{2S}{2Ag^+} + \underset{S}{HCO_3^-} + \underset{S}{OH^-}$$

Proceeding as in Solution 6-35, we obtain

$$K = \frac{K_{sp}K_w}{K_2} = \frac{(8.2 \times 10^{-12})(1.00 \times 10^{-14})}{4.8 \times 10^{-11}} = 1.71 \times 10^{-15} = (2S)^2 \cdot S \cdot S = 4S^4$$

$$\therefore \quad S = \sqrt[4]{\frac{1.71 \times 10^{-15}}{4}} = 1.44 \times 10^{-4} \text{ mol/L}$$

6-37.

$$NH_4^+ + CO_3^{2-} \rightleftharpoons NH_3 + HCO_3^- \qquad (1)$$

The equilibrium constant (hydrolysis constant) for Reaction (1) is equal to

$$K_h = \frac{[NH_3][HCO_3^-]}{[NH_4^+][CO_3^{2-}]} = \frac{K_w}{K_b K_2} = \frac{1.00 \times 10^{-14}}{(1.8 \times 10^{-5})(4.8 \times 10^{-11})} = 11.6$$

For precipitation of $MgCO_3$,

$[CO_3^{2-}] > 4 \times 10^{-5}/0.0125$ or $[CO_3^{2-}] > 3.2 \times 10^{-3}$ $\underline{M}$

The required NH_4^+ concentration to reduce $[CO_3^{2-}]$ to this value is equal to

$$[NH_4^+] = \frac{[NH_3]\,[HCO_3^-]}{[CO_3^{2-}]\quad K_h} = \frac{0.30 \times 0.080}{3.2 \times 10^{-3} \times 11.6} = 0.65\ \underline{M}$$

$\therefore$ an NH_4^+ concentration in excess of 0.65 $\underline{M}$ will prevent precipitation of $MgCO_3$.

6-38. (a) $[Mg^{2+}] = \dfrac{0.020\ g/L}{24.30\ g/mol} = 8.23 \times 10^{-4}\ \underline{M}$

To prevent precipitation of $Mg(OH)_2$, we should have

$[OH^-] \leq \sqrt{8.9 \times 10^{-12} / 8.23 \times 10^{-4}} = 1.04 \times 10^{-4}\ \underline{M}$

$[H^+] \geq 1.00 \times 10^{-14} / 1.04 \times 10^{-4} = 9.62 \times 10^{-11}\ \underline{M}$

$\therefore$ pH $\leq -\log(9.62 \times 10^{-11}) = 10.02$

(b) At pH = 10.50

$[OH^-] = 10^{-3.50} = 3.16 \times 10^{-4}\ \underline{M}$

$[Mg^{2+}] = 8.9 \times 10^{-12}/(3.16 \times 10^{-4})^2 = 0.89 \times 10^{-4}\ \underline{M}$

$\therefore \dfrac{(8.23 \times 10^{-4}) - (0.89 \times 10^{-4})}{8.23 \times 10^{-4}} \times 100 = 89\%$ of Mg^{2+} will be precipitated.

6-39. To reduce $[Fe^{3+}]$ to $(0.010 \times 0.001) = 1.0 \times 10^{-5}\ \underline{M}$, we should have

$[OH^-] \geq \sqrt[3]{6 \times 10^{-38} / 1.0 \times 10^{-5}} = 1.8 \times 10^{-11}\ \underline{M}$

To prevent precipitation of $Mg(OH)_2$, we should have

$[OH^-] \leq \sqrt{8.9 \times 10^{-12} / 0.010} = 3.0 \times 10^{-5}\ \underline{M}$

$\therefore$ we should have $1.8 \times 10^{-11}\ \underline{M} < [OH^-] < 3.0 \times 10^{-5}\ \underline{M}$.

6-40. (a) $[CrO_4^{2-}]$ required to start precipitation of 1) $BaCrO_4 = 1.2 \times 10^{-10}/0.030 = 4.0 \times 10^{-9}\ \underline{M}$, 2) $SrCrO_4 = 3.6 \times 10^{-5}/0.00030 = 1.2 \times 10^{-1}\ \underline{M}$, 3) $CaCrO_4 = 7.1 \times 10^{-4}/0.010 = 7.1 \times 10^{-2}\ \underline{M}$. Hence, $BaCrO_4$ is precipitated first, subsequently $CaCrO_4$, and finally $SrCrO_4$.

(b) When $[CrO_4^{2-}] > 7.1 \times 10^{-2}\ \underline{M}$, $CaCrO_4$ is coprecipitated with $BaCrO_4$. At the start of $CaCrO_4$ precipitation, $[Ba^{2+}] = 1.2 \times 10^{-10}/7.1 \times 10^{-2} = 1.7 \times 10^{-9}\ \underline{M}$, i.e., equal to $(1.7 \times 10^{-9}/0.030)\,100 = 5.7 \times 10^{-6}\%$ of the initial concentration. Hence, 99.999994% of Ba^{2+} ions have been precipitated. When $SrCrO_4$ starts to coprecipitate with $CaCrO_4$, $[Ca^{2+}] = 7.1 \times 10^{-4}/1.2 \times 10^{-1} = 5.9 \times 10^{-3}\ \underline{M}$, i.e., equal to $(5.9 \times 10^{-3}/0.010)\,100 =$ 59% of the initial concentration. Hence, only 41% of Ca^{2+} ions have been precipitated.

6-41. At $[Cl^-] > \sqrt{1.6 \times 10^{-5}/0.010} = 4.0 \times 10^{-2}$ $\underline{M}$, $PbCl_2$ starts to precipitate, whereupon $[Ag^+] = 1.8 \times 10^{-10}/4.0 \times 10^{-2} = 4.5 \times 10^{-9}$ $\underline{M}$.

6-42. (a) $[Ag^+]$ required to start precipitation of 1) AgCl $= 1.8 \times 10^{-10}/0.090 = 2.0 \times 10^{-9}$ $\underline{M}$, 2) $Ag_2CrO_4 = \sqrt{1.9 \times 10^{-12}/0.0020} = 3.1 \times 10^{-5}$ $\underline{M}$ $\therefore$ AgCl will be precipitated first

(b) At the start of Ag_2CrO_4 precipitation, $[Cl^-] = 1.8 \times 10^{-10}/3.1 \times 10^{-5} = 5.8 \times 10^{-6}$ $\underline{M}$

$\therefore$ $[(0.090 - 5.8 \times 10^{-6})/0.090]\ 100 = 99.994$ % of Cl^- ions have been precipitated.

6-43. (a) $[CrO_4^{2-}]/[Cl^-] = 1250 = 0.0010/[Cl^-]$ $\therefore$ $[Cl^-] = 8.0 \times 10^{-7}$ $\underline{M}$

$[Ag^+]$ required to start precipitation of 1) AgCl $= 1.8 \times 10^{-10}/8.0 \times 10^{-7} = 2.25 \times 10^{-4}$ $\underline{M}$, 2) $Ag_2CrO_4 = \sqrt{1.9 \times 10^{-12}/0.0010} = 4.4 \times 10^{-5}$ $\underline{M}$

$\therefore$ Ag_2CrO_4 will be precipitated first

(b) $[CrO_4^{2-}]/[Cl^-] = 1250 = 0.10/[Cl^-]$ $\therefore$ $[Cl^-] = 8.0 \times 10^{-5}$ $\underline{M}$

$[Ag^+]$ required to start precipitation of 1) AgCl $= 1.8 \times 10^{-10}/8.0 \times 10^{-5} = 2.25 \times 10^{-6}$ $\underline{M}$, 2) $Ag_2CrO_4 = \sqrt{1.9 \times 10^{-12}/0.10} = 4.4 \times 10^{-6}$ $\underline{M}$

$\therefore$ AgCl will be precipitated first.

6-44. $K_{sp(XS)}/K_{sp(Y_2S)} = [X^{2+}][S^{2-}]/[Y^+]^2[S^{-2}] = 0.010/(1.0 \times 10^{-6})^2 = 1.0 \times 10^{10}$

6-45. $[Ba^{2+}]/[Ca^{2+}] = [Ba^{2+}][CrO_4^{2-}]/[Ca^{2+}][CrO_4^{2-}] = 1.2 \times 10^{-10}/7.1 \times 10^{-4} = 1.7 \times 10^{-7}$

6-46. $K_{sp(XS)} = [X^{2-}][S^{2-}]$ (1)

$K_{sp(ZS)} = [Z^{2+}][S^{2-}]$ (2)

Dividing Equations (1) and (2),

$$\frac{K_{sp(XS)}}{K_{sp(ZS)}} = [X^{2+}]/[Z^{2+}] = 0.050/1.00 \times 10^{-6} = 5.0 \times 10^{4}$$

6-47. At the start of $Fe(OH)_3$ precipitation, $[OH^-] = \sqrt[3]{6 \times 10^{-38}/0.010} = 1.8 \times 10^{-12}$ $\underline{M}$

$\therefore$ pH $= -\log(1.00 \times 10^{-14}/1.8 \times 10^{-12}) = 2.26$

For $[Fe^{3+}] = 1.0 \times 10^{-6}$ $\underline{M}$, $[OH^-] = \sqrt[3]{6 \times 10^{-38}/1.0 \times 10^{-6}} = 3.9 \times 10^{-11}$ M $\therefore$ pH = 3.59

At the start of $Ni(OH)_2$ precipitation, $[OH^-] = \sqrt{1.6 \times 10^{-16}/0.010} = 1.26 \times 10^{-7}$ $\underline{M}$

$\therefore$ pH = 7.10

For $[Ni^{2+}] = 1.0 \times 10^{-6}$ $\underline{M}$, $[OH^-] = \sqrt{1.6 \times 10^{-16}/1.00 \times 10^{-6}} = 1.26 \times 10^{-5}$ $\therefore$ pH = 9.10

At the start of $Mg(OH)_2$ precipitation, $[OH^-] = \sqrt{8.9 \times 10^{-12}/0.010} = 2.98 \times 10^{-5}$ M $\therefore$ pH=9.47

For $[Mg^{2+}] = 1.0 \times 10^{-6}$ M, $[OH^-] = \sqrt{8.9 \times 10^{-12}/1.0 \times 10^{-6}} = 2.98 \times 10^{-3}$ M $\therefore$ pH = 11.47

$\therefore$ It is possible to separate the three cations.

6-48. (a) See Solution 6-37.

$$[CO_3^{2-}] = \frac{[NH_3][HCO_3^-]}{[NH_4^+] K_h} = \frac{(0.10)(0.10)}{(0.50)(11.6)} = 1.7 \times 10^{-3} \text{ M}$$

(b) $[Mg^{2+}][CO_3^{2-}] = (0.020)(1.7 \times 10^{-3}) = 3.4 \times 10^{-5} < 4 \times 10^{-5} = K_{sp(MgCO_3)}$

$\therefore$ $MgCO_3$ will not be precipitated

$[Ba^{2+}][CO_3^{2-}] = (0.020)(1.7 \times 10^{-3}) = 3.4 \times 10^{-5} > 1.6 \times 10^{-9} = K_{sp(BaCO_3)}$

$\therefore$ $BaCO_3$ will be precipitated

$[OH^-] = 1.8 \times 10^{-5}(0.10/0.50) = 3.6 \times 10^{-6}$ M

$[Mg^{2+}][OH^-]^2 = (0.020)(3.6 \times 10^{-6})^2 = 2.6 \times 10^{-13} < 8.9 \times 10^{-12} = K_{sp[Mg(OH)_2]}$

$\therefore$ $Mg(OH)_2$ will not be precipitated.

6-49. $$[CrO_4^{2-}] = [Ba^{2+}] + [Ca^{2+}] = \frac{K_{sp(BaCrO_4)}}{[CrO_4^{2-}]} + \frac{K_{sp(CaCrO_4)}}{[CrO_4^{2-}]}$$

or $[CrO_4^{2-}] = \sqrt{K_{sp(BaCrO_4)} + K_{sp(CaCrO_4)}}$

$\therefore$ $[CrO_4^{2-}] = \sqrt{1.2 \times 10^{-10} + 7.1 \times 10^{-4}} = 2.66 \times 10^{-2}$ M

$[Ba^{2+}] = 1.2 \times 10^{-10}/2.66 \times 10^{-2} = 4.5 \times 10^{-9}$ M

$[Ca^{2+}] = 7.1 \times 10^{-4}/2.66 \times 10^{-2} = 2.66 \times 10^{-2}$ M

6-50. (a) To reduce $[Zn^{2+}]$ to less than 1.0×10^{-6} M, we should have

$[S^{-2}] > 1.6 \times 10^{-23}/1.0 \times 10^{-6} = 1.6 \times 10^{-17}$ M

$$\therefore [H^+] < \sqrt{\frac{K_1 K_2 [H_2S]}{[S^{2-}]}} = \sqrt{\frac{(1.0 \times 10^{-7})(1.0 \times 10^{-14})(0.10)}{1.6 \times 10^{-17}}} = 2.5 \times 10^{-3} \text{ M},$$

pH $> -\log(2.5 \times 10^{-3}) = 2.60$

To prevent coprecipitation of MnS, we should have

$[S^{2-}] < 8 \times 10^{-14}/0.0010 = 8 \times 10^{-11}$ M

$$\therefore [H^+] > \sqrt{\frac{(1.0 \times 10^{-7})(1.0 \times 10^{-14})(0.10)}{8 \times 10^{-11}}} = 1.1_2 \times 10^{-6} \text{ M}, \quad \text{pH} < 5.95$$

$\therefore$ we should have $2.60 < \text{pH} < 5.95$

(b) To reduce $[Mn^{2+}]$ to less than 1.0×10^{-6} M, we should have

$[S^{2-}] > 8 \times 10^{-14} / 1.0 \times 10^{-6} = 8 \times 10^{-8}\ \underline{M}$

$\therefore\ [H^+] < \sqrt{\dfrac{(1.0 \times 10^{-7})(1.0 \times 10^{-14})(0.10)}{8 \times 10^{-8}}} = 3.5_4 \times 10^{-8}\ \underline{M}\ ,\ pH_{minimum} = 7.45$

6-51. $[S^{2-}] = \dfrac{K_1 K_2 [H_2S]}{[H^+]^2} = \dfrac{(1.0 \times 10^{-7})(1.0 \times 10^{-14})(0.10)}{(0.30)^2} = 1.1_1 \times 10^{-21}\ \underline{M}$

$\therefore [Cu^{2+}] = 4.0 \times 10^{-36}/1.1_1 \times 10^{-21} = 3.6 \times 10^{-15}\ \underline{M} \equiv$

$(3.6 \times 10^{-15}\ mol/L)(63.54 \times 10^3\ mg\ Cu^{2+}/mol) = 2.3 \times 10^{-10}\ mg\ Cu^{2+}/L$

$[Zn^{2+}] = 1.6 \times 10^{-23}/1.1_1 \times 10^{-21} = 1.44 \times 10^{-2} \equiv$

$(1.44 \times 10^{-2}\ mol/L)(65.37 \times 10^3\ mg\ Zn^{2+}/mol) = 9.4 \times 10^2\ mg\ Zn^{2+}/L$

6-52. $CaC_2O_4 + CO_3^{2-} \rightleftharpoons CaCO_3 + C_2O_4^{2-}$

$[0.100\ g\ CaC_2O_4/(0.1281\ g/mmol)](1\ mmol\ C_2O_4^{2-}/mmol\ CaC_2O_4) = 0.7806\ mmol\ C_2O_4^{2-}$

Let y mL be the required volume of Na_2CO_3. Then,

$[C_2O_4^{2-}] = 0.7806 / y$

$[CO_3^{2-}] = \dfrac{\text{initial mmol } CO_3^{2-} - \text{mmol } C_2O_4^{2-}}{y} = \dfrac{0.50\,y - 0.7806}{y}$

$\dfrac{[C_2O_4^{2-}]}{[CO_3^{2-}]} = \dfrac{K_{sp(CaC_2O_4)}}{K_{sp(CaCO_3)}} = \dfrac{1.3 \times 10^{-9}}{6.9 \times 10^{-9}} = \dfrac{0.7806/y}{(0.50\,y - 0.7806)/y}$

y = 9.8 mL 0.50 $\underline{M}$ Na_2CO_3

6-53. $PbS + CO_3^{2-} \rightleftharpoons PbCO_3 + S^{2-}$

y 1.5 - y y

$K = \dfrac{[S^{2-}]}{[CO_3^{2-}]} = \dfrac{K_{sp(PbS)}}{K_{sp(PbCO_3)}} = \dfrac{8 \times 10^{-28}}{1.5 \times 10^{-13}} = \dfrac{y}{(1.5 - y)}$

$y = 8 \times 10^{-15}\ \underline{M} \equiv (8 \times 10^{-15}\ mol/L)(239.25\ g\ PbS/mol)(10.0\ mL)(10^{-3}\ L/mL) =$

1.9×10^{-14} g PbS / 10.0 mL

6-54. 2.00 g $BaSO_4$/(0.2334 g/mmol) = 8.57 mmol $BaSO_4$

Let y be the mmol of $BaSO_4$ converted to $BaCO_3$

$BaSO_4$	+	CO_3^{2-}	$\rightleftharpoons$	$BaCO_3$	+	SO_4^{2-}
(8.57 - y) mmol		(15 - y) mmol		y mmol		y mmol

$$\frac{[SO_4^{2-}]}{[CO_3^{2-}]} = \frac{K_{sp(BaSO4)}}{K_{sp(BaCO_3)}} = \frac{1.5 \times 10^{-9}}{1.6 \times 10^{-9}} = \frac{y/10}{(15-y)/10}$$

$y = 7.26$ mmol $BaSO_4$ $\therefore$ $(7.26/8.57)\,100 = 84.7\ \%$ of $BaSO_4$ is converted to $BaCO_3$.

6-55. $$\frac{2.00 \text{ g } BaSO_4}{(233.40 \text{ g/mol})(0.020 \text{ L})} = 0.4284 = [SO_4^{2-}]$$

Let y be the required concentration of Na_2CO_3

$$BaSO_4 + CO_3^{2-} \rightleftharpoons BaCO_3 + SO_4^{2-}$$

$$y - 0.4284 \qquad\qquad 0.4284$$

$$\frac{[SO_4^{2-}]}{[CO_3^{2-}]} = \frac{K_{sp(BaSO4)}}{K_{sp(BaCO3)}} = \frac{1.5 \times 10^{-9}}{1.6 \times 10^{-9}} = \frac{0.4284}{y - 0.4284}$$

$y = 0.89\ \underline{M}\ Na_2CO_3$

6-56. $$Ag_2CO_3 + 2\,I^- \rightleftharpoons 2\,AgI + CO_3^{2-}$$

$$K = \frac{[CO_3^{2-}]}{[I^-]^2} = \frac{[CO_3^{2-}]}{[I^-]^2} \cdot \frac{[Ag^+]^2}{[Ag^+]^2} = \frac{K_{sp(Ag2CO3)}}{K^2_{sp(AgI)}} = \frac{8.2 \times 10^{-12}}{(8.5 \times 10^{-17})^2} = 1.1 \times 10^{21}$$

7-1. $[Ag(CN)_2]^- \rightleftharpoons Ag^+ + 2CN^-$

$0.10 - y \qquad y \qquad 2y$

$$\frac{y(2y)^2}{0.10 - y} = 1 \times 10^{-20}$$

$y = [Ag^+] = 6.3 \times 10^{-8}$ $\underline{M}$, $[Cl^-] = 1.8 \times 10^{-10}/6.3 \times 10^{-8} = 2.86 \times 10^{-3}$ $\underline{M}$

$\therefore$ $(2.86 \times 10^{-3}$ mol/L)(0.250 L)(74.45 g KCl/mol) = 0.053 g KCl must be added.

7-2. $[Ag(NH_3)_2]^+ \rightleftharpoons Ag^+ + 2NH_3$

$0.0010 - y \simeq 0.0010 \qquad y \qquad 10 - [2(0.0010 - y)] \simeq 10$

$K_{inst} = 5.9 \times 10^{-8} = y(10)^2/0.0010$

$y = [Ag^+] = 5.9 \times 10^{-13}$

$\therefore$ $[Ag^+][Cl^-] = (5.9 \times 10^{-13})(0.0005) = 2.95 \times 10^{-16} < 1.8 \times 10^{-10} = K_{sp(AgCl)}$

Hence, AgCl will not precipitate.

7-3. $[Cd(NH_3)_4]^{2+} \rightleftharpoons Cd^{2+} + 4NH_3$

$0.600 - y \simeq 0.600 \qquad y \qquad 4y$

$K_{inst} = 1.9 \times 10^{-7} = y(4y)^4/0.600$

$y = [Cd^{2+}] = 1.35 \times 10^{-2}$ $\underline{M}$ $\therefore$ $[S^{2-}] = 6 \times 10^{-27}/1.35 \times 10^{-2} = 4._4 \times 10^{-25}$ $\underline{M}$

7-4. $[Ag(NH_3)_2^+] + [Ag(NH_3)^+] = 0.00400$

$2[Ag(NH_3)_2^+] + [Ag(NH_3)^+] = 0.00400 \times 1.40 = 0.00560$

Solving the system of the above equations, $[Ag(NH_3)_2^+] = 0.00160$ $\underline{M}$, $[Ag(NH_3)^+] =$ 0.00240 $\underline{M}$.

$$K_{inst_1} = \frac{[Ag(NH_3)^+][NH_3]}{[Ag(NH_3)_2^+]} = 1.18 \times 10^{-4}$$

$[NH_3] = (1.18 \times 10^{-4})(0.00160)/(0.00240) = 7.87 \times 10^{-5}$ $\underline{M}$

$\therefore$ $[NH_4^+] = 1.8 \times 10^{-5}[NH_3]/[OH^-] = (1.8 \times 10^{-5})(7.87 \times 10^{-5})/(1.0 \times 10^{-4}) = 1.4 \times 10^{-5}$ $\underline{M}$

7-5. (a) Substituting in Equations (7-7), (7-8), (7-9), and (7-10) (n = 4), we obtain the following data, which are plotted in Figure 7S-1.

I^-	pI	β_0	β_1	β_2	β_3	β_4
1	0.00	-	-	0.006	0.073	0.921
0.1	1.00	0.003	0.058	0.253	0.304	0.382
0.01	2.00	0.260	0.495	0.216	0.026	0.003
0.001	3.00	0.834	0.159	0.007	-	-
0.0001	4.00	0.981	0.019	-	-	-

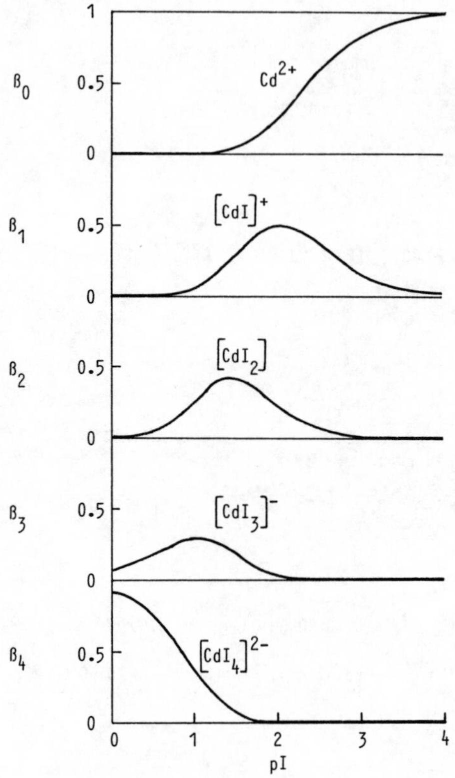

Figure 7S-1. Fraction of cadmium present as each of the complexes, as a function of pI.

(b) For the construction of the distribution diagram we obtain from part (a) the following data, which are plotted in Figure 7S-2.

pI	0	1	2	3	4
β_4	0.921	0.382	0.003	-	-
$\beta_3 + \beta_4$	0.994	0.686	0.029	-	-
$\beta_2 + \beta_3 + \beta_4$	1.000	0.939	0.245	0.007	-
$\beta_1 + \beta_2 + \beta_3 + \beta_4$	1.000	0.997	0.740	0.166	0.019

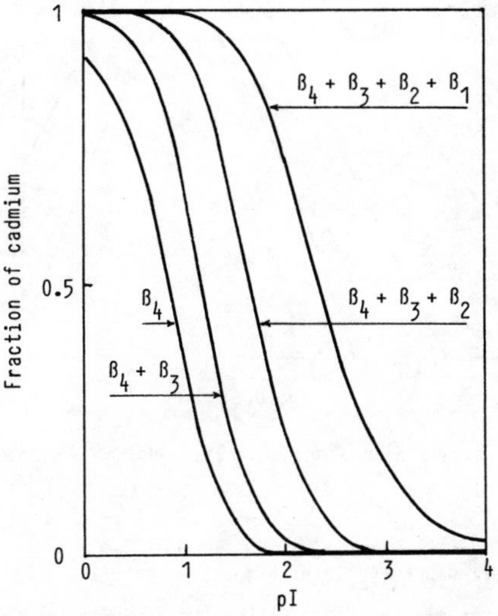

Figure 7S-2. Distribution diagram for cadmium iodide complexes.

7-6. Substituting in Equations (7-7), (7-8), (7-9), and (7-10) (n = 4), we obtain the following data, which are plotted in Figure 7S-3.

$\log[NH_3]$	$\log[Cd^{2+}] = \beta_0 C_M$	$\log[Cd(NH_3)^{2+}]$	$\log[Cd(NH_3)_2^{2+}]$	$\log[Cd(NH_3)_3^{2+}]$	$\log[Cd(NH_3)_4^{2+}]$
-5	-2.00	-4.49	-7.53	-11.23	-15.44
-4	-2.01	-3.50	-5.54	-8.24	-11.45
-3	-2.13	-2.62	-3.66	-5.36	-7.57
-2	-2.89	-2.38	-2.42	-3.12	-4.33
-1	-5.11	-3.60	-2.64	-2.34	-2.55
0	-8.63	-6.12	-4.16	-2.86	-2.07

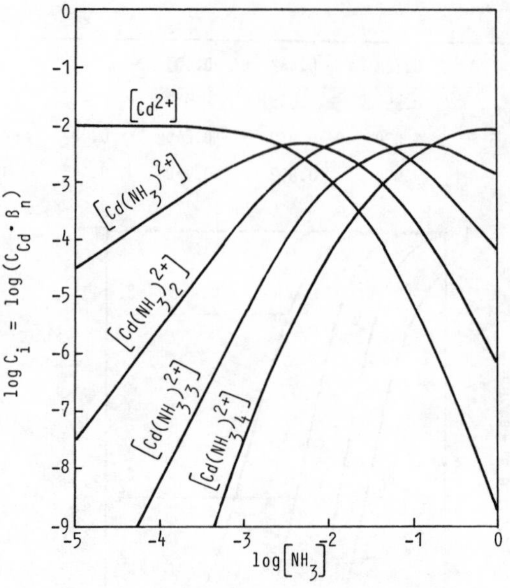

Figure 7S-3. Logarithmic diagram of the cadmium-ammonia system.

7-7. The concentration of all copper containing species are calculated using Equations (7-7), (7-8), and (7-9). However, simpler equations can be used for the calculations, as follows:

1. For $10^{-14} < [en] \ll 10^{-10.7}$, from Equation (7-7),

$$[Cu^{2+}] = \frac{C_{Cu}}{1 + K_1[en] + K_1K_2[en]^2} \simeq C_{Cu} \quad \therefore \quad \log[Cu^{2+}] = \log C_{Cu} = -2.00 \,.$$

From Equation (7-8),

$$[Cu(en)^{2+}] = \frac{C_{Cu}K_1[en]}{1 + K_1[en] + K_1K_2[en]^2} \simeq C_{Cu}K_1[en]$$

$\therefore \log[Cu(en)^{2+}] = \log C_{Cu} + \log K_1 + \log[en]$, that is, a line with a slope of +1.
For $[en] = 1.00 \times 10^{-14}$ $\underline{M}$, $\log[Cu(en)^{2+}] = -2.00 + 10.7 - 14.00 = -5.3$
From Equation (7-9),

$$[Cu(en)_2^{2+}] = \frac{C_{Cu}K_1K_2[en]^2}{1 + K_1[en] + K_1K_2[en]^2} \simeq C_{Cu}K_1K_2[en]^2$$

$\therefore \log[Cu(en)_2^{2+}] = \log C_{Cu} + \log K_1 + \log K_2 + 2\log[en]$, that is, a line with a slope of +2. For $[en] = 1.00 \times 10^{-14}\underline{M}$, $\log[Cu(en)_2^{2+}] = -2.00+10.7+8.9-28.00 = -10.4$.

2. For $10^{-8.9} \ll [en] < 10^{-7}$,

$$[Cu^{2+}] = \frac{C_{Cu}}{1 + K_1[en] + K_1K_2[en]^2} \simeq \frac{C_{Cu}}{K_1K_2[en]^2} \quad \therefore \quad \log[Cu^{2+}] =$$

$\log C_{Cu} - \log K_1 - \log K_2 - 2\log[en]$, that is, a line with a slope of -2. For $[en] = 1 \times 10^{-7}\ \underline{M}$, $\log[Cu^{2+}] = -2.00 - 10.7 - 8.9 + 14.0 = -7.6$.

$$[Cu(en)^{2+}] = \frac{C_{Cu}K_1[en]}{1 + K_1[en] + K_1K_2[en]^2} \simeq \frac{C_{Cu}}{K_2[en]} \quad \therefore \quad \log[Cu(en)^{2+}] =$$

$\log C_{Cu} - \log K_2 - \log[en]$, that is, a line with a slope of -1. For $[en] = 1 \times 10^{-7}\ \underline{M}$, $\log[Cu(en)^{2+}] = -2.00 - 8.9 + 7.0 = -3.9$.

$$[Cu(en)_2^{2+}] = \frac{C_{Cu}K_1K_2[en]^2}{1 + K_1[en] + K_1K_2[en]^2} \simeq C_{Cu} \quad \therefore \log[Cu(en)_2^{2+}] = \log C_{Cu} =$$

-2.00.

Useful points for the completion of the logarithmic diagram are points A and B (Figure 7S-4). Point A has an abscissa equal to $\log[en] = pK_1 = -10.7$. At point A, $[Cu^{2+}] = [Cu(en)^{2+}] \simeq C_{Cu}/2$

$\therefore \log[Cu^{2+}] = \log[Cu(en)^{2+}] = \log(0.0100/2) = -2.3$. Point B has an abscissa equal to $\log[en] = pK_2 = -8.9$, and an ordinate equal to -2.3.

By increasing [en] from the range $10^{-14} - 10^{-10.7}$ to the range $10^{-10.7} - 10^{-8.9}$, that is, for $10^{-10.7} < [en] < 10^{-8.9}$, the slope of the curve for Cu^{2+} changes from 0 to -1, for $[Cu(en)]^{2+}$ from +1 to -1, and for $[Cu(en)_2]^{2+}$ from +2 to +1.

The above data are used to construct the logarithmic diagram of Figure (7S-4).

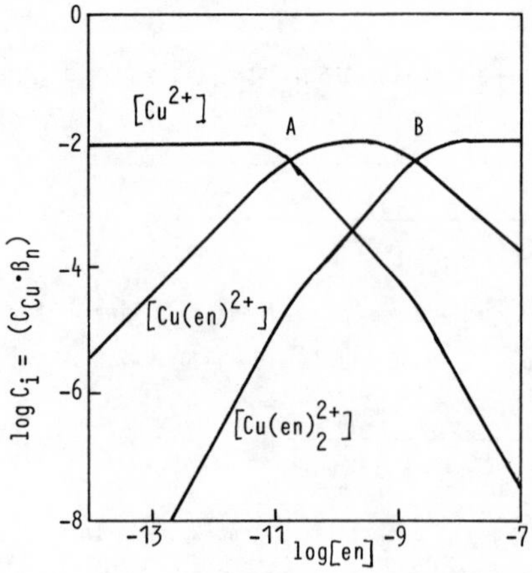

Figure 7S-4. Logarithmic diagram for the copper-ethylenediamine system.

7-8. $M_{NH_3} = \dfrac{(1000\text{ mL/L})(0.898\text{ g soln/mL})(0.280\text{ g }NH_3/\text{g soln})}{17.03\text{ g }NH_3/\text{mol}} = 14.8\text{ mol/L}$

14.33 g AgCl/(143.32 g AgCl/mol) = 0.1000 mol AgCl

If x liters NH_3 are required, then $[Ag(NH_3)_2^+] = [Cl^-] = 0.1000/x$, $[NH_3] = 14.8 - (0.2000/x)$

$$[Ag^+] = \frac{K_{sp(AgCl)}}{[Cl^-]} = \frac{[Ag(NH_3)_2^+]K_{inst}}{[NH_3]^2}$$

or $$\frac{1.8 \times 10^{-10}}{0.1000/x} = \frac{(0.1000/x)(5.9 \times 10^{-8})}{[14.8 - (0.2000/x)]^2}$$

$x = 0.135$ L $\equiv$ 135 mL NH_3 .

7-9. We have $K_1' = 10^{4.75}$, $K_2' = 10^{8.23}$, $K_3' = 10^{9.45}$, $K_4' = 10^{9.67}$. Substituting these values in Equation (7-37), for $[SCN^-] = 10^{-6}$ $\underline{M}$

$S = 1 \times 10^{-12}\left[1/10^{-6} + 10^{4.75} + 10^{8.23}(10^{-6}) + 10^{9.45}(10^{-6})^2 + 10^{9.67}(10^{-6})^3\right] =$ 1.1×10^{-6} $\underline{M}$.

Similarly, for $[SCN^-] = 10^{-5}$, 10^{-4}, 10^{-3}, 10^{-2}, and 10^{-1} $\underline{M}$, $S = 1.6 \times 10^{-7}$, 8.3×10^{-8} , 2.3×10^{-7} , 2.0×10^{-6} and 5.0×10^{-5} $\underline{M}$, respectively. These data are plotted in Figure 7S-5, from which it is seen that the solubility S is minimal for $[SCN^-] \simeq 8 \times 10^{-5}$ $\underline{M}$. The exact value is obtained by differentiating Equation (7-37) with respect to [X] and setting the first derivative equal to zero, whereupon we have

$$3K_4'[X]^4 + 2K_3'[X]^3 + K_2'[X]^2 - 1 = 0 \tag{1}$$

Substituting the data in Equation (1) and solving by the Newton - Raphson method, we obtain $[X] = [SCN^-] = 7.66 \times 10^{-5}$ $\underline{M}$.

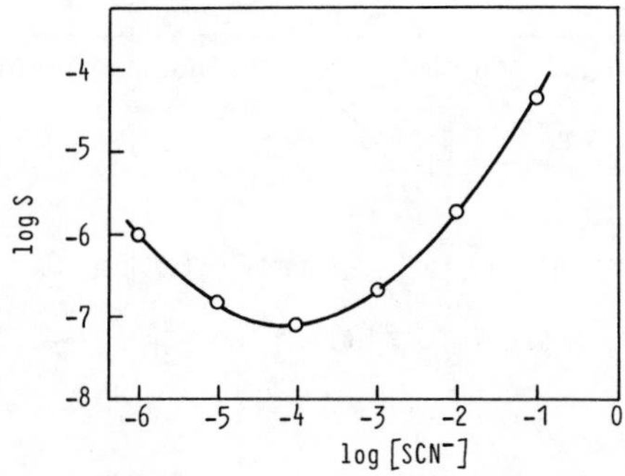

Figure 7S-5. Log solubility of AgSCN as a function of $\log[SCN^-]$.

7-10. $AgBr + 2NH_3 \rightleftharpoons [Ag(NH_3)_2]^+ + Br^-$

0.0050 mol $AgBr/0.500$ L $= 0.0100$ mol/L $= [Ag(NH_3)_2^+] = [Br^-]$

$[Ag^+] = K_{sp(AgBr)}/[Br^-] = 5 \times 10^{-13}/0.0100 = 5 \times 10^{-11}$ $\underline{M}$

$$\therefore \quad \frac{[Ag^+][NH_3]^2}{[Ag(NH_3)_2^+]} = \frac{(5 \times 10^{-11})[NH_3]^2}{0.0100 - 5 \times 10^{-11}} = 5.9 \times 10^{-8}$$

$[NH_3] = 3.44$ $\underline{M}$ = concentration of free (uncomplexed) ammonia. Since 0.0100 mol $[Ag(NH_3)_2]^+$ contains 0.0200 mol NH_3, the molarity of the ammonia solution should be equal to $3.44 + 0.02 = 3.46$ $\underline{M}$.

7-11. $AgBr + 2S_2O_3^{2-} \rightleftharpoons [Ag(S_2O_3)_2]^{3-} + Br^-$

0.0939 g AgBr/(187.77 g/mol) $= 5.00 \times 10^{-4}$ mol AgBr. Let y L be the volume of 1 $\underline{M}$ $Na_2S_2O_3$ required to dissolve AgBr. Then, $[Ag(S_2O_3)_2^{3-}] = [Br^-] = 5.00 \times 10^{-4}$ $\underline{M}$.

$$\frac{[Ag(S_2O_3)_2^{3-}][Br^-]}{[S_2O_3^{2-}]^2} \cdot \frac{[Ag^+]}{[Ag^+]} = \frac{K_{sp(AgBr)}}{K_{inst}} = \frac{5 \times 10^{-13}}{1 \times 10^{-13}} = \frac{(5.00 \times 10^{-4})^2}{(y - 0.00100)^2}$$

$y = 0.00122$ L 1 $\underline{M}$ $Na_2S_2O_3 \equiv 12.2$ mL 0.100 $\underline{M}$ $Na_2S_2O_3$.

7-12. $[S^{2-}] = 1.00 \times 10^{-22}/(0.3)^2 = 1.1 \times 10^{-21}$ $\underline{M}$ $\therefore$ $[Cd^{2+}] = 6 \times 10^{-27}/1.1 \times 10^{-21} = 5.5 \times 10^{-6}$ $\underline{M}$.
Hence, in the 0.3 $\underline{M}$ HI solution in which a trace of CdS precipitates, we have $[CdI_4^{2-}] = 0.060 - 5.5 \times 10^{-6} \simeq 0.060$ $\underline{M}$.

$$\therefore K_{inst} = \frac{[Cd^{2+}][I^-]^4}{[CdI_4^{2-}]} = \frac{(5.5 \times 10^{-6})(0.3)^4}{0.060} = 7 \times 10^{-7}$$

7-13. $$\beta_0 = \frac{[Ag^+]}{0.00494} = \frac{1}{1 + (2.0 \times 10^3)(0.089) + (2.0 \times 10^3)(8.5 \times 10^3)(0.089)^2} = 7.4 \times 10^{-6}$$

$$\therefore [Ag^+] = (0.00494)(7.4 \times 10^{-6}) = 3.7 \times 10^{-8}\ \underline{M}$$

7-14. $[OH^-] = \sqrt{1.8 \times 10^{-5}} = 4.24 \times 10^{-3}\ \underline{M}$ $\therefore [H^+] = 1.00 \times 10^{-14}/4.24 \times 10^{-3} = 2.36 \times 10^{-12}\ \underline{M}$.

$$K_{sp(Ag_2S)} = [Ag^+]^2[S^{2-}] = (2\beta_0 S)^2(\alpha_2 S) = 4\beta_0^2\alpha_2 S^3$$

$$S = \sqrt[3]{\frac{K_{sp(Ag_2S)}}{4\alpha_2}\left(\frac{1}{\beta_0}\right)^2} \qquad (1)$$

From Equation (5-56), for $[H^+] = 2.36 \times 10^{-12}\ \underline{M}$,

$$\alpha_2 = \frac{(1.0 \times 10^{-7})(1.0 \times 10^{-14})}{(2.36 \times 10^{-12})^2 + (1.0 \times 10^{-7})(2.36 \times 10^{-12}) + (1.0 \times 10^{-7})(1.0 \times 10^{-14})} = 4.22 \times 10^{-3}$$

From Equation (7-7), $1/\beta_0 = 1 + (2.0 \times 10^3)(1.00) + (2.0 \times 10^3)(8.5 \times 10^3)(1.00)^2 = 1.7 \times 10^7$.

Substituting the values of K_{sp}, α_2 and β_0 in Equation (1), we obtain

$$S = \sqrt[3]{\frac{1 \times 10^{-50}}{4 \times 4.22 \times 10^{-3}}(1.7 \times 10^7)^2} = 5.6 \times 10^{-12}\ \text{mol/L}$$

7-15. (a) See Example 7-9.

$$\frac{S^2}{(0.100 - S)^2} = \frac{K_{sp(AgBr)}}{K_{inst}} = \frac{5 \times 10^{-13}}{5.9 \times 10^{-8}}$$

$$S = 2.75 \times 10^{-3}\ \text{mol/L}$$

(b) Similarly,

$$\frac{S^2}{(0.100 - S)^2} = \frac{K_{sp(AgI)}}{K_{inst}} = \frac{8.5 \times 10^{-17}}{5.9 \times 10^{-8}}, \quad S = 3.80 \times 10^{-6}\ \text{mol/L}$$

8-1. $S_2O_8^{2-}$, H_2O_2 , MnO_4^- , $HClO$, $Cr_2O_7^{2-}$, Cu^{2+} , Cd^{2+} , K^+

8-2. Ce^{3+} , Cl^- , Br^- , H_3AsO_3 , I^- , H_2S , Ni , K

8-3. (a) $E = E^o_{[Zn(CN)_4]^{2-},Zn} - \frac{0.05916}{2}\log\frac{[CN^-]^4}{[Zn(CN)_4^{2-}]}$

(b) $E = E^o_{PbO_2,Pb} - \frac{0.05916}{2}\log\frac{[Pb^{2+}]}{[H^+]^4}$

(c) $E = E^o_{CuBr,Cu} - 0.05916\log\frac{1}{[Cu^{2+}][Br^-]}$

(d) $E = E^o_{NO_2^-,NO} - 0.05916\log\frac{P_{NO}[OH^-]^2}{[NO_2^-]}$

(e) $E = E^o_{CdS,Cd} - \frac{0.05916}{2}\log\frac{P_{H_2S}}{[H^+]^2}$

(f) $E = E^o_{Hg_2Cl_2,Hg} - \frac{0.05916}{2}\log[Cl^-]^2 = E^o_{Hg_2Cl_2,Hg} - 0.05916\log[Cl^-]$

8-4. (a) $E^o_{H_2O_2,H_2O} = +1.77 \gg +0.5355 = E^o_{I_2,I^-}$ ∴ the reaction will proceed from right to left. This can also be deduced from the value of the equilibrium constant which is equal to $K = 10^{16.903 \times 2(0.5355 - 1.77)} = 1.8 \times 10^{-42}$.

(b) $E^o_{AgBr,Ag} = +0.095 \gg -0.763 = E^o_{Zn^{2+},Zn}$ ∴ the reaction will proceed from left to right.

(c) $E^o_{Ag^+,Ag} = +0.7994 \gg -0.255 = E^o_{V^{3+},V^{2+}}$ ∴ the reaction will proceed from right to left.

(d) $E^o_{Ce^{4+},Ce^{3+}\ (H_2SO_4)} = +1.74 \gg 0.356 = E^o_{[Fe(CN)_6]^{3-},[Fe(CN)_6]^{4-}}$ ∴ the reaction will proceed from right to left.

8-5. (a) $E = E^o_{Ni^{2+},Ni} - \frac{0.05916}{2}\log\frac{1}{[Ni^{2+}]} = -0.250 - \frac{0.05916}{2}\log\frac{[NH_3]^4}{[Ni(NH_3)_4^{2+}] \times K_{inst}}$ (1)

For $[NH_3] = [Ni(NH_3)_4^{2+}] = 1.00\ \underline{M}$, Equation (1) becomes

$E^o_{[Ni(NH_3)_4^{2+}],Ni} = -0.250 - \frac{0.05916}{2}\log\frac{1^4}{1 \times (1 \times 10^{-8})} = -0.487$ V

(b) $E^0_{Mn(OH)_2,Mn} = E^0_{Mn^{2+},Mn} + \frac{0.05916}{2}\log[Mn^{2+}] = -1.18 + \frac{0.05916}{2}\log\frac{K_{sp[Mn(OH)2]}}{[OH^-]^2} =$

$-1.18 + \frac{0.05916}{2}\log\frac{2 \times 10^{-13}}{1^2} = -1.56\ V$

8-6. See Example 8-15 .

In order for the reaction to be completed by 99.9%, the equilibrium constant should be equal to at least

$$K = \frac{[A_{red}][B_{ox}]^5}{[A_{ox}][B_{red}]^5} = \frac{(0.999)(0.999)^5}{(0.001)(0.001)^5} = 9.94 \times 10^{17}$$

Substituting the value of K in Equation (8-11), we have

$\log(9.94 \times 10^{17}) = 16.903 \times 5 \times (E^0_A - E^0_B)$, from which $E^0_A - E^0_B = 0.213\ V$

8-7. $E = E^0_{AgI,Ag} - 0.05916\log[I^-] = E^0_{AgI,Ag} - 0.05916\log(8.5 \times 10^{-17}) + 0.05916\log[Ag^+]$ (1)

$E = E^0_{Ag^+,Ag} + 0.05916\log[Ag^+] = +0.7994 + 0.05916\log[Ag^+]$ (2)

Combining Equations (1) and (2), we have

$E^0_{AgI,Ag} = +0.7994 + 0.05916\log(8.5 \times 10^{-17}) = -0.151\ V$

8-8. $E = E^0_{PbSO_4,Pb} - \frac{0.05916}{2}\log[SO_4^{2-}] = E^0_{PbSO_4,Pb} - \frac{0.05916}{2}\log(1.3 \times 10^{-8}) +$

$\frac{0.05916}{2}\log[Pb^{2+}]$ (1)

$E = E^0_{Pb^{2+},Pb} + \frac{0.05916}{2}\log[Pb^{2+}] = -0.126 + \frac{0.05916}{2}\log[Pb^{2+}]$ (2)

Combining Equations (1) and (2), we have

$E^0_{PbSO_4,Pb} = -0.126 + \frac{0.05916}{2}\log(1.3 \times 10^{-8}) = -0.359\ V$

8-9. $E = +0.7994 + \frac{0.05916}{2}\log[Ag^+]^2 = +0.7994 + \frac{0.05916}{2}\log\frac{K_{sp(Ag_2S)}}{[S^{2-}]}$ (1)

For $[S^{2-}] = 1.00\ \underline{M}$, Equation (1) becomes

$E^0_{Ag_2S,Ag} = +0.7994 + \frac{0.05916}{2}\log(1 \times 10^{-50}) = -0.680\ V$

8-10. $+0.2412 = 0.2801 - 0.05916\log[Cl^-]$ or $[Cl^-] = 4.55\ \underline{M}$

∴ The molar solubility of KCl is equal to 4.55 mol/L .

8-11. $E = +0.337 + \frac{0.05916}{2} \log [Cu^{2+}] = +0.337 + \frac{0.05916}{2} \log \frac{K_{sp[Cu(OH)_2]}}{[OH^-]^2}$ (1)

For $[OH^-] = 1.00$ M, Equation (1) becomes

$$E_{Cu(OH)_2,Cu} = +0.337 + \frac{0.05916}{2} \log (1.6 \times 10^{-19}) = -0.219 \text{ V}$$

8-12. (a) The half-reaction $ClO_4^- + 8H^+ + 7e \rightleftharpoons \frac{1}{2}Cl_2 + 4H_2O$ is the sum of the other two half reactions.

$$\therefore \quad E^0_{ClO_4^-,Cl_2} = \frac{(2 \times 1.19) + (5 \times 1.49)}{7} = +1.40 \text{ V}$$

(b) $E = E^0_{Hg^{2+}, Hg} - \frac{0.05916}{2} \log \frac{1}{[Hg^{2+}]} = +0.854 - \frac{0.05916}{2} \log \frac{[CH_3COO^-]^2}{[(CH_3COO)_2Hg] \times K_{inst}}$ (1)

For $[CH_3COO^-] = [(CH_3COO)_2Hg] = 1.00$ M, Equation (1) becomes

$$E^0_{[(CH_3COO)_2Hg], Hg} = +0.854 - \frac{0.05916}{2} \log \frac{1^4}{1 \times (4.0 \times 10^{-9})} = +0.606 \text{ V}$$

(c) $E = E^0_{Hg^{2+}, Hg} - \frac{0.05916}{2} \log \frac{1}{[Hg^{2+}]} = +0.854 - \frac{0.05916}{2} \log \frac{[HgY^{2-}] \times K_f}{[Y^{4-}]}$ (2)

For $[Y^{4-}] = [HgY^{2-}] = 1.00$ M, Equation (2) becomes

$$E^0_{[HgY]^{2-}, Hg} = +0.854 - \frac{0.05916}{2} \log \frac{1 \times (6.3 \times 10^{21})}{1} = 0.209 \text{ V}$$

8-13. (a) $E = E^0_{Ag^+,Ag} + 0.05916 \log a_{Ag^+} = +0.7994 + 0.05916 \log 0.100 + 0.05916 \log f_{Ag^+} =$
$+0.7402 + 0.05916 \log f_{Ag^+}$ (1)

$-\log f_{Ag^+} = 0.51 (1)^2 \sqrt{0.100} / (1 + \sqrt{0.100}) = 0.1225$ or $f_{Ag^+} = 0.754$

$\therefore$ Equation (1) becomes $E = +0.7402 + 0.05916 \log 0.754 = +0.7330$ V

(b) $\mu = 0.100 + 0.175 = 0.275 \quad \therefore \quad -\log f_{Ag^+} = 0.51 (1)^2 \sqrt{0.275} / (1 + \sqrt{0.275}) = 0.1754$

or $f_{Ag^+} = 0.668$. Substituting this value in Equation (1), we have

$E = +0.7402 + 0.05916 \log 0.668 = +0.7298$ V

8-14. $+1.14 = +1.09 + \frac{0.05916}{6} \log \frac{(0.200)(1.00)^{14}}{[Cr^{3+}]^2}$ or $[Cr^{3+}] = 0.001303$ M

$\equiv 0.001303 \text{ mol } CrCl_3/L \times 158.36 \text{ g/mol} = 0.206 \text{ g } CrCl_3/L$.

8-15. (a) $E = -0.151 - 0.05916 \log (0.00500) = -0.015$ V

(b) After mixing, $[Ag^+] = (50.0 \times 0.0800 - 50.00 \times 0.0500)$ mmol/ 90.0 mL = 0.01667 M

$\therefore \quad E = +0.7994 + 0.05916 \log (0.01667) = +0.6942$ V

(c) After mixing, $[I^-] = (50.0 \times 0.0800 - 50.0 \times 0.0500)$ mmol/ 90.0 mL = 0.01667 M

$\therefore \quad E = -0.151 - 0.05916 \log (0.01667) = -0.046$ V

(d) $E = E^0_{Ag^+,Ag} - 0.05916 \log \dfrac{1}{[Ag^+]} = +0.7994 - 0.05916 \log \dfrac{[S_2O_3^{2-}]^2}{[Ag(S_2O_3)_2^{3-}] \times K_{inst}} =$

$+0.7994 - 0.05916 \log \dfrac{(1.00)^2}{(0.00100)(1 \times 10^{-13})} = -0.14$ V

8-16. (a) $Ce^{4+} + Fe^{2+} \rightleftharpoons Ce^{3+} + Fe^{3+}$

25.0 mL Ce^{4+} X 0.100 mmol/mL = 2.50 mmol Ce^{4+} react with Fe^{2+} forming 2.50 mmol of Fe^{3+} $\therefore$ the mixture contains 2.50 mmol of Fe^{3+} and (50 mL X 0.100 mmol/mL) - 2.50 = 2.50 mmol Fe^{2+}. Hence,

$E = +0.771 - 0.05916 \log \dfrac{2.50/75.0}{2.50/75.0} = +0.771$ V .

(b) Since there is a large excess of KI, the following reaction takes place :

$H_2O_2 + 3I^- + 2H^+ \rightleftharpoons [I_3]^- + 2H_2O$

10.0 mL H_2O_2 X 0.0100 mmol/mL = 0.100 mmol H_2O_2 reacts with 0.300 mmol of I^- forming 0.100 mmol of $[I_3]^-$ $\therefore$ the mixture contains 0.100 mmol of $[I_3]^-$ and (40.0 mL X 0.250 mmol/mL) - 0.300 = 9.70 mmol of I^-. Hence,

$E = +0.536 - \dfrac{0.05916}{2} \log \dfrac{(9.70/50.0)^3}{(0.100/50.0)} = +0.519$ V .

8-17. (a) E^0 vs. SCE = $-0.763 - 0.2412 = -1.004$ V

(b) $E^{0\prime}$ vs. SCE = $+1.28 - 0.2412 = +1.04$ V

(c) E^0 vs. SCE = $-0.136 - 0.2412 = -0.377$ V

8-18. $2AgCl + H_2 \rightleftharpoons 2Ag + 2H^+ + 2Cl^-$ (cell reaction) (1)

$E_{cell} = +0.2224 - 0.000 - \dfrac{0.05916}{2} \log \dfrac{(0.0100)^2(0.100)^2}{0.50} = +0.391$ V

$K = 10^{16.903 \times 2 \times 0.2224} = 3.3 \times 10^7$

The positive E_{cell} denotes that Equation (1) represents the spontaneous cell reaction, and that the silver electrode is the positive electrode of the galvanic cell, whereas the platinum electrode is the negative electrode.

8-19. (a) $E_{cell} = +0.337 - 0.7994 - \frac{0.05916}{2} \log \frac{(0.050)^2}{0.200} = -0.406$ V

(b) $E_{cell} = +0.2224 - \left[-0.356 - \frac{0.05916}{2} \log(0.050)\right] = +0.540$ V

(c) $E_{cell} = \left[0.000 - \frac{0.05916}{2} \log \frac{0.50}{(0.200)^2}\right] - (0.2224 - 0.05916 \log 0.100) = -0.314$ V

(d) $E_{cell} = \left[0.000 - \frac{0.05916}{2} \log \frac{1.00}{(1.00)^2}\right] - \left[0.000 - \frac{0.05916}{2} \log \frac{1.00}{(1.00 \times 10^{-3})^2}\right] = +0.177$ V

(e) $E_{cell} = \left[1.33 - \frac{0.05916}{6} \log \frac{(0.100)^2}{(0.100)(1.00)^{14}}\right] - (-0.763 - \frac{0.05916}{2} \log \frac{1}{0.100}) = +2.13$ V

(f) $E_{cell} = (+0.7994 + 0.05916 \log \sqrt{\frac{1 \times 10^{-11}}{1.00}}) - 0.2412 = +0.233$ V

(g) At the platinum electrode, $[H^+] = 1.8 \times 10^{-5}(0.100/0.100) = 1.8 \times 10^{-5}$ M

$\therefore E_{cell} = 0.2412 - \left[0.000 - \frac{0.05916}{2} \log \frac{1}{(1.8 \times 10^{-5})^2}\right] = +0.522$ V

8-20. $E_{cell} = -0.438 = (0.000 - \frac{0.05916}{2} \log \frac{1.00}{[H^+]^2}) - 0.2224$ or $[H^+] = 2.27 \times 10^{-4}$ M

$\therefore$ pH $= -\log(2.27 \times 10^{-4}) = 3.64$

8-21. Let y be the normality of the reducing solution. Initially, each beaker contains 100 mL X 0.100 meq/mL = 10.0 meq Fe^{2+} and 10.0 meq Fe^{3+}. After the addition of the reducing solution to one of the two beakers, that beaker contains (10.0 + 10.0 y) meq of Fe^{2+} and (10.0 - 10.0 y) meq of Fe^{3+}

$\therefore +0.1183 = (+0.771 - 0.05916 \log \frac{0.100}{0.100}) - \left[+0.771 - 0.05916 \log \frac{(10.0 + 10.0\,y)/110}{(10.0 - 10.0\,y)/110}\right]$

or y = 0.98 . Hence, the reducing solution is 0.98 N .

8-22. $E_{cell} = E_{Pt} - E_{SCE} = (+0.699 - \frac{0.05916}{2} \log \frac{[H_2Q]}{[Q][H^+]^2}) - 0.2412$

or $E_{cell} = 0.458 - 0.05916\,\text{pH}$ (1)

Substituting pH in Equation (1) with integer values between 0 and 8, we obtain the following results :

pH :	0	1	2	3	4	5	6	7	8
E, V:	+0.458	+0.399	+0.340	+0.281	+0.221	+0.162	+0.103	+0.044	-0.015

8-23. $E_{cell} = 0 = E_{Hg} - E_{Ag} = +0.280 - (-0.151 - 0.05916 \log [I^-])$ or $[I^-] = 5.18 \times 10^{-8}$ M .

8-24. The potentials of the half reactions which take place at the electrodes are equal to

$E_{Cu^{2+},Cu} = +0.337 - \frac{0.05916}{2} \log \frac{1}{0.0200} = +0.287$ V for the cathode, and

$E_{O_2,H_2O} = +1.229 - \frac{0.05916}{4} \log \frac{1}{(1.00 \times 10^{-3})^4(1.00)} = +1.052$ V for the anode.

∴ the voltage E required to initiate the deposition of copper, according to the overall reaction $2Cu^{2+} + 2H_2O \rightleftharpoons 2Cu + 4H^+ + O_2$, should be greater than $(+1.052 - 0.287)$ V, that is $E > +0.765$ V.

8-25. Since $[M^{2+}] / [X^{2+}] = 10.0$, we have

$+0.150 = E^0_{cell} - \frac{0.05916}{2} \log 10$ or $E^0_{cell} = +0.180$ V

∴ $E_{cell} = +0.180 - \frac{0.05916}{2} \log \frac{0.100}{1.00 \times 10^{-5}} = +0.062$ V

8-26. (a) $E_{cell} = E^0_{Cu^{2+},Cu} - E^0_{Zn^{2+},Zn} - \frac{0.05916}{2} \log \frac{[Zn^{2+}]}{[Cu^{2+}]} = +0.337 - (-0.763) - \frac{0.05916}{2} \log \frac{0.200}{0.0200} = 1.070$ V

(b) The copper electrode is the positive electrode (cathode) of the cell, whereas the zinc electrode is the negative electrode (anode)

(c) $Zn + Cu^{2+} \rightleftharpoons Zn^{2+} + Cu$ (1)

(d) For the cell reaction (1) we have $K = 10^{16.903 \times 2 \times [0.337 - (-0.763)]} = 1.5 \times 10^{37}$.

Since $K \gg 1$, reaction (1) is quantitative. Hence, at equilibrium we have

$E_{Zn} = -0.763 + \frac{0.05916}{2} \log (0.200 + 0.0200) = -0.782 \text{ V} = E_{Cu}$

8-27. For the two galvanic cells, we have

$+0.4010 = (+0.7994 + 0.05916 \log x) - 0.2801$, from which $x = 0.01000$ M ;

$+0.4601 = (+0.7994 + 0.05916 \log y) - 0.2801$, from which $y = 0.1000$ M

Suppose that a mL of 0.01000 M Ag^+ should be mixed with b mL of 0.1000 M Ag^+.

We have $(0.01000\,a + 0.1000\,b)/(a+b) = 0.0400$ or $a : b = 2 : 1$.

8-28. (a) $E_{cell} = [+0.7994 + 0.05916 \log (0.100)] - 0.000 = +0.740$ V

(b) $1/\beta_0 = 1.7 \times 10^5$ [Example 7-9] ∴ $[Ag^+] = \beta_0 (0.100) = 0.100/1.7 \times 10^5 = 5.88 \times 10^{-7}$ M, and $E_{cell} = [+0.7994 + 0.05916 \log (5.88 \times 10^{-7})] - 0.000 = +0.431$ V.

8-29. $+0.0784 = (+0.7994 + 0.05916 \log x) - (+0.7994 + 0.05916 \log 0.0100)$ or $x = [AgNO_3] = 0.212$ M .

8-30. See Example (8-29). For the right-hand and left-hand half-cells, we have

$$E_1 = +1.51 - \frac{0.05916}{5} \log \frac{0.00100}{(0.0100)(1.00)^8} = +1.52 \text{ V}$$

$$E_2 = +0.771 - 0.05916 \log (0.100/0.0100) = +0.712 \text{ V}$$

$$\therefore E_{cell} = +1.52 - 0.712 = +0.81 \text{ V}$$

The equilibrium constant for the cell-reaction

$$MnO_4^- + 5Fe^{2+} + 8H^+ \rightleftharpoons Mn^{2+} + 5Fe^{3+} + 4H_2O \qquad (1)$$

is equal to $K = 2.9 \times 10^{62}$ [Example (8-29)] ∴ Reaction (1) is quantitative. Initially, the Fe^{2+} is in excess relative to MnO_4^- ∴ $[MnO_4^-]$ will be reduced practically by 0.0100 M, $[Fe^{2+}]$ by $5 \times 0.0100 = 0.0500$ M becoming 0.0500 M , while $[Fe^{3+}]$ will be increased by 0.0500 M becoming 0.0600 M. Hence, at equilibrium the potential of the left-hand half-cell is equal to $E_1' = +0.771 - 0.05916 \log (0.0500/0.0600) = +0.776$ V, and this is also the value of the potential E_2' of the right-hand half-cell. At equilibrium $E_{cell} = E_1' - E_2' = 0$ V .

8-31. $$pH = 9.4 = pK_a + \log \frac{[CN^-]}{[HCN]} = 9.4 + \log \frac{[CN^-]}{[HCN]} \text{ or } \frac{[CN^-]}{[HCN]} = 1 \qquad (1)$$

$$[CN^-] + [HCN] = 0.20 \qquad (2)$$

Solving the simultaneous Equations (1) and (2) gives $[CN^-] = [HCN] = 0.100$ M . The cell reaction is $2[Ag(CN)_2^-] + Cu \rightleftharpoons 2Ag + Cu^{2+} + 4CN^-$

$$\therefore E_{cell} = E^0_{[Ag(CN)_2]^-,Ag} - E^0_{Cu^{2+},Cu} - \frac{0.05916}{2} \log \frac{[Cu^{2+}][CN^-]^4}{[Ag(CN)_2^-]^2} =$$

$$-0.31 - 0.337 - \frac{0.05916}{2} \log \frac{(0.040)(0.100)^4}{(0.020)^2} = -0.59 \text{ V}$$

8-32. $$AgBr + e \rightleftharpoons Ag + Br^- , \quad E^0_{AgBr,Ag} = +0.095 \text{ V} \qquad (1)$$

$$V^{3+} + e \rightleftharpoons V^{2+} , \quad E^0_{V^{3+},V^{2+}} = -0.255 \text{ V} \qquad (2)$$

Subtracting Equation (2) from Equation (1), we have

$$AgBr + V^{2+} \rightleftharpoons Ag + V^{3+} + Br^- , \quad E^0_{cell} = +0.350 \text{ V}$$

Hence, $K = 10^{16.903 \times 1 \times 0.350} = 8.2 \times 10^5$

8-33. (a) $K = 10^{16.903 \times 2\,(0.536\,-\,0.559)} = 0.167$

(b) $K = 10^{16.903 \times 2\,(0.771\,-\,0.141)} = 2.0 \times 10^{21}$

(c) $K = 10^{16.903 \times 5\,(1.51\,-\,0.771)} = 3 \times 10^{62}$

(d) $K = 10^{16.903 \times 2\,(0.403\,-\,0.000)} = 4.2 \times 10^{13}$

(e) $K = 10^{16.903 \times 2\,[0.7994\,-\,(-0.403)]} = 4.4 \times 10^{40}$

(f) $K = 10^{16.903 \times 2\,[-0.151\,-\,(-0.763)]} = 4.9 \times 10^{20}$

(g) $K = 10^{16.903 \times 2\,[0.771\,-\,(-0.44)]} = 9 \times 10^{40}$

8-34. The equilibrium constant for the reaction $2Cu^+ \rightleftharpoons Cu^{2+} + Cu$ is equal to

$K = 10^{16.903 \times 1\,(0.521\,-\,0.153)} = 1.66 \times 10^{6}$

$\therefore\ [Cu^{2+}]/(7.76 \times 10^{-4})^2 = 1.66 \times 10^{6}$ or $[Cu^{2+}] = 1.00\ \underline{M}$

8-35. The reaction $2H_2 + O_2 \rightleftharpoons 2H_2O\ (l)$ takes place in the cell

$Pt, H_2 \mid H^+ \mid O_2, Pt$

right-hand half-cell : $O_2 + 4H^+ + 4e \rightleftharpoons 2H_2O\ (l),\qquad E^0_{O_2,H_2O} = +1.229\ V$ (1)

left-hand half-cell : $2H^+ + 2e \rightleftharpoons H_2,\qquad E^0_{H^+,H_2} = 0.000\ V$ (2)

By multiplying Equation (2) by 2 and subtracting the result from Equation (1), we have

$2H_2 + O_2 \rightleftharpoons 2H_2O\ (l),\qquad E^0_{cell} = +1.229\ V$

$\therefore\ K = 10^{16.903 \times 4 \times 1.229} = 1.2 \times 10^{83}$

8-36. $K = 10^{16.903 \times 2\,[0.771\,-\,(-0.440)]} = 8.7 \times 10^{40}$

8-37. $K = 10^{16.903 \times 6\,(1.33\,-\,0.771)} = 5 \times 10^{56}$

8-38. $O_2 + 2H_2O + 4e \rightleftharpoons 4\,OH^-,\qquad E^0_1 = +0.401\ V$ (1)

$O_2 + 4H^+ + 4e \rightleftharpoons 2H_2O,\qquad E^0_2 = +1.229\ V$ (2)

Subtracting Equation (2) from Equation (1), we have

$4H_2O \rightleftharpoons 4H^+ + 4\,OH^-,\qquad E^0_{1-2} = -0.828\ V$ (3)

At equilibrium, we have

$$E_{1-2} = 0 = E^o_{1-2} - \frac{0.05916}{4} \log [H^+]^4[OH^-]^4 = -0.828 - 0.05916 \log K_w \quad \text{or} \quad K_w = 1.0 \times 10^{-14}$$

8-39. We have

$$+0.6506 = \left[0.00 - \frac{0.05916}{2} \log \frac{0.90}{(0.100)^2}\right] - \left[0.00 - \frac{0.05916}{2} \log \frac{0.90}{(K_w/0.0100)^2}\right]$$

from which $K_w = 1.00 \times 10^{-14}$

8-40. (a) See Example 8-16, 3rd method.

$$+0.268 = +0.789 - (0.05916/2) \log (1/[Hg_2^{2+}]) \quad \text{or} \quad [Hg_2^{2+}] = 2.4 \times 10^{-18}\ \underline{M}$$

$$\therefore K_{sp(Hg_2Cl_2)} = 2.4 \times 10^{-18}\ (1.00)^2 = 2.4 \times 10^{-18}$$

(b) $+0.2224 = +0.7994 - 0.05916 \log (1/[Ag^+])$ or $[Ag^+] = 1.8 \times 10^{-10}\ \underline{M}$

$$\therefore K_{sp(AgCl)} = 1.8 \times 10^{-10}\ (1.00) = 1.8 \times 10^{-10}$$

(c) $+0.446 = +0.7994 - 0.05916 \log (1/[Ag^+])$ or $[Ag^+] = 1.06 \times 10^{-6}\ \underline{M}$

$$\therefore K_{sp(Ag_2CrO_4)} = (1.06 \times 10^{-6})^2\ (1.00) = 1.1 \times 10^{-12}$$

(d) $-0.185 = +0.521 - 0.05916 \log (1/[Cu^+])$ or $[Cu^+] = 1.2 \times 10^{-12}\ \underline{M}$

$$\therefore K_{sp(CuI)} = 1.2 \times 10^{-12}\ (1.00) = 1.2 \times 10^{-12}$$

(e) $-1.44 = -0.763 - (0.05916/2) \log (1/[Zn^{2+}])$ or $[Zn^{2+}] = 1.3 \times 10^{-23}\ \underline{M}$

$$\therefore K_{sp(ZnS)} = (1.3 \times 10^{-23})(1.00) = 1.3 \times 10^{-23}$$

(f) $-1.55 = -1.18 - (0.05916/2) \log (1/[Mn^{2+}])$ or $[Mn^{2+}] = 3.1 \times 10^{-13}\ \underline{M}$

$$\therefore K_{sp[Mn(OH)_2]} = 3.1 \times 10^{-13}\ (1.00)^2 = 3.1 \times 10^{-13}$$

(g) $-0.356 = -0.126 - (0.05916/2) \log (1/[Pb^{2+}])$ or $[Pb^{2+}] = 1.7 \times 10^{-8}\ \underline{M}$

$$\therefore K_{sp(PbSO_4)} = 1.7 \times 10^{-8}\ (1.00) = 1.7 \times 10^{-8}$$

8-41. We have $[OH^-] = 1.00 \times 10^{-5}\ \underline{M}$, and

$$+0.164 = 0.2412 - \left(+0.337 - \frac{0.05916}{2} \log \frac{1}{[Cu^{2+}]}\right) \quad \text{or} \quad [Cu^{2+}] = 1.6 \times 10^{-9}\ \underline{M}$$

$$\therefore K_{sp[Cu(OH)_2]} = (1.6 \times 10^{-9})(1.00 \times 10^{-5})^2 = 1.6 \times 10^{-19}$$

8-42. The emf of the cell is equal to

$$E_{cell} = +0.331 = E_{Hg_2Cl_2,Hg} - E_{AgI,Ag} = 0.2412 - E_{AgI,Ag}, \quad \text{whereupon}$$

$E_{AgI,Ag} = -0.090$ V. Hence, $-0.090 = +0.7994 - 0.05916 \log (1/[Ag^+])$ or

$[Ag^+] = 9.3 \times 10^{-16}$ $\underline{M}$ $\therefore$ $K_{sp(AgI)} = (9.3 \times 10^{-16})(0.100) = 9.3 \times 10^{-17}$

8-43. $-0.151 = +0.7994 - 0.05916 \log (1/[Ag^+])$ or $[Ag^+] = 8.6 \times 10^{-17}$ $\underline{M}$

$\therefore K_{sp(AgI)} = 8.6 \times 10^{-17}(1.00) = 8.6 \times 10^{-17}$

8-44. $+0.4982 = (+0.7994 + 0.05916 \log [Ag^+]) - E_{ref} = [+0.7994 +$

$0.05916 \log (\frac{25.00 \times 0.100 - 1.00 \times 0.100}{26.00})] - E_{ref}$ or $E_{ref} = +0.240$ V

Hence, $+0.1037 = [+0.7994 + 0.05916 \log K_{sp(AgCl)} - 0.05916 \log(\frac{30.00 \times 0.100 - 25.00 \times 0.100}{55.00})]$

-0.240, from which $K_{sp(AgCl)} = 1.8 \times 10^{-10}$

8-45. $E_{cell} = 0.458 - 0.05916$ pH [Solution 8-22] (1)

Hence, $+0.329 = 0.458 - 0.05916$ pH or pH = 2.18 $\therefore$ $[H^+] = 10^{-2.18} = 6.6 \times 10^{-3}$ $\underline{M}$.

We have a $H_3PO_4 - NaH_2PO_4$ buffer. Using Equation (5-84), we obtain

$$K_1 = [H^+] \frac{C_{H_2PO_4^-} + [H^+] - [OH^-]}{C_{H_3PO_4} - [H^+] + [OH^-]} \simeq 6.6 \times 10^{-3} \times \frac{0.100 + 0.0066}{0.100 - 0.0066} = 7.5 \times 10^{-3}$$

8-46. See Example 8-18.

The emf of the cell is equal to $E_{cell} = +0.420 = +0.280 - E_{H^+,H_2}$, whereupon

$E_{H^+,H_2} = -0.140 = 0.000 - \frac{0.05916}{2} \log \frac{1}{[H^+]^2}$, from which $[H^+] = 4.3 \times 10^{-3}$ $\underline{M}$

Hence, $K_{HA} = \frac{(4.3 \times 10^{-3})^2}{1.00 - 0.0043} = 1.9 \times 10^{-5}$

8-47. See Example 8-19.

The emf of the cell is equal to $E_{cell} = +0.582 = 0.280 - E_{H^+,H_2}$, whereupon

$E_{H^+,H_2} = -0.302 = 0.000 - \frac{0.05916}{2} \log \frac{1}{[H^+]^2}$, from which $[H^+] = 7.86 \times 10^{-6}$ $\underline{M}$.

Hence, $[NH_3] \simeq 7.86 \times 10^{-6}$ $\underline{M}$, $[NH_4^+] = (0.100 - 7.86 \times 10^{-6})$ $\underline{M} \simeq 0.100$ $\underline{M}$,

$[OH^-] = 1.00 \times 10^{-14}/7.86 \times 10^{-6} = 1.27 \times 10^{-9}$ $\underline{M}$

Hence, $K_{NH_3} = \frac{(0.100)(1.27 \times 10^{-9})}{7.86 \times 10^{-6}} = 1.6 \times 10^{-5}$

8-48. From Appendix B, we have

$$[Ag(CN)_2]^- + e \rightleftharpoons Ag + 2CN^- \quad , \quad E_1^o = -0.31\ V \qquad (1)$$

$$Ag^+ + e \rightleftharpoons Ag \quad , \quad E_2^o = +0.7994\ V \qquad (2)$$

Subtracting Equation (2) from Equation (1), we have

$$Ag(CN)_2^- \rightleftharpoons Ag^+ + 2CN^- \quad , \quad E_{1-2}^o = E_1^o - E_2^o = -1.1094\ V$$

We have

$$E_{1-2} = E_{1-2}^o - 0.05916 \log \frac{[Ag^+][CN^-]^2}{[Ag(CN)_2^-]} = -1.1094 - 0.05916 \log K_{inst}$$

At equilibrium, we have $E_{1-2} = 0$. Hence, $0 = -1.1094 - 0.05916 \log K_{inst}$, from which $K_{inst} = 1.8 \times 10^{-19}$.

8-49. $E_{cell} = +0.267 = +0.280 - (+0.170 - \frac{0.05916}{2} \log \frac{1}{[M^{2+}]})$ or $[M^{2+}] = 4.9 \times 10^{-6}$ $\underline{M}$.

$$\text{Hence,}\ K_{inst\,[MA]^+} = \frac{[M^{2+}][A^-]}{[MA^+]} = \frac{(4.9 \times 10^{-6})^2}{0.00500} = 4.8 \times 10^{-9}$$

8-50. From Appendix B, we have

$$2Fe^{3+} + 2e \rightleftharpoons 2Fe^{2+} \quad (HCl\ 1\underline{M}) \quad , \quad E^{o\prime}_{Fe^{3+},Fe^{2+}} = +0.700\ V$$

$$[SnCl_6]^{2-} + 2e \rightleftharpoons [SnCl_4]^{2-} + 2Cl^- \quad (HCl\ 1\underline{M}) \quad , \quad E^{o\prime}_{[SnCl_6]^{2-},[SnCl_4]^{2-}} = +0.14\ V$$

At equilibrium, we have $E_{Fe^{3+},Fe^{2+}} = E_{[SnCl_6]^{2-},[SnCl_4]^{2-}}$. Hence,

$$E^{o\prime}_{Fe^{3+},Fe^{2+}} - \frac{0.05916}{2} \log \frac{[Fe^{2+}]^2}{[Fe^{3+}]^2} = E^{o\prime}_{[SnCl_6]^{2-},[SnCl_4]^{2-}} - \frac{0.05916}{2} \log \frac{[SnCl_4^{2-}][Cl^-]^2}{[SnCl_6^{2-}]}$$

$$\text{or} \quad \frac{0.05916}{2} \log \frac{[Fe^{2+}]^2[SnCl_6^{2-}]}{[Fe^{3+}]^2[SnCl_4^{2-}][Cl^-]^2} = +0.700 - 0.14 = 0.56$$

or $(0.05916/2) \log K = 0.56$ or $K = 8.5 \times 10^{18}$

After mixing, the solution contains

(19.0 mL)(0.0050 mmol Fe(III)/mL) = 0.095 mmol Fe(III) and

(1.00 mL)(0.050 mmol Sn(II)/mL) = 0.050 mmol Sn(II),

which react quantitatively, according to the reaction

$$2Fe^{3+} + [SnCl_4]^{2-} + 2Cl^- \rightleftharpoons 2Fe^{2+} + [SnCl_6]^{2-} \quad , \quad K = 8.5 \times 10^{18} \qquad (1)$$

∴ practically 0.095 mmol of Fe^{2+} and 0.095/2 = 0.0475 mmol of Sn(IV) are formed, and 0.050 - 0.0475 = 0.0025 mmol of Sn(II) remains unreacted. At equilibrium, let $y = [Fe^{3+}]$, whereupon $[SnCl_6^{2-}] = (0.0025\ mmol/20.0\ mL) + (y/2) \simeq 1.25 \times 10^{-4}$ $\underline{M}$,

$[Fe^{2+}] = (0.095\text{ mmol}/20.0\text{ mL}) - y \simeq 4.75 \times 10^{-3}$ $\underline{M}$, $[SnCl_6^{2-}] = (0.0475\text{ mmol}/20.0\text{ mL}) = 2.37 \times 10^{-3}$ $\underline{M}$. Substituting the above values in the equilibrium constant expression, we have

$$K = 8.5 \times 10^{18} = \frac{(4.75 \times 10^{-3})^2 (2.37 \times 10^{-3})}{y^2 (1.25 \times 10^{-4})(1.00)^2}$$, from which $y = [Fe^{3+}] = 7.1 \times 10^{-12}$ $\underline{M}$.

8-51. After mixing, the solution contains

$(50.00\text{ mL})(0.1000\text{ mmol } Ce^{4+}/\text{mL}) = 5.00\text{ mmol } Ce^{4+}$ and

$(50.00\text{ mL})(0.1000\text{ mmol } Fe^{2+}/\text{mL}) = 5.00\text{ mmol } Fe^{2+}$,

which react quantitatively, according to the reaction

$$Ce^{4+} + Fe^{2+} \rightleftharpoons Ce^{3+} + Fe^{3+}, \quad K = 8.9 \times 10^{12}$$ [Example 8-24]

∴ practically 5.00 mmol of Fe^{3+} and 5.00 mmol of Ce^{3+} are formed. At equilibrium, let $y = [Ce^{4+}] = [Fe^{2+}]$, whereupon $[Fe^{3+}] = [Ce^{3+}] = (5.00\text{ mmol}/100.0\text{ mL}) - y \simeq 0.0500$ $\underline{M}$. Hence, we have

$$K = 8.9 \times 10^{12} = \frac{[Ce^{3+}][Fe^{3+}]}{[Ce^{4+}][Fe^{2+}]} = \frac{(0.0500)^2}{y^2}$$, from which $y = [Ce^{4+}] = [Fe^{2+}] = 1.68 \times 10^{-8}$ $\underline{M}$.

8-52. After mixing, the solution contains

$(25.00\text{ mL})(0.03333\text{ mmol } K_2Cr_2O_7/\text{mL}) = 0.8332_5\text{ mmol } K_2Cr_2O_7$ and

$(25.00\text{ mL})(0.2000\text{ mmol } Fe^{2+}/\text{mL}) = 5.000\text{ mmol } Fe^{2+}$

which react quantitatively, according to the reaction

$$Cr_2O_7^{2-} + 6Fe^{2+} + 14H^+ \rightleftharpoons 2Cr^{3+} + 6Fe^{3+} + 7H_2O, \quad K = 10^{16.903 \times 6\,(1.33 - 0.771)} = 4.9 \times 10^{56}$$

∴ practically 5.000 mmol of Fe^{3+} and 1.665 mmol of Cr^{3+} are formed.

At equilibrium, let $y = [Fe^{2+}]$, whereupon $[Cr_2O_7^{2-}] = y/6$, $[Cr^{3+}] = (1.665\text{ mmol}/50.00\text{ mL}) - (y/3) \simeq 0.03333$ $\underline{M}$, $[Fe^{3+}] = (5.00\text{ mmol}/50.00\text{ mL}) - y \simeq 0.1000$ $\underline{M}$. Hence,

$$K = 4.9 \times 10^{56} = \frac{[Cr^{3+}]^2 [Fe^{3+}]^6}{[Cr_2O_7^{2-}][Fe^{2+}]^6 [H^+]^{14}} = \frac{(0.03333)^2 (0.1000)^6}{(y/6)\, y^6 (1.00)^{14}}$$,

from which $y = [Fe^{2+}] = 5.4 \times 10^{-10}$ $\underline{M}$. Hence, $[Cr_2O_7^{2-}] = 5.4 \times 10^{-10}/6 = 9.0 \times 10^{-11}$ $\underline{M}$.

8-53. $+0.412 = (+0.771 + 0.05916 \log \frac{[Fe^{3+}]}{[Fe^{2+}]}) - 0.2412$,

or $[Fe^{3+}]/[Fe^{2+}] = 0.0102 = x/(0.100 - x)$, from which $x = 1.00 \times 10^{-3}$ $\underline{M}$

$\therefore$ $(1.00 \times 10^{-3}/0.100)\,100 = 1.00\ \%$ of Fe^{2+} has been oxidized to Fe^{3+} .

8-54. $+0.0089 = (E^0_{Cu^{2+},Cu} + \frac{0.05916}{2} \log x) - [E^0_{Cu^{2+},Cu} + \frac{0.05916}{2} \log(0.100)] =$

$- \frac{0.05916}{2} \log \frac{x}{0.100}$, from which $x = 0.200$ $\underline{M}$.

8-55. $Fe + Cu^{2+} \rightleftharpoons Fe^{2+} + Cu$ (1)

At equilibrium, let x g be the amount of copper plated on the iron sheet, and y g the amount of Fe^{2+} formed according to Reaction (1). We have

$10.10 = 10.00 + x - y$ or $x - y = 0.10$ (2)

$x/y = 63.55/55.85$ (3)

Solving the simultaneous Equations (2) and (3) gives $x = 0.825$ g .

8-56. $Zn + Fe^{2+} \rightleftharpoons Zn^{2+} + Fe$, $K = 10^{16.903 \times 2[-0.440 - (-0.763)]} = 8.3 \times 10^{10}$

At equilibrium, let $y = [Fe^{2+}]$, whereupon $[Zn^{2+}] = 0.100 - y$. Hence,

$K = 8.3 \times 10^{10} = [Zn^{2+}]/[Fe^{2+}] = (0.100 - y)/y$, or $y = [Fe^{2+}] = 1.20 \times 10^{-12}$ $\underline{M}$.

8-57. $Fe + 2Ag^+ \rightleftharpoons Fe^{2+} + 2Ag$, $K = 10^{16.903 \times 2[0.7994 - (-0.440)]} = 7.9 \times 10^{41}$

At equilibrium, let $y = [Ag^+]$, whereupon $[Fe^{2+}] = (0.100 - y)/2$. Hence,

$K = 7.9 \times 10^{41} = \frac{(0.100 - y)/2}{y^2} \simeq \frac{0.050}{y^2}$, from which $y = [Ag^+] = 2.5 \times 10^{-22}$ $\underline{M}$

$\therefore$ $[Fe^{2+}] = (0.100 - 2.5 \times 10^{-22})/2 \simeq 0.050$ $\underline{M}$.

8-58. Right-hand half-cell : $PbO_2 + 4H^+ + 2SO_4^{2-} + 2e \rightleftharpoons PbSO_4 + 2H_2O$

Left-hand half-cell : $PbSO_4 + 2e \rightleftharpoons Pb + SO_4^{2-}$

Cell reaction : $PbO_2 + Pb + 4H^+ + 2SO_4^{2-} \rightleftharpoons 2PbSO_4 + 2H_2O$

The density of the electrolyte affects the operation of the battery. During discharge, H_2SO_4 is replaced by H_2O , and the density decreases.

8-59. (a) $H_3AsO_4 + 2[Fe(CN)_6]^{4-} + 2H^+ \rightleftharpoons H_3AsO_3 + 2[Fe(CN)_6]^{3-} + H_2O$,

$K = 10^{16.903 \times 2(0.559 - 0.356)} = 7.3 \times 10^6$

At equilibrium, $[Fe(CN)_6^{3-}] = 2\,[H_3AsO_3]$, $[Fe(CN)_6^{4-}] = 2\,[H_3AsO_4]$

$$\therefore\ 7.3\times10^6 = \frac{[H_3AsO_3]\,[Fe(CN)_6^{3-}]^2}{[H_3AsO_4][Fe(CN)_6^{4-}]^2[H^+]^2} = \frac{[H_3AsO_3]\ (2\,[H_3AsO_3])^2}{[H_3AsO_4]\ (2\,[H_3AsO_4])^2\,[H^+]^2}$$

or $[H_3AsO_3]/[H_3AsO_4] = \sqrt[3]{7.3\times10^6\,[H^+]^2}$ (1)

$\therefore$ at pH = 2.00 , $[H_3AsO_3]/[H_3AsO_4] = \sqrt[3]{7.3\times10^6\,(0.010)^2} = 9.0$

(b) At pH = 6.00, $[H_3AsO_3]/[H_3AsO_4] = \sqrt[3]{7.3\times10^6\,(1.0\times10^{-6})^2} = 1.94\times10^{-2}$.

CHAPTER 9

9-1. $F = \dfrac{As_2S_3}{6AgCl}$

9-2. (a) $F = \dfrac{P}{PbMoO_4} = \dfrac{30.97}{367.13} = 0.08436$

(b) g P = 0.1000 X 0.08436 = 0.00844

9-3. (a) $g\ Fe = 0.3117\ g\ Fe_2O_3 \times \dfrac{(2 \times 55.85)\ g\ Fe}{159.69\ g\ Fe_2O_3} = 0.2180$

(b) $g\ FeO = 0.3117\ g\ Fe_2O_3 \times \dfrac{(2 \times 71.85)\ g\ FeO}{159.69\ g\ Fe_2O_3} = 0.2805$

(c) $g\ FeS_2 = 0.3117\ g\ Fe_2O_3 \times \dfrac{(2 \times 119.98)\ g\ FeS_2}{159.69\ g\ Fe_2O_3} = 0.4684$

9-4. $$\frac{0.3227\ g\ Al(C_9H_6ON)_3 \times \dfrac{26.98\ g\ Al}{459.46\ g\ Al(C_9H_6ON)_3}}{0.2970\ g\ sample} \times 100 = 6.380\ \%\ Al$$

9-5. (a) $$\frac{0.3016\ g\ Fe_2O_3 \times \dfrac{(2 \times 392.14)\ g\ FeSO_4 \cdot (NH_4)_2SO_4 \cdot 6H_2O}{159.69\ g\ Fe_2O_3}}{1.5000\ g\ sample} \times 100 = 98.75\ \%\ FeSO_4 \cdot (NH_4)_2SO_4 \cdot 6H_2O$$

(b) $$\frac{0.3016\ g\ Fe_2O_3 \times \dfrac{(2 \times 55.85)\ g\ Fe}{159.69\ g\ Fe_2O_3}}{1.5000\ g\ sample} \times 100 = 14.06\ \%\ Fe$$

9-6. $$\frac{0.0589\ g\ Al_2O_3 \times \dfrac{(2 \times 26.98)\ g\ Al}{101.96\ g\ Al_2O_3}}{0.5874\ g\ sample} \times 100 = 5.31\ \%\ Al$$

$$\frac{0.0589\ g\ Al_2O_3 \times \dfrac{(2 \times 39.10)\ g\ K}{101.96\ g\ Al_2O_3}}{0.5874\ g\ sample} \times 100 = 7.69\ \%\ K$$

9-7. Mol. weight of $Na_2S_xO_6 = 141.98 + 32.06\,x$

$$\frac{0.3570\ g\ BaSO_4}{233.40\ g/mol} = 0.001530\ mol\ BaSO_4 \equiv \frac{0.001530}{x}\ mol\ Na_2S_xO_6$$

$$\therefore \frac{0.1028 \text{ g } Na_2S_xO_6}{(141.98 + 32.06\,x) \text{ g/mol}} = \frac{0.001530}{x}, \text{ from which } x \simeq 4$$

9-8. $$\% \; Fe_2O_3 = \frac{\text{g } O_2 \times \frac{6Fe_2O_3}{O_2}}{\text{g sample}} \times 100 = \frac{(0.9996 - 0.9784) \times \frac{6 \times 159.69}{32.00}}{0.9996} \times 100 = 63.50$$

9-9. The sample contains

$$\frac{250 \text{ mg NaCl}}{58.44 \text{ mg/mmol}} = 4.28 \text{ mmol NaCl} \equiv \frac{4.28 \text{ mmol } AgNO_3}{0.200 \text{ mmol/mL}} = 21.4 \text{ mL}$$

$\therefore$ 21.4 X 1.1 = 23.5 mL of 0.200 $\underline{M}$ $AgNO_3$ are required .

9-10. 1 mol $CaCO_3$ $\equiv$ 1 mol $(NH_4)_2C_2O_4 \cdot H_2O$ $\therefore$ the maximum weight of ammonium oxalate (for a 100% pure sample) is equal to

$$\left[0.500 \text{ g } CaCO_3 \times \frac{142.12 \text{ g } (NH_4)_2C_2O_4 \cdot H_2O}{100.09 \text{ g } CaCO_3}\right] \times 1.1 = 0.781 \text{ g } (NH_4)_2C_2O_4 \cdot H_2O$$

9-11. $2H_nA + nCa(OH)_2 \rightleftharpoons Ca_nA_2 + 2nH_2O$

300.0 mg Ca_nA_2 $\equiv$ 25.00 mL $Ca(OH)_2$ X 0.1000 mmol/mL = 2.500 mmol $Ca(OH)_2$ $\equiv$

5.000 meq H^+ $\equiv$ 5.000 meq H^+ X 1.008 mg/meq = 5.04 mg H^+ $\equiv$ 2.500 mmol Ca =

2.500 mmol Ca X 40.08 mg/mmol = 100.2 mg Ca $\equiv$ 300.0 - 100.2 = 199.8 mg A

$\therefore$ x = 5.04 + 199.8 = 204.84 mg

$$\therefore \% \; H = \frac{5.04 \text{ mg H}}{204.84 \text{ mg sample}} \times 100 = 2.46$$

9-12. $$KClO_4 \xrightarrow{\Delta} KCl + 2\,O_2\uparrow$$

$$KCl \xrightarrow{Ag^+} AgCl$$

$$\therefore 0.1280 \text{ g } O_2 \times \frac{143.32 \text{ g AgCl}}{(4 \times 16.00) \text{ g } O_2} = 0.2866 \text{ g AgCl}$$

The amount of evolved oxygen does not depend on the nature of the salt $MClO_4$, because regardless of the nature of M the ratio of Cl to O is always the same, 1:4 .

9-13. $$0.4994 \text{ g } CuSO_4 \cdot xH_2O \cdot \frac{159.60 \text{ g } CuSO_4}{(159.60 + 18.02\,x) \text{ g } CuSO_4 \cdot xH_2O} = 0.3184 \text{ g } CuSO_4 \text{ or } x \simeq 5 .$$

9-14. $(M/MCl_x)\,100 = 22.55$ (1)

$(M/MCl_{x+2})\,100 = 14.87$ (2)

Dividing Equations (1) and (2), we have

$$\frac{MCl_{x+2}}{MCl_x} = \frac{22.55}{14.87} = \frac{MCl_x + 2\,Cl}{MCl_x} = \frac{MCl_x + (2 \times 35.45)}{MCl_x} \quad \text{or} \quad MCl_x = 137.28$$

$\therefore$ the atomic weight of M is $137.28 \times (22.55/100) = 30.96$ and

$x = (137.28 - 30.96)/35.45 = 3.00$.

From the table of atomic weights, we find that the element M is P .

9-15. $CaCO_3 \xrightarrow{\Delta} CaO + CO_2\uparrow$

$MgCO_3 \xrightarrow{\Delta} MgO + CO_2\uparrow$

Suppose that the 0.3200 - g sample and consequently the residue contains x mmol of CaO and y mmol of MgO. Hence, the sample contains (x + y) mmol CO_2. We have

$(x + y)$ mmol CO_2 (44.01 mg CO_2/mmol) = (320.0 - 166.4) mg CO_2 or $x + y = 3.490$ (1)

$56.08\,x + 40.30\,y = 166.4$ (2)

Solving the simultaneous equations gives $x = 1.632$, $y = 1.858$.

Hence, the residue contains

[(1.632 mmol CaO)(56.08 mg/mmol)/166.4 mg] 100 = 55.00 % CaO, and

[(1.858 mmol MgO)(40.30 mg/mmol)/166.4 mg] 100 = 45.00 % MgO

9-16. Suppose that the 0.2000-g sample contains y mmol of chlorides and z mmol of iodides. We have

$143.32\,y + 234.77\,z = 378.0$ (1)

$(234.77 - 143.32)\,z = 48.8$ (2)

Solving the simultaneous equations gives $z = 0.5336$, $y = 1.763$.

Hence, the sample contains

[(1.763 mmol Cl)(35.45 mg/mmol)/200.0 mg] 100 = 31.25 % Cl , and

[(0.5336 mmol I)(126.90 mg/mmol)/200.0 mg] 100 = 33.86 % I

9-17. The sample contains

$$(3.9996 - 3.7113)\text{g } H_2O \times \frac{244.28 \text{ g } BaCl_2\cdot 2H_2O}{36.04 \text{ g } H_2O} = 1.9541 \text{ g } BaCl_2\cdot 2H_2O \text{ ,}$$

and $3.9996 - 1.9541 = 2.0455$ g NaCl .

Let V mL be the required volume of $AgNO_3$. We have

$$\left(\frac{2045.5 \text{ mg NaCl}}{58.44 \text{ mg/mmol}} + \frac{1954.1 \text{ mg } BaCl_2 \cdot 2H_2O}{244.28 \text{ mg/mmol}} \times \frac{2 \text{ mmol Cl}}{\text{mmol } BaCl_2 \cdot 2H_2O}\right) \times \frac{10.00}{250.0} = V \text{ mL} \times 0.1000 \text{ mmol/mL},$$

from which V = 20.40 mL 0.1000 M $AgNO_3$

9-18. Suppose that the 0.3697-g sample contains x mmol of NaCl, y mmol of NaBr, and z mmol of NaI. We have

$$25.00 \text{ mL A} \equiv (z/4) \text{ mmol NaI} \equiv (z/8) \text{ mmol } PdI_2 = \frac{45.0 \text{ mg } PdI_2}{360.2 \text{ mg/mmol}}$$, from

which z = 0.9994 mmol NaI,

50.00 mL A ≡ (x/2) mmol AgCl (143.32 mg/mmol) + (y/2) mmol AgBr (187.77 mg/mmol) + (0.9994/2) mmol AgI (234.77 mg/mmol) = 355.1 mg, or

$71.66\,x + 93.88\,y = 237.8$ (1)

$71.66\,(x + y + 0.9994) = 286.6$ or $71.66\,x + 71.66\,y = 215.0$ (2)

Solving the simultaneous equations gives x = 1.974, y = 1.026. Hence, the sample contains

[(1.974 mmol Cl)(35.45 mg/mmol)/369.7 mg]100 = 18.93 % Cl

[(1.026 mmol Br)(79.90 mg/mmol)/369.7 mg]100 = 22.17 % Br

[(0.9994 mmol I)(126.90 mg/mmol)/369.7 mg]100 = 34.30 % I

9-19. $CaC_2O_4 \xrightarrow{900^o} CaO + CO\uparrow + CO_2\uparrow$

Suppose that the 1.2000-g sample contains y g of CaC_2O_4 and consequently (1.200 - y) g CaO. We have

$$y \text{ g } CaC_2O_4 \times \frac{56.08 \text{ g CaO}}{128.10 \text{ g } CaC_2O_4} + (1.200 - y) = 0.8400, \text{ or } y = 0.6403$$

Hence, the sample contains (0.6403/1.2000) 100 = 53.36 % CaC_2O_4, and

[(1.200 - 0.6403)/1.2000]100 = 46.64 % CaO.

9-20. Suppose that the 0.3527-g sample contains y mmol of CaC_2O_4 and z mmol of MgC_2O_4. We have

$128.10\,y + 112.32\,z = 352.7$ (1)

$100.09\,y + 40.30\,z = 180.7$ (2)

Solving the simultaneous Equations (1) and (2) gives y = 1.000, z = 2.000.

Hence, the sample contains

[(1.000 mmol Ca)(40.08 mg/mmol)/352.7 mg]100 = 11.36 % Ca, and

$[(2.000 \text{ mmol Mg})(24.30 \text{ mg/mmol})/352.7 \text{ mg}]100 = 13.78 \% \text{ Mg}$

9-21. Suppose that the 0.2660 - g sample contains y mmol of KCl and z mmol of NaCl. We have

$74.56\,y + 58.44\,z = 266.0$ (1)

$35.45\,(y + z) = 141.8$ (2)

Solving the simultaneous equations gives $y = z = 2.000$. Hence, the sample contains

$[(2.000 \text{ mmol K})(39.10 \text{ mg/mmol})/266.0 \text{ mg}]100 = 29.40 \% \text{ K}$, and

$[(2.000 \text{ mmol Na})(22.99 \text{ mg/mmol})/266.0 \text{ mg}]100 = 17.29 \% \text{ Na}$

9-22. Suppose that the mixture contains y g of KCl and consequently (100.00 - y) g of NaBr per 100.00 g of sample. We have

$$y \text{ g KCl} \times \frac{174.27 \text{ g } K_2SO_4}{(2 \times 74.56) \text{ g KCl}} + (100.00 - y) \text{ g NaBr} \times \frac{142.04 \text{ g } Na_2SO_4}{(2 \times 102.90) \text{ g NaBr}} = 100.00 ,$$

from which $y = 64.75$. Hence, the sample contains 64.75% KCl.

9-23. Suppose that the sample contains y % KCl and z % $KClO_3$. We have

$y + z = 100.00$ (1)

$$y \text{ g KCl} \times \frac{35.45 \text{ g Cl}}{74.56 \text{ g KCl}} + z \text{ g } KClO_3 \times \frac{35.45 \text{ g Cl}}{122.55 \text{ g } KClO_3} = 35.97 \quad \text{or}$$

$0.47546\,y + 0.28927\,z = 35.97$ (2)

Solving the two simultaneous equations gives $y = 37.83$, $z = 62.17$. Hence, the sample contains 37.83 % KCl and 62.17 % $KClO_3$.

9-24. Suppose that the 0.7500 - g sample contains y mmol of KCl and z mmol of KBr. We have

$y + z = (32.00 \text{ mL})(0.1250 \text{ mmol/mL}) = 4.000$ (1)

$(143.32\,y + 187.78\,z)(0.2500/0.7500) = 220.7$ (2)

Solving the two simultaneous equations gives $y = 2.002$, $z = 1.998$. Hence, the sample contains

$[(2.002 \text{ mmol KCl})(74.56 \text{ mg/mmol})/750.0 \text{ mg}]100 = 19.90 \% \text{ KCl}$

$[(1.998 \text{ mmol KBr})(119.01 \text{ mg/mmol})/750.0 \text{ mg}]100 = 31.70 \% \text{ KBr}$

9-25. Suppose that the mixture contains y g of $PbSO_4$/100.0 g of sample. We have

$y + y\,(Pb/PbSO_4)(0.6629)(BaSO_4/Ba) = 100.00$, or

$y + y\,(207.19/303.25)(0.6629)(233.40/137.34) = 100.00$, or $y = 56.51$.

Hence, the mixture contains 56.51 % $PbSO_4$.

9-26. Let y be the atomic weight of M. We have

$$0.4828 \text{ g sample} \times \frac{78.11 \text{ g NaCl}}{100.00 \text{ g sample}} \times \frac{143.32 \text{ g AgCl}}{58.44 \text{ g NaCl}} +$$

$$0.4828 \text{ g sample} \times \frac{21.89 \text{ g MCl}}{100.00 \text{ g sample}} \times \frac{143.32 \text{ g AgCl}}{(y + 35.45) \text{ g MCl}} = 1.1280 \text{ g AgCl}$$, from which

y = 39.11 . Hence, the atomic weight of M is 39.11 ($M \equiv K$)

9-27. $C_6H_5OH + 7.5\,O_2 \longrightarrow 6CO_2 + 3H_2O$

$C_6H_{12}O_6 + 6\,O_2 \longrightarrow 6CO_2 + 6H_2O$

Suppose that the 0.2743 - g sample contains y g of C_6H_5OH and z g of $C_6H_{12}O_6$. We have

$$y + z = 0.2473 \quad (1)$$

$$y \text{ g } C_6H_5OH \times \frac{(6 \times 44.01) \text{ g } CO_2}{94.11 \text{ g } C_6H_5OH} + z \text{ g } C_6H_{12}O_6 \times \frac{(6 \times 44.01) \text{ g } CO_2}{180.16 \text{ g } C_6H_{12}O_6} = 0.5281 \quad (2)$$

Solving the simultaneous Equations (1) and (2) gives y = 0.0941 , z = 0.1802. Hence, the sample contains

(0.0941/0.2743) 100 = 34.31 % C_6H_5OH , and

(0.1802/0.2743) 100 = 65.69 % $C_6H_{12}O_6$.

9-28. (a) See Example 9-4 . We have

$$\% \; KClO_3 = \frac{\text{g AgCl} \times F}{\text{g sample}} \times 100 \quad (1)$$

where $F = KClO_3/AgCl = 122.55/143.32 = 0.8551$

For a given sample weight, the minimum amount of AgCl will be obtained from the sample that contains the least $KClO_3$ (20 %). Hence, the minimum sample weight that must be taken to assure at least 0.500 g of AgCl is calculated by Equation (1), as follows :

$$20.0 = \frac{0.500 \times 0.8551}{\text{g sample}} \times 100$$, or g sample = 2.14 .

(b) The maximum weight of AgCl from 2.14 g of sample will be obtained from the sample that contains the most $KClO_3$ (25.0 %). Hence, we will obtain

$$2.14 \text{ g sample} \times \frac{25.0 \text{ g } KClO_3}{100.0 \text{ g sample}} \times \frac{143.32 \text{ g AgCl}}{122.55 \text{ g } KClO_3} = 0.626 \text{ g AgCl}$$

9-29. We have

$$0.100 \;\% \; S = \frac{0.00100 \text{ g } BaSO_4 \times \frac{32.06 \text{ g S}}{233.40 \text{ g } BaSO_4}}{\text{g sample}} \times 100$$

or g sample = 0.137 .

9-30. Substituting the data in Equation (9-1), we have

$$0.200\ \%\ Fe = \frac{0.00100\ g\ Fe_2O_3 \times \dfrac{2 \times 55.85\ g\ Fe}{159.69\ g\ Fe_2O_3} \times 100}{S}$$

or S = 0.350 g of sample .

9-31. (a) The lower limit of sample size is determined from the smallest weight of $BaSO_4$ (0.250 g) and K_2SO_4, which has the smallest percentage of sulfate. 0.250 g of $BaSO_4$ is obtained from

$$0.250\ g\ BaSO_4 \times \frac{174.27\ g\ K_2SO_4}{233.40\ g\ BaSO_4} = 0.187\ g\ K_2SO_4\ ,$$

whereas 0.500 g of $BaSO_4$ is obtained from

$$0.500\ g\ BaSO_4 \times \frac{142.04\ g\ Na_2SO_4}{233.40\ g\ BaSO_4} = 0.304\ g\ Na_2SO_4$$

Hence, the sample weight should lie between 0.187 and 0.304 g .

(b) Suppose that the sample consists of Na_2SO_4 which contains the larger percentage of sulfate and ∴ requires the largest amount of $BaCl_2$. Let V mL be the volume of $BaCl_2$ equivalent to y g of sample, whereupon

$$\frac{(y\ g\ Na_2SO_4)(1000\ mg/g)}{142.04\ mg/mmol} = V\ mL \times 0.200\ mmol/mL$$

or V = 35.2 y mL . Since a 10 % excess of $BaCl_2$ is desired , a total of (35.2 y)(1.1) = 38.7 y mL of 0.200 M $BaCl_2$ is required.

9-32. Let y g be the weight of sample. We have

$$\frac{0.200\,y\ g\ Br^-}{79.90\ g/mol} = \frac{0.3876\ g\ AgBr}{187.78\ g/mol} \quad \text{or} \quad y = 0.825$$

∴ we should take a 0.825 - g sample .

9-33. Substituting the data in Equation (9-6), we have

$$21.70 = \frac{\%\ Zn_{a.r.} \times 100}{100 - 1.80} \quad \text{or} \quad \%\ Zn_{a.r.} = 21.31$$

9-34. Substituting the data in Equation (9-6), we have

$$48.10 = \frac{47.08 \times 100}{100.00 - \%M} \quad \text{or} \quad \%\ M = 2.12$$

9-35. (a) $$\% \, Cl_d = \frac{0.3810 \text{ g AgCl} \times \dfrac{35.45 \text{ g Cl}}{143.32 \text{ g AgCl}}}{(0.4000 \times 0.9875) \text{ g}} \times 100 = 23.86$$

(b) $$\% \, Cl_{a.r.} = \frac{0.3810 \text{ g AgCl} \times \dfrac{35.45 \text{ g Cl}}{143.32 \text{ g AgCl}}}{0.4000 \text{ g}} \times 100 = 23.56$$

9-36. The compound contains

$$\frac{0.6324 \text{ g } CO_2 \times \dfrac{12.01 \text{ g C}}{44.01 \text{ g } CO_2}}{0.7821 \text{ g sample}} \times 100 = 22.07 \% \text{ C },$$

$$\frac{0.3222 \text{ g } H_2O \times \dfrac{(2 \times 1.008) \text{ g H}}{18.02 \text{ g } H_2O}}{0.7821 \text{ g sample}} \times 100 = 4.609 \% \text{ H}$$

$$\frac{0.2586 \text{ g AgBr} \times \dfrac{79.90 \text{ g Br}}{187.78 \text{ g AgBr}}}{0.1500 \text{ g sample}} \times 100 = 73.36 \% \text{ Br}$$

We have 22.07 + 4.609 + 73.36 = 100.04 %. Hence, the compound contains only C, H, and Br. We have

$$C = \frac{22.07}{12.01} = 1.838 \ , \quad H = \frac{4.609}{1.008} = 4.572 \ , \quad Br = \frac{73.36}{79.90} = 0.918 \ .$$

Dividing by 0.918, we have C = 2.002 , H = 4.98 , Br = 1.00 . Hence the empirical formula of the compound is $(C_2H_5Br)_n$.

9-37. Since the analyst used a common filter, the weight of the initial residue was equal to

$$0.6225 \text{ g} \times \frac{12.69}{100.00} \times \frac{159.69}{2 \times 55.85} = 0.1129 \text{ g}$$

$\therefore$ real weight of Fe_2O_3 = 0.1129 - 0.0029 = 0.1100 g

Hence, the real percentage of iron in the sample is equal to

$$\% \, Fe = \frac{0.1100 \text{ g } Fe_2O_3 \times \dfrac{(2 \times 55.85) \text{ g Fe}}{159.69 \text{ g } Fe_2O_3}}{0.6225 \text{ g sample}} \times 100 = 12.36$$

9-38. (a) Let y = g BaS in the precipitate. We have

$$y \text{ g BaS} \times \frac{233.40 \text{ g } BaSO_4}{169.40 \text{ g BaS}} + (0.4604 - y) \text{ g } BaSO_4 = 0.2841 \text{ g } Na_2SO_4 \times \frac{233.40 \text{ g } BaSO_4}{142.04 \text{ g } Na_2SO_4} =$$

0.4668 g $BaSO_4$,

or y = 0.0169 $\therefore$ % BaS = (0.0169/0.4604) 100 = 3.68

(b) $$\frac{0.4604 - 0.4668}{0.4668} \times 100 = -1.37 \% \text{ error}$$

9-39. $\% \text{ Fe calculated} = \dfrac{0.2922 \text{ g } Fe_2O_3 \times \dfrac{(2 \times 55.85) \text{ g Fe}}{159.69 \text{ g } Fe_2O_3}}{1.5584 \text{ g sample}} \times 100 = 13.11_5$

$\therefore \text{ relative error } = \dfrac{13.11_5 - 12.85}{13.11_5} \times 100 = +2.0\ \%$

9-40. $6Fe_2O_3 \xrightarrow{\Delta} 4Fe_3O_4 + O_2\uparrow$ (1)

$6 \times 159.69 = 958.14 \qquad 4 \times 231.54 = 926.16$

$30\ Fe_3O_4 \equiv (30.00 \times 958.14)/926.16 \equiv 31.036\ Fe_2O_3$

Because of Reaction (1), the precipitate weighs 70.00 + 30.00 = 100.00 instead of 70.00 + 31.036 = 101.036, that is, we have a loss of 1.036 parts per 101.036 parts of initial Fe_2O_3 $\therefore$ relative error = (- 1.036/101.036) 100 = - 1.02 % .

9-41. $\% \text{ error} = -(Cl_2/2\ AgCl) \times 0.0240 \times 100 = -[(2 \times 35.45)/(2 \times 143.32)] \times 0.0240 \times 100 = -0.59$

9-42. Suppose that the experimental weight of the residue is 1.0000 g. It contains 0.9800 g of $CaCO_3$ and 0.0200 g of CaC_2O_4.

$\therefore$ theoretical weight of residue is

$0.9800 \text{ g } CaCO_3 + 0.0200 \text{ g } CaC_2O_4 \times \dfrac{100.09 \text{ g } CaCO_3}{128.10 \text{ g } CaC_2O_4} = 0.9956 \text{ g}$

Hence, the relative error is $[(1.0000 - 0.9956)/0.9956]100 = +0.442\ \%$

9-43. Substituting the data in Equation (9-6), we have

$20.35 = \dfrac{20.28 \times 100}{100.00 - \%M} \qquad \text{or} \qquad \%M = 0.34$

10-1. 250.0 mL X 0.1000 mmol/mL X 0.05844 g NaCl/mmol = 1.4610 g

10-2. $Cr_2O_7^{2-} + 14H^+ + 6e \rightleftharpoons 2Cr^{3+} + 7H_2O$

$$M = \frac{4.8893 \text{ g } K_2Cr_2O_7/L}{294.19 \text{ g } K_2Cr_2O_7/\text{mol}} = 0.01662 \text{ mol/L}$$

$$N = 6\,M = 6 \text{ eq/mol} \times 0.01662 \text{ mol/L} = 0.0997 \text{ eq/L}$$

10-3. The titration reaction is $(CH_2OH)_3CNH_2 + H^+ \rightleftharpoons (CH_2OH)_3CNH_3^+$

$$\therefore\ 45.18 \text{ mL} \times N \text{ meq HCl/mL} = \frac{538.4 \text{ mg THAM}}{121.14 \text{ mg THAM/meq}} \quad \text{or} \quad N_{HCl} = 0.09837 \text{ meq/mL}$$

10-4. The normality of oxalic acid as an acid is equal to its normality as a reductant ($C_2O_4^{2-} \longrightarrow 2CO_2 + 2e$)

$$\therefore\ N_{NaOH} \times V_{NaOH} = N_{H_2C_2O_4} \times V_{H_2C_2O_4} \qquad (1)$$

$$N_{KMnO_4} \times V_{KMnO_4} = N_{H_2C_2O_4} \times V'_{H_2C_2O_4} \qquad (2)$$

Combining Equations (1) and (2), we have

$$N_{KMnO_4} = N_{H_2C_2O_4} \times \frac{V'_{H_2C_2O_4}}{V_{KMnO_4}} = \frac{N_{NaOH} \times V_{NaOH}}{V_{H_2C_2O_4}} \times \frac{V'_{H_2C_2O_4}}{V_{KMnO_4}} =$$

$$\frac{0.1800 \times 30.00}{25.00} \times \frac{20.50}{44.28} = 0.1000 \text{ meq/mL}$$

Since the change in oxidation number is 5 per MnO_4^- ion, we have

$M = (0.1000 \text{ meq } KMnO_4/\text{mL}) / (5 \text{ meq/mmol}) = 0.02000 \text{ mmol/ml}$

10-5. $\frac{0.5870 \text{ g } BaSO_4}{0.23340 \text{ g/mmol}} = 25.00 \text{ mL} \times M \text{ mmol } H_2SO_4/\text{mL}$,

from which $M_{H_2SO_4} = 0.1006$ mmol/mL

10-6. $$\% \ NaHC_2O_4 = \frac{12.50 \text{ mL} \times 0.0999 \text{ mmol/mL} \times 0.11202 \text{ g } NaHC_2O_4/\text{mmol}}{0.3750 \text{ g sample}} \times 100 = 37.30$$

$$\%_{Na_2C_2O_4} = \frac{(20.10 \text{ mL} \times 0.1200 \text{ meq/mL}) - (12.50 \text{ mL} \times 0.0999 \text{ mmol/mL} \times 2 \text{ meq/mL})/2}{0.1875 \text{ g sample}} \times$$

$$(0.06700 \text{ g } Na_2C_2O_4/\text{meq}) \times 100 = 41.57$$

10-7. $\% NaCl = \frac{V\,mL \times N\,meq/mL \times 0.05844\,g\,NaCl/meq}{1.0580\,g\,sample} \times 100 = 200\,N$,

from which $V = 36.21$ mL of $AgNO_3$

10-8. $\% KCl = \frac{V\,mL \times N\,meq/mL \times 0.07456\,g\,KCl/meq}{0.3728\,g\,sample} \times 100 = \frac{V}{2}$,

from which $N_{AgNO_3} = 0.02500$ meq/mL

10-9. The normality of KHC_2O_4 as an acid, N_a, is one-half its normality as a reductant. Let V mL be the required volume of NaOH. We have

$$N_a = \frac{(34.02\,mL \times 0.1003\,meq/mL)/25.00\,mL}{2} = 0.06824\,meq/mL$$

$\therefore$ V mL X 0.1000 meq/mL = 25.00 mL X 0.06824 meq/mL , or V = 17.06 mL

10-10. The normality of the initial H_2SO_4 solution is equal to

$$N_{H_2SO_4} = \frac{1000\,mL/L \times 1.835\,g\,solution/mL \times 0.931\,g\,H_2SO_4/g\,solution}{(98.08/2)\,g\,H_2SO_4\,/\,eq} = 34.84\,eq/mL$$

Let V mL be the required volume of H_2SO_4 . We have

V mL X 34.84 meq/mL = 1000 mL X 1.00 meq/mL , or V = 28.7 mL .

10-11. $MnO_2 + 2Fe^{2+} + 4H^+ \longrightarrow Mn^{2+} + 2Fe^{3+} + 2H_2O$

$$\% MnO_2 = \frac{[(50.00\,mL \times 0.1000\,meq/mL) - (13.31\,mL \times 0.1002\,meq/mL)](86.94/2)\,mg\,MnO_2/meq}{210.8\,mg\,sample} \times 100 =$$

75.6

10-12. $$\% NaCl = \frac{[(50.00\,mL \times 0.1006\,mmol/mL) - (9.58\,mL \times 0.0998\,mmol/mL)] \times 58.44\,mg\,NaCl/mmol}{240.0\,mg\,sample} \times 100 =$$

99.2

10-13. $$\% N = \frac{[(50.00\,mL \times 0.1000\,mmol/mL) - (22.36\,mL \times 0.1064\,mmol/mL)] \times 14.01\,mg\,N/mmol}{587.4\,mg\,sample} \times 100 =$$

6.25

10-14. $$\% Fe_2O_3 = \frac{(50.00 \times 0.0512 - 17.16 \times 0.0504)\,mmol\,Fe \times \frac{1\,mmol\,Fe_2O_3}{2\,mmol\,Fe} \times 159.69\,\frac{mg\,Fe_2O_3}{mmol}}{235.2\,mg\,sample} \times 100 =$$

57.5

10-15. (a) The titration reaction is $CO_3^{2-} + 2H^+ \rightleftharpoons H_2CO_3$

$\therefore$ 1 meq $Na_2CO_3 \equiv 0.10599/2 = 0.05300$ g Na_2CO_3

Hence, from $(35 \times 0.1000 \times 0.05300)$ to $(45 \times 0.1000 \times 0.05300) = 0.1855 - 0.2385 \simeq$ 0.19 to 0.24 g of Na_2CO_3 should be taken.

(b) From (0.1855/0.50) to (0.2385/0.50) $\simeq$ 0.37 to 0.48 g of sample should be taken.

10-16. $$\% \text{KCl} = \frac{\text{mL AgNO}_3 \times 0.1000 \text{ meq/mL} \times 0.07456 \text{ g KCl/meq}}{\text{g sample}} \times 100 \quad (1)$$

Since $(\% \text{KCl}) \times 2 = \text{mL AgNO}_3$, Equation (1) is simplified to

g sample $= (0.1000 \times 0.07456 \times 100)/2 = 0.3728$

10-17. Suppose that the 0.2284 - g sample contains y mmol of $NaHCO_3$ and z mmol of MgO. We have

$(20.00 \text{ mL} \times 0.5000 \text{ mmol/mL}) - (40.00 \text{ mL} \times 0.1500 \text{ mmol/mL}) = 4.000 \text{ mmol} = y + 2z$ (1)

$25.00 \text{ mL} \times 0.02000 \text{ mmol/mL} = 0.5000 \text{ mmol} = z\,(0.1142/0.2284)$ (2)

Solving the two simultaneous equations gives z = 1.000 , y = 2.000. Hence, the preparation contains

$[(2.000 \text{ mmol NaHCO}_3)(84.01 \text{ mg/mmol})/228.4 \text{ mg}]\,100 = 73.56\ \%\ NaHCO_3$,

$[(1.000 \text{ mmol MgO})(40.31 \text{ mg/mmol})/228.4 \text{ mg}]\,100 = 17.65\ \%$ MgO ,

and $\therefore$ 100.00 - (73.56 + 17.65) = 8.79 % inert materials.

10-18. $$\% \text{Ba} = \frac{(32.17 \text{ mL})(0.1001 \text{ mmol Fe}^{2+}/\text{mL})(\frac{1 \text{ mmol Cr(VI)}}{3 \text{ mmol Fe}^{2+}})(\frac{1 \text{ mmol Ba}}{\text{mmol Cr(VI)}})(137.34 \text{ mg Ba/mmol})}{250.8 \text{ mg sample}} \times 100 =$$

58.78

10-19. Suppose that the 0.2500 - g sample contains y mg of SO_3 and $\therefore$ (250.0 - y) mg of H_2SO_4. We have

$$\frac{y \text{ mg SO}_3}{(86.06/2) \text{ mg/meq}} + \frac{(250.0 - y) \text{ mg H}_2\text{SO}_4}{(98.08/2) \text{ mg/meq}} = 26.74 \text{ mL} \times 0.2000 \text{ meq/mL}$$

or y = 87.82 . Hence, the sample contains (87.82/250.0) 100 = 35.13 % SO_3

10-20. Suppose that the 0.2958 - g sample contains y g of $NaHC_2O_4$ and $\therefore$ (0.2958 - y) g of $Na_2C_2O_4$. We have

$$\frac{y \text{ g NaHC}_2\text{O}_4}{(0.11202/2) \text{ g/meq}} + \frac{(0.2958 - y) \text{ g Na}_2\text{C}_2\text{O}_4}{(0.13400/2) \text{ g/meq}} = 40.00 \text{ mL} \times 0.1206 \text{ meq/mL}$$

or y = 0.1397 . Hence, the sample contains (0.1397/0.2958) 100 = 47.22 % $NaHC_2O_4$ and (100 - 47.22) = 52.78 % $Na_2C_2O_4$.

10-21. Let V mL be the volume of HCl added until the end point. We have

$$[OH^-] = 1.0 \times 10^{-4} = \frac{(50.00\text{ mL} \times 0.1000\text{ mmol/mL}) - (V\text{ mL} \times 0.1000\text{ mmol/mL})}{(50.00 + V)\text{ mL}}$$

or V = 49.90 mL . Hence, the titration error is equal to $[(49.90 - 50.00)/50.00]100$ = - 0.2 % .

10-22. Let V mL be the volume of NaOH added until the end point. We have

$$[H^+] = 10^{-3.80} = \frac{(25.00\text{ mL} \times 0.1000\text{ mmol/mL}) - (V\text{ mL} \times 0.1000\text{ mmol/mL})}{(25.00 + V)\text{ mL}}$$

or V = 24.92 mL . Hence, the experimental value of the concentration of HCl is equal to (0.1000)(24.92/25.00) = 0.0997 .

10-23. $$\text{real \% } Fe_2O_3 = 25.80 \times \frac{Na_2C_2O_4}{H_2C_2O_4 \cdot 2H_2O} = 25.80 \times \frac{134.00}{126.07} = 27.42$$

CHAPTER 11

11-1. $$\% \, Na_2CO_3 = \frac{\text{mL HCl} \times 0.1000 \text{ meq/mL} \times (0.10599/2) \text{ g } Na_2CO_3\text{/meq}}{\text{g sample}} \times 100 \qquad (1)$$

Since $\% \, Na_2CO_3$ = mL HCl , Equation (1) is simplified to

g sample = 0.1000 X (0.10599/2) X 100 = 0.530

11-2. The titration reaction is $CO_3^{2-} + 2H^+ \rightleftharpoons H_2CO_3$. We have

$$\% \, Na_2CO_3 = \frac{\text{mL HCl} \times 0.1000 \text{ meq/mL} \times (0.10599/2) \text{ g } Na_2CO_3\text{/meq}}{\text{g sample}} \times 100 \qquad (1)$$

$\therefore$ maximum sample size = [48 X 0.1000 X (0.10599/2) X 100] /40 = 0.64 g

minimum sample size = [24 X 0.1000 X (0.10599/2) X 100] /25 = 0.51 g

Hence, the sample size should lie in the range 0.51 to 0.64 g.

11-3. $$\% \, CH_3COOH = \frac{\text{mL NaOH} \times 0.1000 \text{ mmol/mL} \times 60.05 \text{ mg } CH_3COOH\text{/mmol}}{\text{mg sample}} \times 100 \qquad (1)$$

Since $(\% \, CH_3COOH) \times 5$ = mL NaOH, Equation (1) is simplified to

mg sample = 5 X 0.1000 X 60.05 X 100 = 3002

11-4. $N_{NaOH} = (50.00/25.00) \times N_{HCl}$

$$\therefore \frac{212.0 \text{ mg } Na_2CO_3}{(105.99/2) \text{ mg/meq}} = 50.00 \text{ mL} \times N_{HCl} - 5.00 \text{ mL} \times (50.00/25.00) \times N_{HCl}$$

or N_{HCl} = 0.1000 meq/mL $\therefore$ N_{NaOH} = (50.00/25.00) X 0.1000 = 0.2000 meq/mL

11-5. $N_{NaOH} = (25.00/20.25) \times N_{HCl}$

$$\therefore \frac{297.0 \text{ mg } CaCO_3}{(100.09/2) \text{ mg/meq}} = 30.00 \text{ mL} \times N_{HCl} - 3.36 \text{ mL} \times (25.00/20.25) \times N_{HCl}$$

or N_{HCl} = 0.2296 meq/mL

11-6. (a) 21.20 mL X N meq/mL = 20.00 mL X 0.1260 meq/mL , or N_{NaOH} = 0.1189 meq/mL

(b) $\frac{570.0 \text{ mg } H_nA}{\text{EW (mg/meq)}}$ = 23.04 mL X 0.1189 meq/mL , or EW = 208.1

(c) $\frac{23.04 \text{ mL} \times 0.1189 \text{ meq/mL} \times 1.008 \text{ mg H/meq}}{570.0 \text{ mg sample}} \times 100$ = 0.484 % H

11-7. (a) 0.1000 $\underline{M}$ Na_2CO_3 is 0.1000 $\underline{N}$ Na_2CO_3 with respect to phenolphthalein

$$\therefore N = \frac{(21.12 \text{ mL} \times 0.0510 \text{ meq/mL}) + (28.28 \text{ mL} \times 0.1000 \text{ meq/mL})}{(21.12 + 28.28) \text{ mL}} = 0.0791 \text{ meq/mL}$$

(b) 0.1000 $\underline{M}$ Na_2CO_3 is 0.2000 $\underline{N}$ Na_2CO_3 with respect to methyl orange

$$\therefore N = \frac{(21.12\text{ mL} \times 0.0510\text{ meq/mL}) + (28.28\text{ mL} \times 0.2000\text{ meq/mL})}{(21.12 + 28.28)\text{ mL}} = 0.1363\text{ meq/mL}$$

11-8. At the equivalence point, $C_{NaA} = 0.1000\ \underline{M}$

$\therefore\ pH_{ep} = (pK_w + pK_a + \log[A^-])/2 = (14.00 + 5.0 - 1.0)/2 = 9.0$

Hence, phenolphthalein is the most suitable indicator.

11-9. (a)

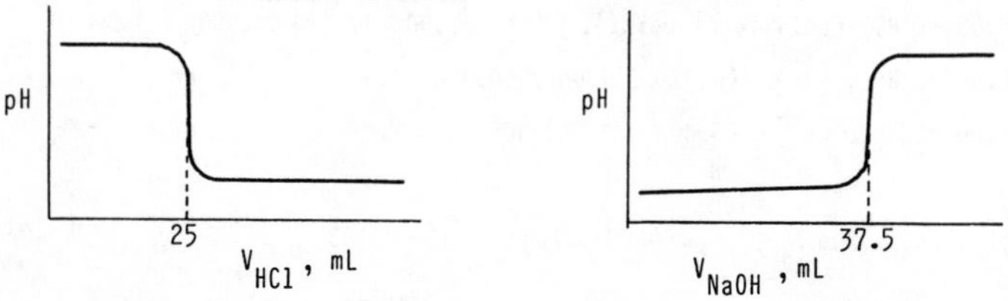

(b)

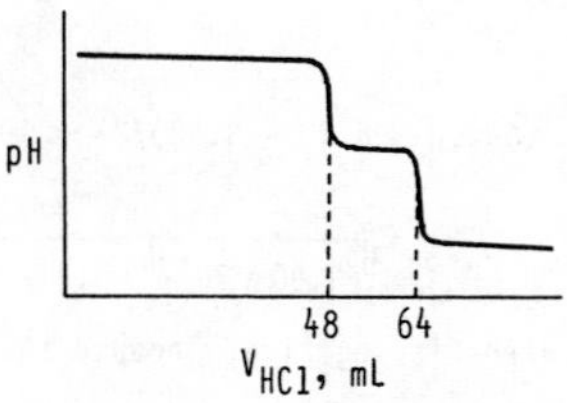

(c)

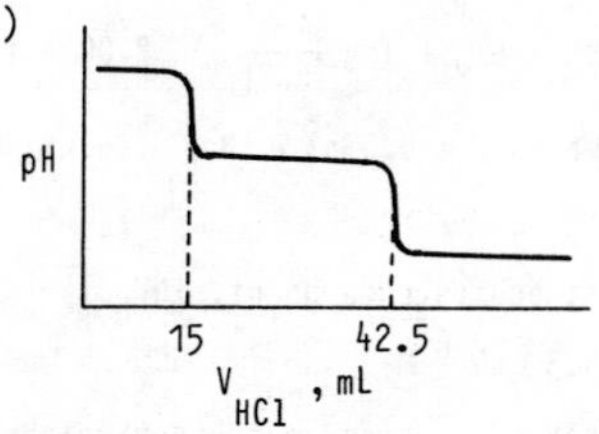

(d)

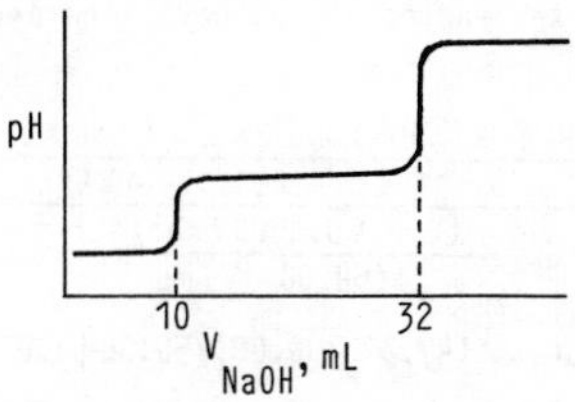

11-10. (a) $C_{HA} = \dfrac{200.0\text{ mg HA}}{(100.0\text{ mg/mmol}) \times 50.0\text{ mL}} = 0.0400\ \underline{M}\ \therefore\ (50.00 \times 0.0400/0.1000) = 20.00$ mL of NaOH are required to reach the equivalence point. At 10% ($V_{NaOH} = 2.00$ mL), $[H^+] =$

$$\frac{(50.00 \times 0.0400) - (2.00 \times 0.1000)}{52.00} = 3.46_2 \times 10^{-2}\ \underline{M}\ ,\ pH = -\log(3.46_2 \times 10^{-2}) = 1.46$$

(b) $$[H^+] = \frac{(50.00 \times 0.0400) - (19.80 \times 0.1000)}{69.80} = 2.86_5 \times 10^{-4}\ \underline{M}\ ,\quad pH = 3.54$$

(c) $[OH^-] = \dfrac{(20.20 \times 0.1000) - (50.00 \times 0.0400)}{70.20} = 2.85 \times 10^{-4}$ $\underline{M}$, pOH = 3.55 , pH = 10.45

11-11. The titration reaction is $A^- + H^+ \rightleftharpoons HA$, $K = 1/K_a = 1/2.00 \times 10^{-11} = 5.00 \times 10^{10}$ (1)

Reaction (1) is quantitative. Before any HCl is added, $A^- + H_2O \rightleftharpoons HA + OH^-$,

$pH = (pK_w + pK_a + \log[A^-])/2 = (14.00 + 10.70 - 1.00)/2 = 11.85$

At 10.00 mL HCl, pH = 10.70 + log(4.000/1.000) = 11.30

At 25.00 mL HCl, $pH = pK_a = 10.70$

At 49.90 mL HCl, pH = 10.70 + log(0.010/4.990) = 8.00

At 50.00 mL HCl (eqivalence point), $[H^+] = \sqrt{2.00 \times 10^{-11} \times 0.0500} = 1.0 \times 10^{-6}$ $\underline{M}$, pH = 6.00

At 50.10 mL HCl, $[H^+] = (0.10 \times 0.1000)/100.10 = 1.0 \times 10^{-4}$ $\underline{M}$, pH = 4.00

At 55.00 mL HCl, $[H^+] = (5.00 \times 0.1000)/105.00 = 4.8 \times 10^{-3}$ $\underline{M}$, pH = 2.32

11-12. (a) $pH = pK_1 + \log\dfrac{[HA^-]}{[H_2A]} = 4.00 + \log\dfrac{2.50}{2.50} = 4.00$

(b) We have a 0.0500 $\underline{M}$ NaHA solution ∴ pH = (4.00 + 8.00)/2 = 6.00

(c) $pH = pK_2 + \log\dfrac{[A^{2-}]}{[HA^-]} = 8.00 + \log\dfrac{2.50}{2.50} = 8.00$

(d) We have a 0.0333 $\underline{M}$ Na_2A solution ∴ pH = (14.00 + 8.00 - 1.48)/2 = 10.26

11-13. (a) At equivalence point, $[NH_4Cl] \simeq 0.0500$ $\underline{M}$ ∴ $[H^+] = \sqrt{(1.00 \times 10^{-14}/1.8 \times 10^{-5})\,0.0500} =$ 5.3×10^{-6} $\underline{M}$, $pH_{eq} = 5.28$. The titration error is negative, because the end-point (pH 8.0) precedes the equivalence point (pH 5.28).

Let V mL be the volume of HCl added until the end point. We have from $K_{NH_4^+}$

$$K_{NH_4^+} = \frac{1.00 \times 10^{-14}}{1.8 \times 10^{-5}} = \frac{(1.0 \times 10^{-8})\dfrac{(50.00\text{ mL} \times 0.1000\text{ mmol/mL}) - (V\text{ mL} \times 0.1000\text{ mmol/mL})}{(50.00 + V)\text{ mL}}}{\dfrac{(V\text{ mL} \times 0.1000\text{ mmol/mL})}{(50.00 + V)\text{ mL}}}$$

from which V = 47.37 mL ∴ titration error = [(47.37 - 50.00)/50.00] 100 = -5.3 %

(b) Let V′ mL be the volume of HCl added until the end point (pH 4.0). We have

$[NH_4^+] + [H^+] = [Cl^-] + [OH^-]$

or $\dfrac{50.00 \times 0.1000}{50.00 + V'} + 1.0 \times 10^{-4} = \dfrac{V' \times 0.1000}{50.00 + V'} + 1.00 \times 10^{-10}$,

from which V′ = 50.10 mL ∴ titration error = [(50.10 - 50.00)/50.00] 100 = +0.2 %

<u>Conclusion</u> . Methyl orange is suitable indicator, whereas phenolphthalein is not.

11-14. % $(NH_4)_2SO_4$ =

$$\frac{[(25.00\text{ mL} \times 0.2020\text{ mmol/mL}) - (16.75\text{ mL} \times 0.1040\text{ mmol/mL})] \times (132.14/2)\text{ mg }(NH_4)_2SO_4/\text{mmol}}{225.0\text{ mg sample}} \times 100 =$$

97.1

11-15. $$\%\text{ protein (w/v)} = \frac{21.18\text{ mL} \times 0.0996\text{ mmol/mL} \times 0.01401\text{ g N/mmol} \times 6.25\text{ g protein/g N}}{2.00\text{ mL}} \times 100 = 9.24$$

11-16. $M_{H_2SO_4} = y$, $M_{H_3PO_4} = z$. We have

$(50.00\text{ mL} \times y\text{ mmol }H_2SO_4/\text{mL} \times 2\text{ meq/mmol}) + (50.00\text{ mL} \times z\text{ meq }H_3PO_4/\text{mL} \times 1\text{ meq/mL}) =$

$32.00\text{ mL} \times 0.2000\text{ meq/mL}$ or

$100.00\,y + 50.00\,z = 6.400$ (1)

$50.00\,z = 11.20 \times 0.2000 = 2.240$ (2)

Solving the two simultaneous equations gives $y = M_{H_2SO_4} = 0.0416$, $z = M_{H_3PO_4} = 0.0448$.

11-17. Suppose that 1 liter of solution contains y mol NaOH and z mol Na_2CO_3. We have

$y + 2z = 0.1000$ (1)

$y + z = 0.0990$ (2)

Solving the two simultaneous equations gives $y = 0.0980$, $z = 0.001000$. Hence, the solution contains 0.0980 mol NaOH/L X 40.00 g/mol = 3.92 g NaOH/L, and 0.001000 mol Na_2CO_3/L X 105.99 g/mol = 0.1060 g Na_2CO_3/L .

11-18. $$\%\,NaHCO_3 = \frac{(24.85 - 9.24)\text{ mL} \times 0.1004\text{ meq/mL} \times 84.01\text{ mg }NaHCO_3/\text{meq} \times (100.0/25.00)}{2023.0\text{ mg sample}} \times 100 = 26.03$$

$$\%\,Na_2CO_3 = \frac{[41.24 - (24.85 - 9.24)]\text{mL} \times 0.1004\text{ meq/mL} \times (105.99/2)\text{mg }Na_2CO_3/\text{meq} \times (100.0/25.00)}{2023.0\text{ mg sample}} \times$$

100 = 26.96

11-19. Suppose that the sample contains y mg Na_2CO_3 . We have

$$\frac{y\text{ mg }Na_2CO_3}{(105.99/1)\text{ mg/meq}} = 100.0\text{ mL} \times 0.0410\text{ meq/mL}$$

or $y = 434.6$ mg Na_2CO_3 $\therefore$ $470.6 - 434.6 = 36.0$ mg $NaHCO_3$. Hence,

$$N = \frac{\dfrac{434.6\text{ mg }Na_2CO_3}{(105.99/2)\text{ mg/meq}} + \dfrac{36.0\text{ mg }NaHCO_3}{84.01\text{ mg/meq}}}{100.0\text{ mL}} = 0.0863\text{ meq/mL}$$

11-20. Solution A contains 0.2650 g Na_2CO_3/(0.10599 g/mmol) = 2.500 mmol Na_2CO_3 and 0.1260 g $NaHCO_3$/(0.08401 g/mmol) = 1.500 mmol $NaHCO_3$

∴ (a) 2.500 mmol/(0.2000 mmol/mL) = 12.50 0.2000 M HCl are required in the presence of phenolphthalein, and

(b) (2 X 2.500 + 1.500) mmol/(0.2000 mmol/mL) = 32.50 mL HCl in the presence of methyl orange as indicator.

11-21. Suppose that the 0.3800-g sample contains y mmol Na_2CO_3, and consequently 3 y mmol $NaHCO_3$. We have

(y mmol Na_2CO_3 X 105.99 mg/mmol) + (3 y mmol $NaHCO_3$ X 84.01 mg/mmol) = 380.0 mg,

or y = 1.061_4 mmol Na_2CO_3

$$\therefore V_p = \frac{1.061_4 \text{ mmol } Na_2CO_3 \times 1 \text{ meq/mmol}}{0.1000 \text{ meq/mL}} = 10.61 \text{ mL},$$

$$V_m = \frac{(1.061_4 \text{ mmol } Na_2CO_3 \times 2 \text{ meq/mmol}) + (3 \times 1.061_4) \text{ meq}}{0.1000 \text{ meq/mL}} = 53.07 \text{ mL}$$

11-22. Suppose that the 0.2400-g sample contains y mmol Na_2CO_3, and consequently 2 y mmol NaOH. We have

(y mmol Na_2CO_3 X 105.99 mg/mmol) + (2y mmol NaOH X 40.00 mg/mmol) = 240.0 mg

or y = 1.290_4 mmol Na_2CO_3

$$\therefore V_p = \frac{(1.290_4 \text{ mmol } Na_2CO_3 \times 1 \text{ meq/mmol}) + (2 \times 1.290_4 \text{ meq } NaHCO_3)}{0.1000 \text{ meq/mL}} = 38.71 \text{ mL},$$

$$V_m = \frac{(1.290_4 \text{ mmol } Na_2CO_3 \times 2 \text{ meq/mmol}) + (2 \times 1.290_4 \text{ meq } NaHCO_3)}{0.1000 \text{ meq/mL}} = 51.62$$

11-23. Suppose that the 0.2000-g sample contains y g Na_2CO_3, and consequently (0.2000 − y) g $NaHCO_3$. We have

$$\frac{y \text{ g } Na_2CO_3}{(0.10599/2)\text{g/meq}} + \frac{(0.2000 - y) \text{ g } NaHCO_3}{0.08401 \text{ g/meq}} = 24.25 \text{ mL} \times 0.1000 \text{ meq/mL}$$

or y = 0.00636 g Na_2CO_3 ∴ the sample contains (0.00636/0.2000) X 100 = 3.18 % Na_2CO_3 and 96.82 % $NaHCO_3$.

11-24. $$\frac{2.80 \text{ mL} \times 0.0250 \text{ meq/mL} \times 60.01 \text{ mg } CO_3^{2-}/\text{meq}}{100.0 \text{ mL}} \times 1000 \text{ mL/L} = 42.0 \text{ mg/L} = 42.0 \text{ ppm } CO_3^{2-}$$

$$\frac{[29.60 - (2 \times 2.80)] \text{ mL} \times 0.0250 \text{ meq/mL} \times 61.02 \text{ mg } HCO_3^-/\text{meq}}{100.0 \text{ mL}} \times 1000 \text{ mL/L} = 366 \text{ mg/L} =$$

366 ppm HCO_3^-

11-25. See Example 11-12. Since $V_m > 2V_p$ (35.68 > 2 X 14.34), the sample contains Na_2CO_3 and $NaHCO_3$

$$\% \ Na_2CO_3 = \frac{14.34 \text{ mL X } 0.0998 \text{ meq/mL X } 105.99 \text{ mg } Na_2CO_3\text{/meq}}{252.8 \text{ mg sample}} \times 100 = 60.0$$

$$\% \ NaHCO_3 = \frac{[35.68 - (2 \times 14.34)] \text{ mL X } 0.0998 \text{ meq/mL X } 84.01 \text{ mg } NaHCO_3\text{/meq}}{252.8 \text{ mg sample}} \times 100 = 23.22$$

11-26. See Example 11-12.

(a) $V_m = V_p$ ∴ it contains only NaOH

g NaOH = 19.76 mL X 0.1000 meq/mL X 0.04000 g NaOH/meq = 0.0790

(b) $V_m > 2V_p$ ∴ it contains Na_2CO_3 and $NaHCO_3$

g Na_2CO_3 = 18.01 mL X 0.1000 meq/mL X 0.10599 g Na_2CO_3/meq = 0.1909

g $NaHCO_3$ = [42.37 - (2 X 18.01)] mL X 0.1000 meq/mL X 0.08401 g $NaHCO_3$/meq = 0.0533

(c) $V_m > V_p = 0$ ∴ it contains only $NaHCO_3$

g $NaHCO_3$ = 32.23 mL X 0.1000 meq/mL X 0.08401 g $NaHCO_3$/meq = 0.2708

(d) $V_m = 2V_p$ ∴ it contains only Na_2CO_3

g Na_2CO_3 = 21.90 mL X 0.1000 meq/mL X 0.10599 g Na_2CO_3/meq = 0.2321

or g Na_2CO_3 = 43.80 mL X 0.1000 meq/mL X (0.10599/2) g Na_2CO_3/meq = 0.2321

(e) $V_m < 2V_p$ ∴ it contains Na_2CO_3 and NaOH

g Na_2CO_3 = (38.24 - 23.72) mL X 0.1000 meq/mL X 0.10599 g Na_2CO_3/meq = 0.1539

g NaOH = [23.72 - (38.24 - 23.72)] mL X 0.1000 meq/mL X 0.04000 g NaOH/meq = 0.0368

11-27. (a) $V_p = 0$, V_m = 1.42 mmol/(0.1000 mmol/mL) = 14.2 mL

(b) $V_p = V_m$ = 2.31 mmol/(0.1000 mmol/mL) = 23.1 mL

(c) V_p = 2.15 mmol/(0.1000 mmol/mL) = 21.5 mL ∴ V_m = 2 X 21.5 = 43.0 mL

(d) $NaOH + NaHCO_3 \rightleftharpoons Na_2CO_3 + H_2O$

1.48 mmol 1.48 mmol 1.48 mmol

∴ we have 2.48 - 1.48 = 1.00 mmol $NaHCO_3$ and 1.48 mmol Na_2CO_3. Hence,

V_p = 1.48 mmol/(0.1000 mmol/mL) = 14.8 mL

V_m = (1.00 + 2 X 1.48) mmol/(0.1000 mmol/mL) = 39.6 mL

(e) $NaOH + NaHCO_3 \rightleftharpoons Na_2CO_3 + H_2O$

1.48 mmol 1.48 mmol 1.48 mmol

∴ we have 2.48 - 1.48 = 1.00 mmol NaOH + 1.48 mmol Na_2CO_3. Hence ,

$V_p = (1.00 + 1.48)\ mmol/(0.1000\ mmol/mL) = 24.8\ mL$

$V_m = (1.00 + 2 \times 1.48)\ mmol/(0.1000\ mmol/mL) = 39.6\ mL$

(f) 1.48 mmol NaOH and 1.48 mmol $NaHCO_3$ react and give 1.48 mmol Na_2CO_3. Hence ,

$V_p = 1.48\ mmol/(0.1000\ mmol/mL) = 14.8\ mL$, $V_m = 29.6\ mL$

(g) $V_p = 1.19\ mmol/(0.1000\ mmol/mL) = 11.9\ mL$

$V_m = (2 \times 1.19 + 0.83)\ mmol/(0.1000\ mmol/mL) = 32.1\ mL$

(h) $V_p = (2.56 + 1.00)\ mmol/(0.1000\ mmol/mL) = 35.6\ mL$

$V_m = (2.56 + 2 \times 1.00)\ mmol/(0.1000\ mmol/mL) = 45.6\ mL$

11-28. Since $pH \simeq 7$, the solution contains NaH_2PO_4 and Na_2HPO_4 .

$$\%\ NaH_2PO_4\ (w/w) = \frac{49.20\ mL \times 0.1000\ meq/mL \times 0.11998\ g\ NaH_2PO_4/meq}{25.00\ mL \times 1.00\ g/mL} \times 100 = 2.36$$

$$\%\ Na_2HPO_4\ (w/w) = \frac{30.90\ mL \times 0.1000\ meq/mL \times 0.14196\ g\ Na_2HPO_4/meq}{25.00\ mL \times 1.00\ g/mL} \times 100 = 1.75$$

$$\therefore\ pH = pK_2 + \log\frac{[HPO_4^{2-}]}{[H_2PO_4^-]} = 7.21 + \log\frac{(17.5\ g/L)/(141.96\ g/mol)}{(23.6\ g/L)/(119.98\ g/mol)} = 7.01$$

11-29. See Example 11-18.

(a) $V_p > 2V_m$ $(49.45 > 2 \times 19.12)$ $\therefore$ it contains H_3PO_4 and NaH_2PO_4 , at concentrations equal to

$$M_{H_3PO_4} = \frac{19.12 \times 0.1000}{25.00} = 0.0765$$

$$M_{NaH_2PO_4} = \frac{[49.45 - (2 \times 19.12)] \times 0.1000}{25.00} = 0.0448$$

(b) $V_p = V_m$ $\therefore$ it contains only HCl, at a concentration of $(37.35 \times 0.1000)/25.00 =$ 0.1494 M

(c) $V_p > V_m = 0$ $\therefore$ it contains only NaH_2PO_4, at a concentration of $(39.16 \times 0.1000)/25.00$ = 0.1566 M

(d) $V_p < 2V_m$ $\therefore$ it contains H_3PO_4 and HCl , at concentrations equal to

$$M_{H_3PO_4} = \frac{(28.77 - 16.92) \times 0.1000}{25.00} = 0.0474$$

$$M_{HCl} = \frac{[16.92 - (28.77 - 16.92)] \times 0.1000}{25.00} = 0.0203$$

(e) $V_p = 2V_m$ $\therefore$ it contains only H_3PO_4, at a concentration of $(22.46 \times 0.1000)/25.00 =$ 0.0898 M .

11-30. See Example 11-17.

(a) $V_m > V_p = 0$ ∴ it contains only Na_2HPO_4

mg NaH_2PO_4 = 19.77 mL X 0.1000 mmol/mL X 141.96 mg Na_2HPO_4/mmol = 280.7

(b) $V_m = 2V_p$ ∴ it contains only Na_3PO_4

mg Na_3PO_4 = 20.05 mL X 0.1000 mmol/mL X 163.94 mg Na_3PO_4/mmol = 328.7

or mg Na_3PO_4 = 40.10 mL X 0.1000 mmol/mL X (163.94/2) mg Na_3PO_4/mmol = 328.7

(c) $V_m < 2V_p$ ∴ it contains Na_3PO_4 and NaOH

mg Na_3PO_4 = (41.28 - 25.74) mL X 0.1000 mmol/mL X 163.94 mg Na_3PO_4/mmol = 254.8

mg NaOH = [25.74 - (41.28 - 25.74)] mL X 0.1000 mmol/mL X 40.00 mg NaOH/mmol = 40.8

(d) $V_m > 2V_p$ ∴ it contains Na_3PO_4 and Na_2HPO_4

mg Na_3PO_4 = 22.49 mL X 0.1000 mmol/mL X 163.94 mg Na_3PO_4/mmol = 368.7

mg Na_2HPO_4 = [48.26 - (2 X 22.49)] mL X 0.1000 mmol/mL X 141.96 mg Na_2HPO_4/mmol = 46.6

11-31. Since volume of acid until the first equivalence point (11.22 mL) is smaller than volume of acid consumed between first and second equivalence point (33.66 - 11.22 = 22.44), solution A contains PO_4^{3-} (≡ 11.22) and HPO_4^{2-} (≡ 22.44)

$$\therefore \quad pH = pK_3 + \log\frac{[PO_4^{3-}]}{[HPO_4^{2-}]} = 12.0 + \log\frac{11.22}{22.44} = 11.7$$

11-32. See Equations (11-38), (11-39), and (11-40). The sample contains

(18.37 - 8.12) mL X 0.5040 mmol/mL X 0.09411 g C_6H_5OH/mmol = 0.4862 g C_6H_5OH

11-33. The following reactions take place ,

$$CH_3OH + (CH_3CO)_2O \rightleftharpoons CH_3OCOCH_3 + CH_3COOH$$

$$CH_3NH_2 + (CH_3CO)_2O \rightleftharpoons CH_3NHCOCH_3 + CH_3COOH$$

$$(CH_3CO)_2O + H_2O \rightleftharpoons 2CH_3COOH$$

$$CH_3NH_2 + HClO_4 \rightleftharpoons CH_3NH_3ClO_4$$

$$HClO_4 + CH_3COONa \rightleftharpoons NaClO_4 + CH_3COOH$$

Suppose that sample A contains y mmol CH_3OH and z mmol CH_3NH_2. We have

y + z = (26.10 - 16.10) mL X 0.5000 mmol/mL X 4 = 20.00 (1)

z = [(25.00 mL X 0.2000 mmol/mL) - (20.00 mL X 0.1250 mmol/mL)] X 4 = 10.00 (2)

Solving the two simultaneous equations gives y = 10.00

∴ sample A contains 10.00 mmol X 0.03204 g CH_3OH/mmol = 0.3204 g CH_3OH

11-34. (a) The titration reaction is $NH_4^+ + OH^- \rightleftharpoons NH_3 + H_2O$, $K = \frac{[NH_3]}{[NH_4^+][OH^-]} = \frac{1}{K_b} =$ $1/(1.8 \times 10^{-5}) = 5.6 \times 10^4$

At equ. point , $C_{NH_3} = 0.0500$ $\underline{M}$, $[NH_3] = 0.0500 - [NH_4^+] \simeq 0.0500$ $\underline{M}$, $[NH_4^+] \simeq [OH^-]$

$\therefore$ $0.0500/[NH_4^+]^2 = 5.6 \times 10^4$, or $[NH_4^+] = 9.4 \times 10^{-4}$ $\underline{M}$. Hence, we have

$(9.4 \times 10^{-4}/0.0500) \times 100 = 1.9\ \%$ of unreacted NH_4^+

(b) The titration reaction is $NH_4^+ + C_2H_5O^- \rightleftharpoons NH_3 + C_2H_5OH$, $K = \frac{[NH_3]}{[NH_4^+][C_2H_5O^-]} \times \frac{[C_2H_5OH_2^+]}{[C_2H_5OH_2^+]} = \frac{1 \times 10^{-10}}{3 \times 10^{-20}} = 3.3 \times 10^9$

At equ. point, $C_{NH_3} = 0.0500$ $\underline{M}$, $[NH_3] \simeq 0.0500$ $\underline{M}$, $[NH_4^+] \simeq [C_2H_5O^-]$

$\therefore$ $0.0500/[NH_4^+]^2 = 3.3 \times 10^9$, or $[NH_4^+] = 3.9 \times 10^{-6}$ $\underline{M}$. Hence, we have

$(3.9 \times 10^{-6}/0.0500) \times 100 = 0.008\ \%$ of unreacted NH_4^+

In the titration of NH_4^+ ions, ethanol is a better solvent than water (0.008 % vs. 1.9 % of unreacted NH_4^+).

11-35. Suppose that the sample contains y mmol CH_3OH and z mmol C_2H_5OH. We have

$$y + z = (45.96 - 20.96)\ \text{mL} \times 0.1000\ \text{mmol/mL} = 2.500 \qquad (1)$$

$$32.04\,y + 46.07\,z = 94.1 \qquad (2)$$

Solving the two simultaneous equations gives $y = 1.502$, $z = 0.998$. Hence, the sample contains

$$\frac{1.502\ \text{mmol}\ CH_3OH \times 32.04\ \text{mg/mmol}}{94.1\ \text{mg sample}} \times 100 = 51.1\ \%\ CH_3OH \text{ , and}$$

$$\frac{0.998\ \text{mmol}\ C_2H_5OH \times 46.07\ \text{mg/mmol}}{94.1\ \text{mg sample}} \times 100 = 48.9\ \%\ C_2H_5OH$$

11-36. See Example 11-24.

Suppose that the titrated 1/4 of the sample contains w mmol $C_6H_5NH_2$, y mmol $C_6H_5NHCH_3$, and z mmol $C_6H_5N(CH_3)_2$. We have

$$w + y + z = (33.25\ \text{mL} \times 0.1000\ \text{mmol/mL}) = 3.325 \qquad (1)$$

$$z = 17.40\ \text{mL} \times 0.1000\ \text{mmol/mL} = 1.740 \qquad (2)$$

$$y + z = 23.25\ \text{mL} \times 0.1000\ \text{mmol/mL} = 2.325 \qquad (3)$$

Solving the system of three equations gives $w = 1.000$, $y = 0.585$, $z = 1.740$. Hence, the sample contains

$[(1.000\ \text{mmol}\ C_6H_5NH_2 \times 93.12\ \text{mg/mmol})/500.0\ \text{mg}] \times 100 = 18.62\ \%\ C_6H_5NH_2$,

$[(0.585\ \text{mmol}\ C_6H_5NHCH_3 \times 107.15\ \text{mg/mmol})/500.0\ \text{mg}] \times 100 = 12.54\ \%\ C_6H_5NHCH_3$,

$[(1.740\ \text{mmol}\ C_6H_5N(CH_3)_2 \times 121.18\ \text{mg/mmol})/500.0\ \text{mg}] \times 100 = 42.17\ \%\ C_6H_5N(CH_3)_2$,

and $100.00-(18.62+12.54+42.17) = 26.67\ \%$ unreactive substances.

11-37. (a) The following reactions take place :

$$CH_3CH(NH_2)COOH + HClO_4 \rightleftharpoons (CH_3CHNH_3COOH)ClO_4$$

$$HClO_4 + CH_3COONa \rightleftharpoons NaClO_4 + CH_3COOH$$

$$CH_3CH(NH_2)COOH + HNO_2 \rightleftharpoons CH_3CHOHCOOH + H_2O + N_2\uparrow$$

$$\therefore \frac{(25.00\ \text{mL} \times 0.2008\ \text{mmol/mL} - 26.89\ \text{mL} \times 0.1004\ \text{mmol}) \times 89.09\ \text{mg alanine/mmol}}{220.8\ \text{mg sample}} \times 100 =$$

93.6 % alanine.

(b) $(25.00 \times 0.2008 - 26.89 \times 0.1004)\ \text{mmol} \times 22.40\ \text{mL}\ N_2/\text{mmol} \times (760/758) \times (298/273) =$

56.9 mL N_2

11-38. $$\frac{0.6486\ \text{g}}{(\text{MW}/1)\ \text{g/mol}} = \frac{(36.20-6.20)\ \text{mL} \times 0.2000\ \text{mmol/mL}}{1000\ \text{mmol/mol}}$$

from which MW = 108.1 ($\equiv C_6H_5CH_2OH$)

11-39. $$\%\ \text{guanine} = \frac{(25.00\ \text{mL} \times 0.1000\ \text{mmol/mL} - 15.32\ \text{mL} \times 0.1000\ \text{mmol/mL}) \times 151.13\ \text{mg guanine/mmol}}{165.0\ \text{mg sample}} \times 100 = 88.7$$

11-40. $$\frac{5.62\ \text{mL} \times 0.01000\ \text{meq/mL} \times (0.06406/2)\ \text{g}\ SO_2/\text{meq}}{10\ \text{L/min} \times 30\ \text{min} \times 2.86\ \text{g}\ SO_2/\text{L}} \times 10^6 = 2.10$$

11-41. $$\%\ \text{HA (w/w)} = \frac{15.00\ \text{mL} \times 0.1000\ \text{mmol/mL} \times 60.0\ \text{mg HA/mmol}}{1800\ \text{mg sample}} \times 100 = 5.00 \quad \therefore \text{(d)}$$

11-42. Suppose that the X-g sample contains a mmol $CaCO_3$ and b mmol $MgCO_3$. We have

$$\frac{a}{2} + \frac{b}{2} = \frac{(40.00\ \text{mL})(0.1500\ \text{meq/mL})}{2\ \text{meq}\ Ca^{2+}\ \text{or}\ Mg^{2+}/\text{mmol}} = 3.000 \qquad (1)$$

$$(a/2)\ \text{mmol} \times 0.05608\ \text{g CaO/mmol} + (b/2)\ \text{mmol} \times 0.04031\ \text{g MgO/mmol} = 0.1525 \qquad (2)$$

Solving the two simultaneous equations gives a = 4.004, b = 1.996

$\therefore$ X = 4.004 mmol $CaCO_3$ × 0.10009 g $CaCO_3$/mmol + 1.996 mmol × 0.08431 g $MgCO_3$/mmol =

0.5690 g

11-43. (a) The 0.9300-g sample contains

18.75 mL × 0.0800 meq/mL × (0.10599/2) g Na_2CO_3/meq × (500.0/50.00) = 0.7950 g Na_2CO_3, and $0.9300 - 0.7950 = 0.1350\ g\ H_2O$

$$\therefore \quad \frac{0.1350\ g\ H_2O}{0.7950\ g\ Na_2CO_3} = \frac{18.01\,y}{105.99}, \quad \text{from which} \quad y \simeq 1$$

(b) Let V mL be the required volume of HCl. We have

$$\frac{0.9300\ g}{(0.28614/2)\ g\ Na_2CO_3\cdot 10H_2O/meq} = V\ mL \times 0.0800\ meq/mL\ ,$$

or $V = 81.3$ mL

11-44. $$\text{Rate} = \frac{(23.31 - 12.17)\ mL \times 0.1250\ meq/mL \times 44.01\ mg\ CO_2/meq \times (100.0/25.00)}{25.00\ g \times 48\ h} =$$

0.204 mg CO_2 per gram soil per hour

11-45. $322.8\ mg/(MW/2)\ mg/meq = 42.67\ mL \times 0.1008\ meq/mL$, or $MW = 150.1$

11-46. $$\%\ H_3BO_3 = \frac{14.75\ mL \times 0.1075\ mmol/mL \times 61.85\ mg\ H_3BO_3/mmol}{875.5\ mg\ sample} \times 100 = 11.20$$

11-47. The following reactions take place :

$$C_6H_5CHO + H_2NOH\cdot HCl \rightleftharpoons C_6H_5CH{=}NOH + H_2O + HCl$$

$$HCl + NaOH \longrightarrow NaCl + H_2O$$

$$\therefore \%\ C_6H_5CHO = \frac{(15.12 - 0.12)\ mL \times 0.5020\ mmol/mL \times 106.12\ mg\ C_6H_5CHO/mmol}{824.2\ mg\ sample} \times 100 = 97.0$$

12-1. $Br_2 + 2Fe^{2+} \rightleftharpoons 2Br^- + 2Fe^{3+}$ (1)

$K = 10^{16.903 \times 2(1.087 - 0.771)} = 4.8 \times 10^{10}$ ∴ reaction (1) is quantitative

$$E_{eq} = E^0_{Fe^{3+},Fe^{2+}} - \frac{RT}{F} \ln \frac{[Fe^{2+}]}{[Fe^{3+}]} \quad (2)$$

or $$E_{eq} = E^0_{Br_2,Br^-} - \frac{RT}{2F} \ln \frac{[Br^-]^2}{[Br_2]} \quad (3)$$

Multiplying Equation (3) by 2 and adding the product to Equation (2), we have

$$3E_{eq} = E^0_{Fe^{3+},Fe^{2+}} + 2E^0_{Br_2,Br^-} - \frac{RT}{F} \ln \frac{[Fe^{2+}][Br^-]^2}{[Fe^{3+}][Br_2]} \quad (4)$$

At the equivalence point, we have $[Fe^{3+}] = [Br^-]$, and $[Fe^{2+}] = 2[Br_2]$. Substituting in Equation (4), we have

$$3E_{eq} = E^0_{Fe^{3+},Fe^{2+}} + 2E^0_{Br_2,Br^-} - \frac{RT}{F} \ln \frac{2[Br_2][Br^-]^2}{[Br^-][Br_2]}$$

or $$E_{eq} = \frac{E^0_{Fe^{3+},Fe^{2+}} + 2E^0_{Br_2,Br^-}}{3} - \frac{RT}{3F} \ln (2[Br^-]_{eq})$$

12-2. (a) $E_{cell} = E_{Pt} - E_{SCE} = (+1.51 - \frac{0.05916}{5} \log \frac{1}{(0.10)^8}) - 0.2412 = +1.17$ V

(b) $E_{cell} = (+0.771 - 0.05916 \log 0.40) - 0.2412 = 0.553$ V

12-3. $2MnO_4^- + 5Sn^{2+} + 16H^+ \rightleftharpoons 2Mn^{2+} + 5Sn^{4+} + 8H_2O$

$K = 10^{16.903 \times 10 \times (1.51 - 0.15)} = 7.6 \times 10^{229}$

∴ 0.140 M $KMnO_4$ ≡ $0.140 \times 5 = 0.700$ N $KMnO_4$, 0.140 M Sn^{2+} ≡ $0.140 \times 2 = 0.280$ N Sn^{2+}.
Hence, $(50.00 \times 0.280/0.700) = 20.0$ mL $KMnO_4$ are consumed till the equivalence point

∴ $V_{eq} = 70.0$ mL .

Let $y = [MnO_4^-]_{eq}$, whereupon $[Sn^{2+}] = (5/2)y = 2.50y$, $[Mn^{2+}] = (20.0 \times 0.140/70.0) - y = 0.0400 - y$, $[Sn^{4+}] = (5/2)[Mn^{2+}] = 2.50 \times (0.0400 - y) = 0.100 - 2.50y$. Substituting in the equilibrium constant expression, we have

$$7.6 \times 10^{229} = \frac{(0.0400 - y)^2 (0.100 - 2.50y)^5}{y^2 \times (2.50y)^5 \times (1.00)^{16}} \quad \text{or} \quad y = 5.8 \times 10^{-35}$$

Hence, $[MnO_4^-] = 5.8 \times 10^{-35}$ M , $[Sn^{2+}] = 2.50 \times 5.8 \times 10^{-35} = 1.45 \times 10^{-34}$ M , $[Mn^{2+}] \simeq 0.0400$ M , $[Sn^{4+}] \simeq 0.100$ M . We have

$$E_{eq} = 1.51 - \frac{0.05916}{5} \log \frac{0.0400}{5.8 \times 10^{-35} \times (1.00)^8} = 1.12 \text{ V}$$

$$\text{or} \quad E_{eq} = 0.15 - \frac{0.05916}{2} \log \frac{1.45 \times 10^{-34}}{0.100} = 1.12 \text{ V}$$

$$\text{or} \quad E_{eq} = \frac{5 E^0_{MnO_4^-,Mn^{2+}} + 2 E^0_{Sn^{4+},Sn^{2+}}}{7} = \frac{(5 \times 1.51) + (2 \times 0.15)}{7} = 1.12 \text{ V}$$

12-4. $N_{KMnO_4} = (0.1005/5) \times 3 = 0.0603$

$$\therefore \% \text{ Mn} = \frac{35.87 \text{ mL} \times 0.0603 \text{ meq/mL} \times (54.94/2) \text{ mg Mn/meq}}{885.7 \text{ mg sample}} \times 100 = 6.71$$

12-5. $238.3 \text{ mg}/(134.00/2) \text{ mg } Na_2C_2O_4/\text{meq} = 35.57 \text{ mL} \times N \text{ meq/mL}$, or $N_{KMnO_4} = 0.1000$. Hence, the sample contains

$$\frac{(36.50 - 0.08) \text{ mL} \times 0.1000 \text{ meq/mL} \times (56.08/2) \text{ mg CaO/meq}}{191.4 \text{ mg sample}} \times 100 = 53.36 \% \text{ CaO}$$

12-6. $\frac{11,740 \text{ mg W}}{(183.85/n) \text{ mg/meq}} \times \frac{25.00}{1000} = 48.00 \text{ mL} \times 0.1000 \text{ meq/mL}$, from which $n = 3.007 \simeq 3$.
Hence, the oxidation number of W in solution A is equal to $6 - 3 = 3$.

12-7. $\frac{(0.2000 \times 0.5104) \text{ g M}}{(50.94/n) \text{ g/eq}} = \frac{40.00 \text{ mL} \times 0.1005 \text{ meq/mL}}{1000 \text{ meq/mL}}$, from which $n = 2.006 \simeq 2$.
Hence, the oxidation number of M in solution A is equal to $5 - 2 = 3$.

12-8. $$\% \ C_2O_4 = \frac{40.00 \text{ mL} \times 0.1000 \text{ meq/mL} \times (88.02/2) \text{ mg } C_2O_4/\text{meq} \times (1000/50.00)}{5084 \text{ mg sample}} \times 100 = 69.25$$

$$\equiv \frac{69.25 \text{ g } C_2O_4/100 \text{ g}}{88.02 \text{ g/gion}} = 0.787 \text{ gion } C_2O_4/100 \text{ g}$$

$$\% \text{ H} = \frac{25.00 \text{ mL} \times 0.1200 \text{ meq/mL} \times 1.008 \text{ g H/meq} \times (1000/50.00)}{5084 \text{ mg sample}} \times 100 = 1.19$$

$$\equiv \frac{1.19 \text{ g H}/100 \text{ g}}{1.008 \text{ g/gion}} = 1.18 \text{ gion H}/100 \text{ g}$$

$\therefore C_2O_4/H = 0.787/1.18 \simeq 2/3$. Hence, the formula of the salt is
$KHC_2O_4 \cdot H_2C_2O_4 \cdot y H_2O$ $\therefore$ we have

$$\% \ C_2O_4 = 69.25 = \frac{2 C_2O_4}{KHC_2O_4 \cdot H_2C_2O_4 \cdot y H_2O} \times 100 = \frac{2 \times 88.02}{218.16 + 18.02 y} \times 100 \quad (1)$$

Solving Equation (1) we find $y = 2$. Hence, the formula of the oxalate salt is
$KHC_2O_4 \cdot H_2C_2O_4 \cdot 2H_2O$.

12-9. $[Fe^{2+}]/C_{Fe} = 36.27/40.89 = 0.8870$. Hence, 88.70% of iron remained as $FeSO_4$

$\therefore$ 100.00 - 88.70 = 11.30% of $FeSO_4$ was oxidized.

12-10. $$N_{KMnO_4} = \frac{286.0 \text{ mg } Na_2C_2O_4}{(134.00/2) \text{ mg/meq} \times 42.68 \text{ mL}} = 0.1000 \text{ meq/mL}$$

$\therefore M_{KMnO_4} = 0.1000/5 = 0.02000$ $\underline{M}$. For the titration of the sample ($MnO_4^- \rightarrow MnO_2$, n=3), $N_{KMnO_4} = 0.02000 \times 3 = 0.0600$. Hence, the sample contains

$$\frac{46.65 \text{ mL} \times 0.0600 \text{ meq/mL} \times (54.94/2) \text{ mg Mn/meq}}{870.0 \text{ mg sample}} \times 100 = 8.84\ \%\ \text{Mn}$$

12-11. $$\%\ Fe = \frac{31.98 \text{ mL} \times 0.1000 \text{ meq/mL} \times 55.85 \text{ mg Fe/meq}}{1000.0 \text{ mg sample}} \times 100 = 17.86$$

$$\%\ FeO = \frac{29.08 \text{ mL} \times 0.1000 \text{ meq/mL} \times 71.85 \text{ mg Fe/meq}}{2500.0 \text{ mg sample}} \times 100 = 8.36$$

$$\%\ Fe_2O_3 = \frac{(31.98 - 29.08 \times \frac{1.0000}{2.5000}) \text{ mL} \times 0.1000 \text{ meq/mL} \times (159.69/2) \text{ mg } Fe_2O_3\text{/meq}}{1000.0 \text{ mg sample}} \times 100 = 16.25$$

12-12. $$\%\ As = \frac{[(50.00 \times 0.2000 - 18.24 \times 0.1000) \text{ meq } As_2S_3/(28 \text{ meq } As_2S_3\text{/mmol})] \times (2 \times 74.92 \text{ mg As/mmol})}{160.4 \text{ mg sample}} \times 100 = 27.28$$

12-13. (a) $$\%\ Fe_3O_4 = \frac{30.00 \text{ mL} \times 0.1250 \text{ meq/mL} \times 231.54 \text{ mg } Fe_3O_4\text{/meq}}{1000.0 \text{ mg sample}} \times 100 = 86.8$$

(b) $3 \times 30.00 = 90.00$ mL

12-14. (a) $$N_{KMnO_4} = \frac{168.3 \text{ mg } Na_2C_2O_4}{(134.00/2) \text{ mg/meq} \times 23.41 \text{ mL}} = 0.1073 \text{ meq/mL}$$

$$\therefore \%\ H_2O_2(w/v) = \frac{[(32.85 - 0.20) \times 0.1073] \text{meq} \times (0.03402/2) \text{g } H_2O_2\text{/meq} \times (100.0/10.00)}{20.00 \text{ mL}} \times 100 = 2.98$$

(b) $(32.85 - 0.20) \text{ mL} \times 0.1073 \text{ meq/mL} \times (22.4/2) \text{ mL } O_2\text{/meq} = 39.2 \text{ mL } O_2$

12-15. N_A as reductant = $(4/3) N_A$ as acid = $(4/3)\, 0.1035 = 0.1380$

$\therefore N_{KMnO_4} = (25.00 \text{ mL} \times 0.1380 \text{ meq/mL})/34.12 \text{ mL} = 0.1011 \text{ meq/mL}$

12-16. $\% \ NaHC_2O_4 = \dfrac{12.00 \text{ mL} \times 0.0950 \text{ meq/mL} \times 112.02 \text{ mg } NaHC_2O_4\text{/meq}}{358.0 \text{ mg sample}} \times 100 = 35.67$

The 0.1790-g sample contains 19.20 mL X 0.1250 meq/mL = 2.400 meq ≡ 1.200 mmol ($Na_2C_2O_4$ + $NaHC_2O_4$),

12.00 mL X 0.0950 meq/mL X (1/2) = 0.5700 meq $NaHC_2O_4$ ≡ 0.5700 mmol $NaHC_2O_4$

∴ it contains 1.200 - 0.5700 = 0.630 mmol $Na_2C_2O_4$. Hence, we have

$$\% \ Na_2C_2O_4 = \frac{0.630 \text{ mmol} \times 134.00 \text{ mg } Na_2C_2O_4\text{/mmol}}{179.0 \text{ g sample}} \times 100 = 47.16$$

12-17. Suppose that the sample contains y g $Na_2C_2O_4$, and consequently (0.1790 - y) g $NaHC_2O_4$. We have

$$\frac{y \text{ g } Na_2C_2O_4}{(134.00/2) \text{ g/eq}} + \frac{(0.1790 - y) \text{ g } NaHC_2O_4}{(112.02/2) \text{ g/eq}} = \frac{24.00 \text{ mL} \times 0.1250 \text{ meq/mL}}{1000 \text{ meq/eq}}$$

from which y = 0.0669. Hence, the sample contains (0.0669/0.1790) X 100 = 37.37 % $Na_2C_2O_4$.

12-18. Suppose that the sample contains y mmol BaC_2O_4 and z mmol CaC_2O_4. We have

$225.36 y + 128.10 z = 480.0$ (1)

$2(y + z) = 49.50 \times 0.1040 = 5.148$ (2)

Solving the two simultaneous equations gives y = 1.545, z = 1.029. Hence, the sample contains

$$\frac{1.545 \text{ mmol} \times 225.36 \text{ mg } BaC_2O_4\text{/mmol}}{480.0 \text{ mg sample}} \times 100 = 72.54 \% \ BaC_2O_4$$

$$\frac{1.029 \text{ mmol} \times 128.10 \text{ mg } CaC_2O_4\text{/mmol}}{480.0 \text{ mg sample}} \times 100 = 27.46 \% \ CaC_2O_4$$

12-19. (a) $N_{KMnO_4} = \dfrac{235.0 \text{ mg Fe}}{55.85 \text{ mg/meq} \times (42.82 - 0.15) \text{ mL}} = 0.0986 \text{ meq/mL}$

(b) The sample contains 235.0 mg X 0.9800 = 230.3 mg Fe, and 235.0 mg X 0.0200 = 4.7 mg Fe_2O_3 ≡ 4.7 mg Fe_2O_3 X (2 X 55.85 mg Fe/159.69 mg Fe_2O_3) = 3.3 mg Fe

∴ the sample is equivalent to 230.3 + 3.3 = 233.6 mg Fe. Hence, we have

$$N_{KMnO_4} = \frac{233.6 \text{ mg Fe}}{55.85 \text{ mg/meq} \times (42.82 - 0.15) \text{ mL}} = 0.0980 \text{ meq/mL}$$

12-20. $\% \ Fe = \dfrac{\text{mL } K_2Cr_2O_7 \times N \text{ meq/mL} \times 55.85 \text{ mg Fe/meq}}{569.7 \text{ mg sample}} \times 100$ (1)

Since % Fe = mL $K_2Cr_2O_7$, Equation (1) is simplified to

$N_{K_2Cr_2O_7} = 569.7/(55.85 \times 100) = 0.1020$ ∴ $M_{K_2Cr_2O_7} = 0.1020/6 = 0.01700$

12-21. $EW = \dfrac{0.2157\ g\ K_2Cr_2O_7}{0.03520\ L \times 0.1250\ eq/L} = 49.02\ g/eq$

12-22. See Example (10-15).

$$\% Cr = \frac{[(50.00 \times 0.1022) - (18.04 \times 0.0999)]\ meq \times (52.00/3)\ mg\ Cr/meq}{268.3\ mg\ \ sample} \times 100 = 21.37$$

12-23. (a) $E_{eq} = (0.674 + 1.44)/2 = 1.06\ V > 0.65\ V$. Hence, we are before the equivalence point.
Let y mL be the volume of added Ce(IV). We have

$$0.65 = 0.674 - 0.05916 \log \frac{(2.50 - 0.1000\,y)/V}{0.1000\,y/V} \quad \text{or} \quad y = 7.1\ mL$$

(b) $1.06 = E_{eq}\ \therefore\ y = 2.50\ mmol/0.1000\ mmol/mL = 25.0\ mL$

(c) $1.39 > 1.06 = E_{eq}$. Hence, we are after the equivalence point. We have

$$1.39 = 1.44 - 0.05916 \log \frac{2.50/V}{(0.1000\,y - 2.50)/V} \quad \text{or} \quad y = 28.6\ mL$$

12-24. (a) Initially, we have $50.00\ mL \times 0.1600\ mmol\ Fe^{2+}/mL = 8.00\ mmol\ Fe^{2+}$

$$\therefore\ E = +0.674 - 0.05916 \log \frac{8.00 - 3.20}{3.20} = +0.664\ V$$

(b) $E = E_{eq} = (0.674 + 1.44)/2 = 1.06\ V$

(c) $E = 1.44 - 0.05916 \log \dfrac{16.00 - 8.00}{8.00} = 1.44\ V$

12-25. $EW = \dfrac{(1.9168 \times 0.990)\ g\ Ce}{0.03000\ L \times 0.1000\ eq/L} = 632.5\ g/eq$

12-26. $2N_3^- + 2Ce(IV) \longrightarrow 3N_2\uparrow + 2Ce(III)$

$$\% NaN_3 = \frac{24.25\ mL \times 0.1064\ meq/mL \times 65.01\ mg\ NaN_3/meq}{215.0\ mg\ sample} \times 100 = 78.0$$

12-27. $K \longrightarrow K_2Na[Co(NO_2)_6] \longrightarrow NO_3^- \quad \therefore\ 1\,K \equiv 3\,NO_2^- \equiv 6\,e$. Hence,

$$\% K = \frac{40.00\ mL \times 0.1050\ meq/mL \times (39.10/6)\ mg\ K/meq}{70.8\ mg\ sample} \times 100 = 38.66$$

12-28. (a) $Sn^{2+} + [I_3]^- \rightleftharpoons Sn^{4+} + 3I^-$ titration reaction (1)

$K = 10^{16.903 \times 2 \times (0.536 - 0.15)} = 1.1 \times 10^{13}\ \therefore$ Reaction (1) is quantitative

Since $V_{eq} = 50.00$ mL, we are before the equivalence point

$$\therefore E = +0.15 - \frac{0.05916}{2} \log \frac{[(50.00 \times 0.1000 - 49.50 \times 0.1000)\text{meq}/(2\ \text{meq/mmol})]/99.50\ \text{mL}}{[(49.50 \times 0.1000)\text{meq}/(2\ \text{meq/mmol})]/99.50\ \text{mL}}$$

$$= +0.209\ \text{V}$$

(b) We are at the equivalence point

$$\therefore E_{eq} = E^0_{Sn^{4+},Sn^{2+}} - \frac{0.05916}{2} \log \frac{[Sn^{2+}]}{[Sn^{4+}]} \quad (2)$$

$$\text{or } E_{eq} = E^0_{I_3^-,I^-} - \frac{0.05916}{2} \log \frac{[I^-]^3}{[I_3^-]} \quad (3)$$

Adding Equations (2) and (3), we have

$$2E_{eq} = E^0_{Sn^{4+},Sn^{2+}} + E^0_{I_3^-,I^-} - \frac{0.05916}{2} \log \frac{[Sn^{2+}][I^-]^3}{[Sn^{4+}][I_3^-]} \quad (4)$$

At the equivalence point, we have $[I^-] = 3[Sn^{4+}]$, and $[I_3^-] = [Sn^{2+}]$. Substituting in Equation (4), we have

$$2E_{eq} = E^0_{Sn^{4+},Sn^{2+}} + E^0_{I_3^-,I^-} - \frac{0.05916}{2} \log \frac{[Sn^{2+}](3[Sn^{4+}])^3}{[Sn^{4+}][Sn^{2+}]}$$

$$\text{or } E_{eq} = \frac{E^0_{Sn^{4+},Sn^{2+}} + E^0_{I_3^-,I^-}}{2} - \frac{0.05916}{4} \log (27[Sn^{4+}]^2) \quad (5)$$

At the equivalence point, $[Sn^{4+}] = (50.00 \times 0.1000)\ \text{meq}/(100.0\ \text{mL} \times 2\ \text{meq/mmol}) =$ 0.0250 $\underline{M}$ $\therefore$ Equation (5) becomes

$$E_{eq} = \frac{+0.15 + 0.536}{2} - \frac{0.05916}{4} \log [27 \times (0.0250)^2] = +0.369\ \text{V}$$

(c) We are after the equivalence point. We have

$$[I_3^-] = \frac{(50.50 \times 0.1000 - 50.00 \times 0.1000)\ \text{meq}}{2\ \text{meq/mmol} \times 100.50\ \text{mL}} = 2.488 \times 10^{-4}\ \underline{M}$$

$$[I^-] = \frac{(50.00 \times 0.1000)\ \text{meq}\ [I_3]^-}{2\ \text{meq/mmol} \times 100.50\ \text{mL}} \times \frac{3\ \text{mmol}\ I^-}{\text{mmol}\ [I_3]^-} = 7.463 \times 10^{-2}\ \underline{M}$$

$$\therefore E = +0.536 - \frac{0.05916}{2} \log \frac{(7.463 \times 10^{-2})^3}{(2.448 \times 10^{-4})} = +0.529\ \text{V}$$

12-29. $$\%\ As_2O_3 = \frac{\text{mL}\ [I_3]^- \times N\ \text{meq/mL} \times (197.84/4)\ \text{mg}\ As_2O_3/\text{meq}}{500.0\ \text{mg sample}} \times 100 \quad (1)$$

Since $\%\ As_2O_3 = \text{mL}\ [I_3]^-$, Equation (1) is simplified to

$N_{[I_3]^-} = 500.0/[(197.84/4) \times 100] = 0.1011$

12-30. $$Cr_2O_7^{2-} + 9I^- + 14H^+ \rightleftharpoons 2Cr^{3+} + 3[I_3]^- + 7H_2O \qquad (n = 6)$$

$$Ca_3(AsO_4)_2 \xrightarrow{H^+} 2AsO_4^{3-} \xrightarrow{I^-} 2AsO_3^{3-} + 2[I_3]^- \xrightarrow{Na_2S_2O_3} 6I^- \qquad (n = 4)$$

$$\therefore \% Ca_3(AsO_4)_2 = \frac{31.14 \text{ mL} \times \frac{1.678 \text{ mg } K_2Cr_2O_7/\text{mL}}{(294.19/6) \text{ mg/meq}} \times \frac{398.06}{4} \frac{\text{mg } Ca_3(AsO_4)_2}{\text{meq}}}{970.3 \text{ mg sample}} \times 100 = 10.93$$

12-31. Suppose that the sample contains y mg KI. We have

$$\frac{y \text{ mg KI}}{166.01 \text{ mg/meq}} + \frac{(570.0 - y) \text{ mg KBr}}{119.01 \text{ mg/meq}} = 40.00 \text{ mL} \times 0.1000 \text{ meq/mL}$$

from which y = 331.9 . Hence, the sample contains

$$\frac{331.9 \text{ mg KI} \times \frac{126.90 \text{ mg I}}{166.01 \text{ mg KI}}}{570.0 \text{ mg sample}} \times 100 = 44.51 \% \text{ I}$$

12-32. $2Cu^{2+} + 5I^- \rightleftharpoons 2CuI + [I_3]^-$

$$\% Cu = \frac{35.66 \text{ mL} \times 0.1004 \text{ meq/mL} \times 63.54 \text{ mg Cu/meq}}{340.7 \text{ mg sample}} \times 100 = 66.8$$

12-33. $$N_{[I_3]^-} = \frac{241.8 \text{ mg } As_2O_3}{(197.84/4) \text{ mg } As_2O_3/\text{meq} \times 43.76 \text{ mL}} = 0.1117 \text{ meq/mL}$$

$$\therefore \% As_2O_3 = \frac{36.09 \text{ mL} \times 0.1117 \text{ meq/mL} \times (197.84/4) \text{ mg } As_2O_3/\text{meq}}{208.4 \text{ mg sample}} \times 100 = 95.67$$

12-34. $$N_{[I_3]^-} = \frac{176.7 \text{ mg } As_2O_3}{(197.84/4) \text{ mg } As_2O_3/\text{meq} \times 35.45 \text{ mL}} = 0.1008 \text{ meq/mL}$$

$$\therefore \% NaAsO_2 = \frac{29.38 \text{ mL} \times 0.1008 \text{ meq/mL} \times (129.91/2) \text{ mg } NaAsO_2/\text{meq}}{940.0 \text{ mg sample}} \times 100 = 20.46$$

12-35. (0.0200×3) mol/L X 34.08 g H_2S/mol = 2.04 g H_2S/L

12-36. Suppose that the substance contains y g $Na_2S_2O_3 \cdot 5H_2O$/g. We have

$$\frac{5.3800 \text{ g } K_2Cr_2O_7/\text{L} \times (25.00/1000.0)}{(294.19/6) \text{ g/eq}} = \frac{12.214\, y \text{ g } Na_2S_2O_3 \cdot 5H_2O \times (28.00/500.0)}{248.18 \text{ g/eq}}$$

from which y = 0.9953. Hence, the substance contains (0.9953/1.0000) X 100 = 99.53 % $Na_2S_2O_3 \cdot 5H_2O$

12-37. $XeO_3 + 9I^- + 6H^+ \rightleftharpoons Xe + 3[I_3]^- + 3H_2O$

$\qquad\qquad\qquad\qquad\qquad\qquad +$

$\qquad\qquad\qquad\qquad\qquad 6S_2O_3^{2-} \rightleftharpoons 9I^- + 3S_4O_6^{2-}$

$\therefore N_{Na_2S_2O_3} = M_{Na_2S_2O_3}$, $N_{XeO_3} = 6\,M_{XeO_3}$. Hence, we have

25.00 mL X M mmol XeO_3/mL X 6 meq/mmol = 44.00 mL X 0.0341 meq/mL, from which M_{XeO_3} = 0.01000 mmol/mL .

12-38. $\dfrac{245.0\text{ mg oxidizing agent}}{(122.55/n)\text{ mg/meq}} = 48.00\text{ mL} \times 0.2500\text{ meq/mL}$, from which $n = 6$

12-39. The following reactions take place during the analysis :

$$IO_4^- + 2H^+ + 3I^- \xrightleftharpoons{pH\ 8} IO_3^- + [I_3]^- + H_2O \qquad (\therefore \text{ mmol } IO_4^- \equiv \text{meq } S_2O_3^{2-}/2)$$

$$IO_4^- + 8H^+ + 11I^- \xrightleftharpoons{pH\ 1} 4[I_3]^- + 4H_2O \qquad (\therefore \text{ mmol } IO_4^- \equiv \text{meq } S_2O_3^{2-}/8)$$

$$IO_3^- + 6H^+ + 8I^- \xrightleftharpoons{pH\ 1} 3[I_3]^- + 3H_2O \qquad (\therefore \text{ mmol } IO_3^- \equiv \text{meq } S_2O_3^{2-}/6)$$

$$[I_3]^- + 2S_2O_3^{2-} \rightleftharpoons 3I^- + S_4O_6^{2-}$$

Let y be the molarity of IO_3^- ions in solution A . We have

$$\frac{(40.00 \times 0.1000)\text{ meq } S_2O_3^{2-} \times \dfrac{1\text{ mmol } IO_4^-}{2\text{ meq } S_2O_3^{2-}}}{25.00\text{ mL}} = 0.0800\text{ mmol } IO_4^-/\text{mL} = M_{IO_4^-}$$

$$\left[(5.00 \times 0.0800)\text{ mmol } IO_4^- \times \frac{8\text{ meq } S_2O_3^{2-}}{\text{mmol } IO_4^-}\right] + \left(5.00\,y\text{ mmol } IO_3^- \times \frac{6\text{ meq } S_2O_3^{2-}}{\text{mmol } IO_3^-}\right) =$$

(47.00×0.100) meq , from which $y = 0.0500\text{ mmol } IO_3^-/\text{mL} = M_{IO_3^-}$

12-40. The following reactions take place during the analysis :

$$H_2NCH_2CH_2OH + HCl \rightleftharpoons H_3N^+CH_2CH_2OH\ Cl^- \qquad (1)$$

$$H_2NCH_2CH_2OH + IO_4^- \rightleftharpoons 2CH_2O + IO_3^- + NH_3 \qquad (2)$$

$$CH_2OHCH_2OH + IO_4^- \rightleftharpoons 2CH_2O + IO_3^- + H_2O \qquad (3)$$

$$IO_4^- + 2H^+ + 3I^- \xrightleftharpoons{pH\ 7} IO_3^- + [I_3]^- + H_2O \qquad (4)$$

$$[I_3]^- + 2S_2O_3^{2-} \rightleftharpoons 3I^- + S_4O_6^{2-} \qquad (5)$$

$\therefore$ 1 mmol $H_2NCH_2CH_2OH \equiv 1$ meq HCl (reaction 1)

1 mmol $H_2NCH_2CH_2OH$ or 1 mmol $CH_2OHCH_2OH \equiv 1$ mmol $IO_4^- \equiv 1$ mmol $[I_3]^- \equiv 2$ meq $S_2O_3^{2-}$ (Reactions 2 - 5)

Suppose that the sample contains y mmol $H_2NCH_2CH_2OH$ and z mmol CH_2OHCH_2OH. We have

$y = 20.85\text{ mL} \times 0.1007\text{ mmol } H_2NCH_2CH_2OH/\text{mL} \times (100.0/50.00) = 4.199$

$y + z = 4.199 + z = [(30.74 - 15.47) \times 0.0983]\text{ meq } S_2O_3^{2-} \times 0.5\text{ mmol } (H_2NCH_2CH_2OH$ or $CH_2OHCH_2OH)/\text{meq } S_2O_3^{2-} \times (100.0/10.00) = 7.505$, from which $z = 3.306$. Hence, the sample contains

$$\frac{4.199 \text{ mmol} \times 61.08 \text{ mg } H_2NCH_2CH_2OH/\text{mmol}}{483.2 \text{ mg sample}} \times 100 = 53.08\ \%\ H_2NCH_2CH_2OH$$

$$\frac{3.306 \text{ mmol} \times 62.07 \text{ mg } CH_2OHCH_2OH/\text{mmol}}{483.2 \text{ mg sample}} \times 100 = 42.47\ \%\ CH_2OHCH_2OH$$

and $100.00 - (53.08 + 42.47) = 4.45\ \%\ H_2O$

12-41. The following reactions take place during the analysis :

$$BrO_3^- + 5Br^- + 6H^+ \rightleftharpoons 3Br_2 + 3H_2O$$

$$C_6H_5OH + 3Br_2 \rightleftharpoons C_6H_2Br_3OH + 3HBr$$

$$Br_2 + 3I^- \rightleftharpoons 2Br^- + [I_3]^-$$

$$[I]_3^- + 2S_2O_3^{2-} \rightleftharpoons 3I^- + S_4O_6^{2-}$$

We have 1 $C_6H_5OH \equiv 3Br_2 \equiv 6$ electrons. Hence, the equivalent weight of C_6H_5OH is equal to MW/6 , and the sample contains

$$\frac{[(20.00 \text{ mL} \times 0.0500 \text{ mmol/mL} \times 6 \text{ meq/mmol})-(27.15 \text{ mL} \times 0.1012 \text{ meq/mL})](94.11/6 \text{ mg } C_6H_5OH/\text{meq})}{55.0 \text{ mg sample}} \times$$

$100 = 92.8\ \%\ C_6H_5OH$

12-42. Let E_1 and E_2 be the potentials before and after the addition of Hg^{2+} ions. We have

$$E_1 = E^o_{Br_2,Br^-} - \frac{0.05916}{2} \log \frac{[Br^-]_1^2}{[Br_2]} \qquad (1)$$

$$E_2 = E^o_{Br_2,Br^-} - \frac{0.05916}{2} \log \frac{[Br^-]_2^2}{[Br_2]} \qquad (2)$$

Subtracting Equation (1) from Equation (2), we obtain

$$E_2 - E_1 = 0.4732 = 0.05916 \log \frac{[Br^-]_1}{[Br^-]_2}$$, from which $[Br^-]_1/[Br^-]_2 = 9.97 \times 10^7$.

Hence, $[Br^-]$ was decreased by a factor of 9.97×10^7.

12-43. (10.55×0.1008) mmol $KBrO_3 \times 6$ meq/mmol $\times \dfrac{1000 \text{ mL/L}}{25.00 \text{ mL}} \times (0.03205/4)$ g N_2H_4/meq $=$ 2.045 g N_2H_4/L

12-44. 1 $Mg^{2+} \equiv 8$ electrons [see Example 12-21]

$N_{KBrO_3} = 6 \times 0.050 = 0.300$

$$\text{meq Mg} = \frac{0.0300 \text{ g Mg}}{(0.02430/8) \text{ g/meq}} = 9.88$$

Let y mL be the required volume of $KBrO_3$. We have y mL X 0.300 meq/mL = 9.88 or y = 32.9 mL .

12-45. $Hg_2^{2+} + 2Cl^- \rightleftharpoons Hg_2Cl_2$ titration reaction

At the equivalence point, we have $[Cl^-] = 2[Hg_2^{2+}]$

$\therefore K_{sp(Hg_2Cl_2)} = [Hg_2^{2+}][Cl^-]^2 = [Hg_2^{2+}](2[Hg_2^{2+}])^2 = 4[Hg_2^{2+}]^3$ or

$[Hg_2^{2+}] = \sqrt[3]{K_{sp(Hg_2Cl_2)}/4}$. Hence, we have

$$E_{eq} = E^o_{Hg_2Cl_2,Hg} + \frac{0.05916}{2}\log[Hg_2^{2+}] = E^o_{Hg_2Cl_2,Hg} + \frac{0.05916}{2}\log\sqrt[3]{\frac{K_{sp(Hg_2Cl_2)}}{4}} =$$

$$E^o_{Hg_2Cl_2,Hg} + \frac{0.05916}{6}\log\frac{K_{sp(Hg_2Cl_2)}}{4}$$

12-46. Initially, each half-cell contains (100 X 0.100) = 10.0 mmol of each Ce^{3+} and Ce^{4+}. Let y meq be the amount of reductant present in 10.00 mL of solution A which was added to one half-cell, reducing Ce^{4+} to Ce^{3+}. After the reaction is complete, the half-cell contains (10.0 + y) mmol Ce^{3+} and (10.0 − y) mmol Ce^{4+}. We have

$$+0.1083 = (E^o - 0.05916\log\frac{0.100}{0.100}) - (E^o - 0.05916\log\frac{[Ce^{3+}]}{[Ce^{4+}]}) = 0.05916\log\frac{[Ce^{3+}]}{[Ce^{4+}]} =$$

$$0.05916\log\frac{10.0+y}{10.0-y} ,$$

from which y = 9.71 . Hence, the normality of solution A is equal to N_A = 9.71 meq/10.00 mL = 0.971 meq/mL .

12-47. Suppose that y mmol $K_2C_2O_4 \cdot H_2O$ should be added. We have

(200 X 0.100) mmol $KHC_2O_4 \cdot H_2C_2O_4 \cdot 2H_2O$ X 4 meq/mmol + y mmol $K_2C_2O_4 \cdot H_2O$ X 2 meq/mmol = 3 X [(200 X 0.100) mmol $KHC_2O_4 \cdot H_2C_2O_4 \cdot 2H_2O$ X 3 meq/mmol]

from which y = 50.0 . Hence, 50.0 mmol X 0.18424 g $K_2C_2O_4 \cdot H_2O$/mmol = 9.2 g $K_2C_2O_4 \cdot H_2O$ should be added.

12-48. (a) $2Fe^{3+} + [SnCl_4]^{2-} + 2Cl^- \rightleftharpoons 2Fe^{2+} + [SnCl_6]^{2-}$ (1)

$$K = 10^{16.903 \times 2 \times (0.700 - 0.14)} = 8._5 \times 10^{18}$$

At equilibrium, we have $[Cl^-] = 6\,\underline{M}$, and $[SnCl_6^{2-}] / [SnCl_4^{2-}] = 1/0.02 = 50$.

Substituting in the equilibrium constant expression for Reaction (1), we have

$$8.5 \times 10^{18} = \frac{[Fe^{2+}]^2\,[SnCl_6^{2-}]}{[Fe^{3+}]\,[SnCl_4^{2-}][Cl^-]^2} = \frac{[Fe^{2+}]^2 \times 50}{[Fe^{3+}]^2 \times (6)^2} ,$$

from which $[Fe^{2+}]/[Fe^{3+}] = 2.47 \times 10^9 = (0.100 - [Fe^{3+}])/[Fe^{3+}]$ or $[Fe^{3+}] = 4.0 \times 10^{-11}$ M , and $[Fe^{2+}] \simeq 0.100$ M. From these values, it can been seen that the reduction of Fe^{3+} is quantitative.

(b) $[SnCl_4]^{2-} + 2\,[HgCl_4]^{2-} \rightleftharpoons [SnCl_6]^{2-} + Hg_2Cl_2 + 4Cl^-$ (2)

$K = 10^{16.903 \times 2 \times (0.69 - 0.14)} = 4 \times 10^{18}$

At equilibrium, we have $[HgCl_4^{2-}] = 0.01$ M , and $[Cl^-] = 6$ M . Substituting in the equilibrium constant expression for Reaction (2), we have

$$K = 4 \times 10^{18} = \frac{[SnCl_6^{2-}]\,[Cl^-]^4}{[SnCl_4^{2-}]\,[HgCl_4^{2-}]} = \frac{[SnCl_6^{2-}]\,(6)^4}{[SnCl_4^{2-}](0.01)^2} ,$$

from which $[SnCl_6^{2-}]/[SnCl_4^{2-}] = 3.1 \times 10^{11}$. We have $C_{Sn} = (0.100/2)\,1.02 \simeq 0.05$ M. Hence, $(0.05 - [SnCl_4^{2-}])/[SnCl_4^{2-}] = 3.1 \times 10^{11}$, from which $[SnCl_4^{2-}] = 1.6 \times 10^{-13}$ M and $[SnCl_6^{2-}] \simeq 0.05$ M. From these values, it can be seen that the oxidation of Sn^{2+} is quantitative.

12-49. $N_{Na_2S_2O_3} = \dfrac{160.0 \text{ mg } KIO_3}{(214.02/6) \text{ mg/meq} \times 40.72 \text{ mL}} = 0.1102$ meq/mL

12-50. $I^- + 3Br_2 + 3H_2O \rightleftharpoons IO_3^- + 6H^+ + 6Br^-$

$IO_3^- + 8\,I^- + 6H^+ \rightleftharpoons 3\,[I_3]^- + 3H_2O$

$[I_3]^- + H_3AsO_3 + H_2O \rightleftharpoons HAsO_4^{3-} + 4H^+ + 3I^-$

∴ 1 mmol KI ≡ 6 meq As. We have

$N_{As} = (0.2563 \text{ mg } As_2O_3/\text{mL})/(197.84/4) \text{ mg/meq} = 0.005182$ meq/mL

$$\therefore \%\ KI = \frac{4.182 \text{ mL} \times 0.005182 \text{ meq/mL} \times (166.01/6) \text{ mg KI/meq}}{897.6 \text{ mg sample}} \times 100 = 0.0668$$

CHAPTER 13

13-1. $\% \text{ Cl}^- = \dfrac{\text{mL AgNO}_3 \times 0.1000 \text{ mmol/mL} \times 0.03545 \text{ g Cl}^-\text{/mmol}}{\text{g sample}} \times 100$

$\therefore$ maximum sample size = (45 X 0.1000 X 0.03545 X 100)/30 = 0.53 g

minimum sample size = (30 X 0.1000 X 0.03545 X 100)/25 = 0.43 g

Hence, the sample size should lie in the range 0.43 - 0.53 g .

13-2. For KCl samples, the sample weight should be from (25.0 mL X 0.2000 mmol/mL X 0.07456 g KCl/mmol) to (45.0 X 0.2000 X 0.07456)= 0.373 to 0.671 g. For $BaCl_2$ samples, it should be from [25.0 mL X 0.2000 mmol/mL X (0.20825/2) g $BaCl_2$/mmol] to (45.0 X 0.2000 X 0.20825/2) = 0.521 - 0.937 g. Hence, for KCl and/or $BaCl_2$ samples, the sample size should lie in the range 0.521 - 0.671 g .

13-3. See Example 13-1.

$$E_{cell} = E_{Ag} - E_{SCE} = (0.7994 + 0.05916 \log[Ag^+]) - 0.2412 = 0.5582 + 0.05916 \log[Ag^+] \quad (1)$$

1. <u>Initially</u>. Before any $AgNO_3$ has been added, the calculation of E_{cell} is impossible.
2. <u>Before the equivalence point</u>, e.g., after 1.00 mL of $AgNO_3$ was added, we have

$$[Ag^+] = \frac{K_{sp(AgCl)}}{[Cl^-]} = \frac{1.8 \times 10^{-10}}{(50.00 \times 0.0500 - 1.00 \times 0.1000)/51.00} = 3.82 \times 10^{-9}\ \underline{M}$$

Substituting in Equation (1), we have $E_{cell} = 0.5582 + 0.05916 \log(3.82 \times 10^{-9}) = 0.060$ V.

3. <u>At the equivalence point</u>, $[Ag^+] = [Cl^-] = \sqrt{1.8 \times 10^{-10}} = 1.34 \times 10^{-5}\ \underline{M}$ $\therefore$ E_{cell} = $0.5582 + 0.05916 \log(1.34 \times 10^{-5}) = 0.270$ V.

4. <u>After the equivalence point</u>, e.g., after 25.10 mL of $AgNO_3$ were added, we have $[Ag^+] = (25.10 \times 0.1000 - 50.00 \times 0.0500)/75.10 = 1.33 \times 10^{-4}\ \underline{M}$ $\therefore$ $E_{cell} = 0.5582 + 0.05916 \log(1.33 \times 10^{-4}) = 0.329$ V.

The results of the calculations and the corresponding titration curve are given below.

$AgNO_3$, mL	E_{cell}, V
1.00	+0.060
5.00	0.067
10.00	0.077
15.00	0.089
20.00	0.109
22.50	0.127
24.90	0.211
25.00	0.270
25.10	0.329
25.50	0.370
27.50	0.411

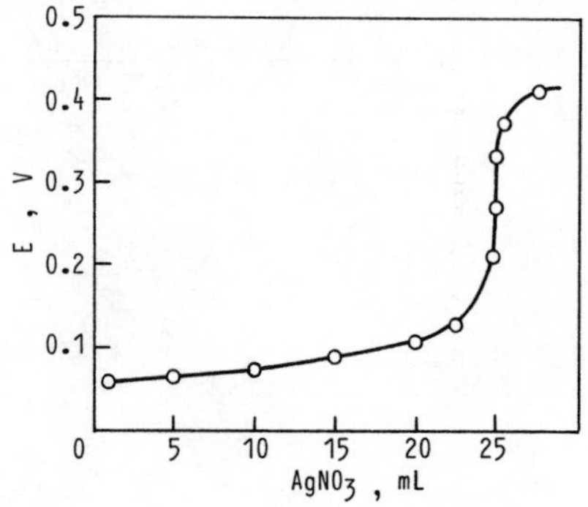

13-4. (a) and (b) $[I^-]_{eq} = K_{sp(AgI)} = \sqrt{8.5 \times 10^{-17}} = 9.2 \times 10^{-9}$ M

(c) $[Cl^-]_{eq} = \sqrt{1.8 \times 10^{-10}} = 1.34 \times 10^{-5}$ M

(d) $[AsO_4^{3-}]_{eq} = S_{Ag_3AsO_4} = \sqrt[4]{1 \times 10^{-22}/27} = 1.4 \times 10^{-6}$ M

13-5. Suppose that the sample contains y g KCl, and consequently (0.5000 - y) g $KClO_4$. We have

$$\frac{y \text{ g KCl}}{0.07456 \text{ g/mmol}} + \frac{(0.5000 - y) \text{ g } KClO_4}{0.13855 \text{ g } KClO_4\text{/mmol}} = 32.00 \text{ mL} \times 0.1377 \text{ mmol/mL} \text{ ,}$$

from which y = 0.1288. Hence, the sample contains (0.1288/0.5000) X 100 = 25.76 % KCl and [(0.5000 - 0.1288)/0.5000] X 100 = 74.24 % $KClO_4$.

13-6. Suppose that the sample contains y g NaCl, and consequently (0.3953 - y) g NaBr. We have

$$\frac{y \text{ g NaCl}}{0.05844 \text{ g/mmol}} + \frac{(0.3953 - y) \text{ g NaBr}}{0.10289 \text{ g/mmol}} = 49.00 \text{ mL} \times 0.1000 \text{ mmol/mL} \text{ ,}$$

from which y = 0.1431. Hence, the sample contains (0.1431/0.3953) X 100 = 36.20 % NaCl, and [(0.3953 - 0.1431)/0.3953] X 100 = 63.80 % NaBr.

13-7. Let y g be the required amount of sample. We have

$$\frac{0.600\,y \text{ g NaCl}}{0.05844 \text{ g/mmol}} + \frac{0.400\,y \text{ g KCl}}{0.07456 \text{ g/mmol}} = (50.00 \times 0.1000 - 8.00 \times 0.1250) \text{ mmol} \text{ ,}$$

from which y = 0.2559 g.

13-8. At the equivalence point, the solution volume is 100.0 mL, and there are (50.00 mL X 0.1000 mmol/mL) = 5.00 mmol of each IO_3^- and Ag^+. For a +0.1% error, we have

$$[Ag^+]_{exc} = \frac{0.1}{100} \times \frac{5.00 \text{ mmol}}{100.0 \text{ mL}} = 5.00 \times 10^{-5} \text{ M}$$

Let S = solubility of $AgIO_3$. We have $K_{sp(AgIO_3)} = 3 \times 10^{-8} = [Ag^+][IO_3^-] = (S + 5.00 \times 10^{-5})S$, or $S = 1.5 \times 10^{-4}$ M $\therefore$ $[Ag^+] = 1.5 \times 10^{-4} + 5.00 \times 10^{-5} = 2.0 \times 10^{-4}$ M, and $[CrO_4^{2-}] = 1.9 \times 10^{-12}/(2.0 \times 10^{-4})^2 = 4.8 \times 10^{-5}$ M.

For a -0.1% error, we have

$$[IO_3^-]_{exc} = \frac{0.1}{100} \times \frac{5.00 \text{ mmol}}{100.0 \text{ mL}} = 5.00 \times 10^{-5} \text{ M}$$

$\therefore$ $3 \times 10^{-8} = S(S + 5.00 \times 10^{-5})$, or $S = 1.5 \times 10^{-4}$ M $= [Ag^+]$, and $[CrO_4^{2-}] = 1.9 \times 10^{-12}/(1.5 \times 10^{-4})^2 = 8.4 \times 10^{-5}$

Hence, we should have $4.8 \times 10^{-5} < [CrO_4^{2-}] < 8.4 \times 10^{-5}$

13-9. $$\% \, CHI_3 = \frac{(8.40 \times 0.1690 - 1.79 \times 0.0950) \text{ mmol } Ag^+ \times \dfrac{1 \text{ mmol } CHI_3}{3 \text{ mmol } Ag^+} \times \dfrac{393.73 \text{ mg } CHI_3}{\text{mmol } CHI_3}}{790.0 \text{ mg sample}} \times 100 = 20.76$$

13-10. $[Ag^+]_{eq} = \sqrt{K_{sp(AgCl)}} = \sqrt{1.8 \times 10^{-10}} = 1.34 \times 10^{-5}$ $\underline{M}$

$\therefore [X^{3-}] = K_{sp(Ag_3X)}/[Ag^+]^3 = 1.8 \times 10^{-18}/(1.34 \times 10^{-5})^3 = 7.5 \times 10^{-4}$ $\underline{M}$

13-11. $$\frac{214.2 \text{ mg } MCl_2}{(36.00 \times 0.1250) \text{ mmol } Ag^+ \times \dfrac{1 \text{ mmol } Cl^-}{\text{mmol } Ag^+} \times \dfrac{1 \text{ mmol } MCl_2}{2 \text{ mmol } Cl^-}} = [M + (2 \times 35.45)] \text{ mg } MCl_2/\text{mmol},$$

from which $M = 24.30$ $(M \equiv Mg^{2+})$.

13-12. $M_{KSCN} = (50.00 \times 0.1000) \text{ mmol}/40.00 \text{ mL} = 0.1250 \text{ mmol/mL}$

$$\therefore \% \, Ag = \frac{31.52 \text{ mL} \times 0.1250 \text{ mmol/mL} \times 107.87 \text{ mg Ag/mmol} \times (100.0/25.00)}{2000.0 \text{ mg sample}} \times 100 = 85.0$$

13-13. (a) $6.000 \text{ meq}/(0.2500 \text{ meq/mL}) = 24.00 \text{ mL } AgNO_3$

(b) $$\frac{40.00 \text{ mL} \times 0.1000 \text{ mmol } CrO_4^{2-}/\text{mL} \times 2 \text{ mmol } Ag^+/\text{mmol } CrO_4^{2-}}{0.2500 \text{ mmol } Ag^+/\text{mL}} = 32.00 \text{ mL } AgNO_3$$

13-14. $$\% \, Br^- = \frac{(V_A M_A - V_I M_I) \text{ mmol} \times 10^{-3} \text{ mol/mmol} \times 79.90 \text{ g } Br^-/\text{mol}}{W \text{ g}} \times 100 = \frac{79.90(V_A M_A - V_I M_I)}{W}$$

13-15. $$\% \, Cl = \frac{\text{mL } AgNO_3 \times M \text{ mmol/mL} \times 35.45 \text{ mg } Cl^-/\text{mmol}}{1000.0 \text{ mg sample}} \times 100 \qquad (1)$$

Since $\% \, Cl = \text{mL } AgNO_3$, Equation (1) is simplified to

$M = 1000.0/(100 \times 35.45) = 0.2821$

13-16. $[Ag^+]_{en} = \sqrt{1.9 \times 10^{-12}/0.0020} = 3.08 \times 10^{-5}$ $\underline{M}$

$\therefore [Cl^-]_{en} = 1.8 \times 10^{-10}/3.08 \times 10^{-5} = 5.8 \times 10^{-6}$ $\underline{M}$

13-17. $$\% \, Br^- = \frac{(25.00 \times 0.1013 - 20.12 \times 0.0502) \text{ mmol } Br^- \times 79.90 \text{ mg } Br^-/\text{mmol}}{416.5 \text{ mg sample}} \times 100 = 29.2$$

13-18. Let y liters be the volume of the reservoir. We have

$$\frac{108.2 \text{ g NaCl} \times (0.1000/y)}{58.44 \text{ g/mol}} = 0.00939 \text{ L} \times 0.1008 \text{ mol/L},$$

from which $y = 195.6$ L .

13-19. $$\% As = \frac{(25.00 \times 0.05000 - 3.85 \times 0.05000)\text{ mmol } Ag^+ \times \frac{1 \text{ mmol As}}{3 \text{ mmol Ag}} \times \frac{0.07492 \text{ g As}}{\text{mmol As}}}{7.150 \text{ g sample}} \times 100 = 0.369$$

13-20. $[Ag^+]_{eq} = \sqrt{1.8 \times 10^{-10}} = 1.34 \times 10^{-5}$ $\underline{M}$ $\therefore [X^-] = 1.34 \times 10^{-8}/1.34 \times 10^{-5} = 1.00 \times 10^{-3}$ $\underline{M}$

Hence, the maximum amount of NaX is equal to (100 mL X 1.00×10^{-3} mmol/mL X 0.120 g NaX/mmol) = 0.0120 g .

13-21. At the equivalence point, there are 4.00 mmol of each A^- and Ag^+. For a + 0.05% error, we have

$$[Ag^+]_{exc} = \frac{0.05}{100} \times \frac{4.00 \text{ mmol}}{100 \text{ mL}} = 2.00 \times 10^{-5} \underline{M} = [Ag^+]_{en} - [A^-]_{en}$$

$\therefore [A^-]_{en} = [Ag^+]_{en} - 2.00 \times 10^{-5}$, and $K_{sp(AgA)} = [Ag^+]_{en}[A^-]_{en} =$

$$\left(\sqrt{\frac{1.9 \times 10^{-12}}{2.50 \times 10^{-3}}}\right)\left(\sqrt{\frac{1.9 \times 10^{-12}}{2.50 \times 10^{-3}}} - 2.00 \times 10^{-5}\right) = 2.1 \times 10^{-10}$$

For a − 0.05% error, we have

$$[A^-]_{exc} = \frac{0.05}{100} \times \frac{4.00 \text{ mmol}}{100 \text{ mL}} = 2.00 \times 10^{-5} \underline{M} = [A^-]_{en} - [Ag^+]_{en}$$

$\therefore [A^-]_{en} = [Ag^+]_{en} + 2.00 \times 10^{-5}$, and $K_{sp(AgA)} = \left(\sqrt{\frac{1.9 \times 10^{-12}}{2.50 \times 10^{-3}}}\right)\left(\sqrt{\frac{1.9 \times 10^{-12}}{2.50 \times 10^{-3}}} + 2.00 \times 10^{-5}\right)$

$= 1.3 \times 10^{-9}$. Hence, we should have $2.1 \times 10^{-10} < K_{sp(AgA)} < 1.3 \times 10^{-9}$

13-22. See Example 13-12.

$$e_{B^-} = \left[\frac{K_{sp(AgC)}}{K_{sp(AgB)}} - \frac{K_{sp(AgB)}}{K_{sp(AgA)}} \times \frac{C_{A^-}}{C_{B^-}}\right] \times 100 = \left(\frac{5.0 \times 10^{-18}}{1.0 \times 10^{-13}} - \frac{1.0 \times 10^{-13}}{1.0 \times 10^{-10}} \times \frac{C_{A^-}}{C_{B^-}}\right) \times 100 = 0,$$

or $C_{A^-} / C_{B^-} = 0.050$

13-23. (a) See Example 13-11.

$$[SCN^-]_{en} = \frac{[Fe(SCN)^{2+}]_{en}}{138 [Fe^{3+}]_{en}} = \frac{6.4 \times 10^{-6}}{138 \times 1.0} = 4.64 \times 10^{-8} \underline{M} \quad \therefore [Ag^+]_{en} = \frac{1 \times 10^{-12}}{4.64 \times 10^{-8}} =$$

2.16×10^{-5} $\underline{M}$

error = total mmol Ag^+ − total mmol SCN^- = $(2.16 \times 10^{-5} - 4.64 \times 10^{-8} - 6.4 \times 10^{-6}) \times 100$ = 1.52×10^{-3} mmol Ag^+. Hence, the end-point precedes the equivalent point

$\therefore$ titration error = − (1.52×10^{-3} mmol/5.00 mmol) X 100 = − 0.03 %.

(b) $$[SCN^-]_{en} = \frac{6.4 \times 10^{-6}}{138 \times 0.1} = 4.64 \times 10^{-7} \underline{M} \quad \therefore [Ag^+]_{en} = \frac{1 \times 10^{-12}}{4.64 \times 10^{-7}} = 2.16 \times 10^{-6} \underline{M}$$

There is $(4.64 \times 10^{-7} + 6.4 \times 10^{-6} - 2.16 \times 10^{-6}) \times 100 = 4.70 \times 10^{-4}$ mmol SCN^- in excess of Ag^+ $\therefore$ titration error = $+(4.70 \times 10^{-4}/5.00) \times 100 = +0.009_4\,\%$.

13-24. From Equation (13-2)

$$10^{-4.20} = 6.31 \times 10^{-5} = \frac{(50.00 - V) \times 0.100}{50.00 + V} + \frac{1.8 \times 10^{-10}}{6.31 \times 10^{-5}}$$

from which V = 49.94 mL. Hence, the percent error is equal to

$$\%\ \text{error} = \frac{49.94 - 50.00}{50.00} \times 100 = -0.12\,\%$$

13-25. $[Ag^+] = (10.00 \times 0.4375 - 2 \times 24.00 \times 0.0531)\ \text{mmol}/34.00\ \text{mL} = 0.0537$ $\therefore$ $pAg = -\log(0.0537) = 1.27$.

Let $[CrO_4^{2-}] = y$. We have $(0.0537 + 2y)^2 y = 1.9 \times 10^{-12}$, or $y = 6.59 \times 10^{-10}$

$\therefore$ $pCrO_4 = -\log(6.59 \times 10^{-10}) = 9.18$.

13-26. $$\frac{5.62\ \text{mL} \times 0.01000\ \text{mmol/mL} \times 0.06406\ \text{g}\ SO_2/\text{mmol}}{20\ \text{L/min} \times 30\ \text{min} \times 2.86\ \text{g}\ SO_2/\text{L}} \times 10^6 = 2.10$$.

CHAPTER 14

14-1. Suppose that the sample contains y g NaCN, and consequently (0.4565 - y) g KCN. We have

$$\frac{y \text{ g NaCN}}{0.04901 \text{ g/mmol}} + \frac{(0.4565 - y) \text{ g KCN}}{0.06512 \text{ g/mmol}} = 40.00 \text{ mL} \times 0.1000 \text{ mmol } Ag^+/\text{mL} \times 2 \text{ mmol } CN^-/\text{mmol } Ag^+,$$

from which y = 0.1961. Hence, the sample contains (0.1961/0.4565) X 100 = 42.96% NaCN, and [(0.4565 - 0.1961)/0.4565] X 100 = 57.04 % KCN.

14-2. $$(20.00 \times 0.1000) \text{ mmol } Ag^+ \times \frac{2 \text{ mmol NaCN}}{\text{mmol } Ag^+} \times \frac{49.01 \text{ mg NaCN}}{\text{mmol NaCN}} = 196.04 \text{ mg NaCN}$$

[(50.00 - 20.00) X 0.1000 - 4.00 X 0.1250] mmol X 58.44 mg NaCl/mmol = 146.1 mg NaCl

Hence, the sample contains (196.04/400.0) X 100 = 49.01% NaCN, (146.1/400.0) X 100 = 36.53% NaCl, and 100.00 - (49.01 + 36.53) = 14.46% inert materials.

14-3. 0.01000 mmol/mL X 100.09 mg $CaCO_3$/mmol = 1.001 mg $CaCO_3$/mL = T

14-4. $K_{ZnY'} = \alpha_4 K_{ZnY} = (4.81 \times 10^{-4})(3.16 \times 10^{16}) = 1.5 \times 10^{13}$. Since $[ZnY^{2-}] = c_{Zn} - [Zn^{2+}] \simeq c_{Zn} = 1.00 \times 10^{-3}$ $\underline{M}$, we have

$$[Zn^{2+}] = \frac{1.00 \times 10^{-3}}{(1.00 \times 10^{-6})(1.5 \times 10^{13})} = 6.7 \times 10^{-11} \ \underline{M}$$

14-5. (a) $K_{ZnY'} = \alpha_4 K_{ZnY} = (2.51 \times 10^{-11})(3.16 \times 10^{16}) = 7.9 \times 10^5 \simeq 1.00 \times 10^{-3}/[Zn^{2+}]^2$

$\therefore [Zn^{2+}] = \sqrt{1.00 \times 10^{-3}/7.9 \times 10^5} = 3.6 \times 10^{-5}$ $\underline{M}$

(b) $K_{ZnY'} = (4.81 \times 10^{-4})(3.16 \times 10^{16}) = 1.5 \times 10^{13} \simeq 1.00 \times 10^{-3}/[Zn^{2+}]^2$, from which $[Zn^{2+}] = 8.2 \times 10^{-9}$ $\underline{M}$

14-6. See Example 14-6.

$$K_{ZnY'} = \frac{[ZnY^{2-}]}{[Zn^{2+}][Y']} = \frac{999}{1.00 \times 10^{-6}} = 1.00 \times 10^9$$

and $\alpha_4 = K_{ZnY'}/K_{ZnY} = 1.00 \times 10^9/3.16 \times 10^{16} = 3.16 \times 10^{-8}$, whereupon $-\log \alpha_4 = -\log(3.16 \times 10^{-8}) = 7.50$. Interpolating in Table 14-1 gives a pH = 4.47 for this α_4.

14-7. $[ML]_{eq} = (99.9/100) \times (0.010/2) = 4.995 \times 10^{-3}$ $\underline{M}$, and $[M^{n+}] = [L^{n-}]_{eq} = (0.1/100) \times (0.010/2) = 5.0 \times 10^{-6}$ $\underline{M}$. Hence, the minimum value for the formation constant is equal to $K_{ML} = [ML]/[M^{n+}][L^{n-}] = 4.995 \times 10^{-3}/(5.0 \times 10^{-6})^2 = 2.0 \times 10^8$

14-8. $[OH^-] = 1.8 \times 10^{-5} \times 0.050/0.090 = 1.0 \times 10^{-5}$ $\underline{M}$. Hence, pOH = 5.00 , pH = 9.00 , and $\alpha_4 = 5.21 \times 10^{-2}$ (Table 14-1). We have

$$\beta_0 = \frac{1}{1 + 10^{2.27}(0.100) + 10^{4.61}(0.100)^2 + 10^{7.01}(0.100)^3 + 10^{9.06}(0.100)^4} = 8.0 \times 10^{-6} .$$

Hence, $K_{Zn'Y'} = \alpha_4 \beta_0 K_{ZnY} = (5.21 \times 10^{-2})(8.0 \times 10^{-6})(3.16 \times 10^{16}) = 1.3 \times 10^{10}$

14-9. 25.00 mL of EDTA are required to reach the equivalence point. After addition of 24.95 mL EDTA, 24.95 X 0.01000 = 0.2495 mmol M^{2+} has been complexed ∴ $[M^{2+}] = 0.00050/49.95 = 1.00 \times 10^{-5}$ $\underline{M}$ and pM = 5.00 . Hence, when 25.05 mL EDTA are added, we have pM = 5.00 + 4.00 = 9.00, and $[M^{2+}] = 1.00 \times 10^{-9}$ $\underline{M}$, $[Y'] = (0.05 \times 0.01000)/50.05 = 1.0 \times 10^{-5}$ $\underline{M}$, and $[MY^{2-}] = 0.250/50.05 = 5.00 \times 10^{-3}$ $\underline{M}$. Hence, we have

$K_{MY'} = 5.00 \times 10^{-3}/(1.0 \times 10^{-9})(1.0 \times 10^{-5}) = 5.0 \times 10^{11}$

14-10. Mass balance : $C_{EDTA} = [Y'] + [BaY^{2-}] + [PbY^{2-}] = 0.050$ $\underline{M}$ (1)

$C_{Ba} = [Ba^{2+}] + [BaY^{2-}] = 0.0200$ $\underline{M}$ (2)

$C_{Pb} = [Pb^{2+}] + [PbY^{2-}] = 0.0100$ $\underline{M}$ (3)

Since both EDTA complexes are very stable, $[Ba^{2+}]$ and $[Pb^{2+}]$ can be considered negligible, whereupon Equations (2) and (3) are simplified to $[BaY^{2-}] = 0.0200$ $\underline{M}$, and $[PbY^{2-}] = 0.0100$ $\underline{M}$. Substituting in Equation (1) we have

$[Y'] = 0.050 - 0.0200 - 0.0100 = 0.0200$ $\underline{M}$ (4)

At pH 7.00 , $\alpha_4 = 4.81 \times 10^{-4}$ (Table 14-1) ∴ we have

$[Y^{4-}] = \alpha_4 [Y'] = 4.81 \times 10^{-4} \times 0.0200 = 9.62 \times 10^{-6}$ $\underline{M}$ (5)

Substituting in the formation constant expressions, we have

$[Ba^{2+}] = 0.0200 / [(5.76 \times 10^7)(9.62 \times 10^{-6})] = 3.61 \times 10^{-5}$ $\underline{M}$

$[Pb^{2+}] = 0.0100 / [(1.10 \times 10^{18})(9.62 \times 10^{-6})] = 9.45 \times 10^{-16}$ $\underline{M}$

The $[SO_4^{2-}]$ required to start the precipitation of each ion is :

for $BaSO_4$: $[SO_4^{2-}] = 1.5 \times 10^{-9}/3.61 \times 10^{-5} = 4.2 \times 10^{-5}$ $\underline{M}$

for $PbSO_4$: $[SO_4^{2-}] = 1.3 \times 10^{-8}/9.45 \times 10^{-16} = 1.4 \times 10^7$ $\underline{M}$

From these two calculated values, it can be seen that it is possible to separate the two cations by precipitating Ba^{2+} as $BaSO_4$, because a sulfate concentration of 1.4×10^7 M can not be achieved experimentally.

14-11. Let $y = [M^{n+}]_{eq}$, whereupon $[L^{n-}]_{eq} = y$, $[ML]_{eq} = 5.00 \times 10^{-3} - y$. Substituting in the formation constant expression, we have $2.0 \times 10^8 = (5.00 \times 10^{-3} - y)/y^2$, or $y = 5.0 \times 10^{-6}$

$\therefore$ $[ML]_{eq} = 5.00 \times 10^{-3} - 5.0 \times 10^{-6} = 4.995 \times 10^{-3}$ $\underline{M}$. Hence, the degree of completion at the equivalence point is equal to $(4.995 \times 10^{-3}/5.00 \times 10^{-3}) \times 100 = 99.9$ %.

14-12. See Example 14-7.

We have $\log K_{CaY} = 10.70$ (Table 14-2), $\log \alpha_4 = -0.45$ (Table 14-1), $\beta_0 = 1$.

$\therefore$ initially, $pCa = -\log(2.00 \times 10^{-3}) = 2.70$ (Equation 14-15)

for 50 % EDTA, $pCa = -\log[0.00200(1-0.50)] = 3.00$ (Equation 14-16)

at equivalence point : $pCa = (10.70 - 0.45 + 2.70)/2 = 6.48$ (Equation 14-17)

for 101 % EDTA, $pCa = \log(1.01-1) + 10.70 - 0.45 = 8.25$ (Equation 14-18)

The results of the calculations and the corresponding titration curve are given below, at the end of Problem 14-13 .

14-13. See Example 14-8.

We have $\log K_{ZnY} = 16.50$ (Table 14-2), $\log \alpha_4 = -1.28$ (Table 14-1), $\beta_0 = 8.0 \times 10^{-6}$ (Problem 14-8), $\log \beta_0 = -5.10$.

$\therefore$ initially, $pZn = 5.10 - \log(2.00 \times 10^{-3}) = 7.80$ (Equation 14-15)

for 50 % EDTA, $pZn = 5.10 - \log(2.00 \times 10^{-3})(1-0.50) = 8.10$ (Equation 14-16)

at equivalence point, $pZn = (16.50 - 1.28 + 2.70 + 5.10)/2 = 11.51$ (Equation 14-17)

for 101 % EDTA, $pZn = \log(1.01-1) + 16.50 - 1.28 = 13.22$ (Equation 14-18)

The results of the calculations and the corresponding titration curve are given below .

% EDTA	pCa	pZn
0	2.70	7.80
50	3.00	8.10
90	3.70	8.80
99	4.70	9.80
99.9	5.70	10.80
100	6.47	11.51
100.1	7.25	12.22
101	8.25	13.22
110	9.25	14.22
200	10.25	15.22

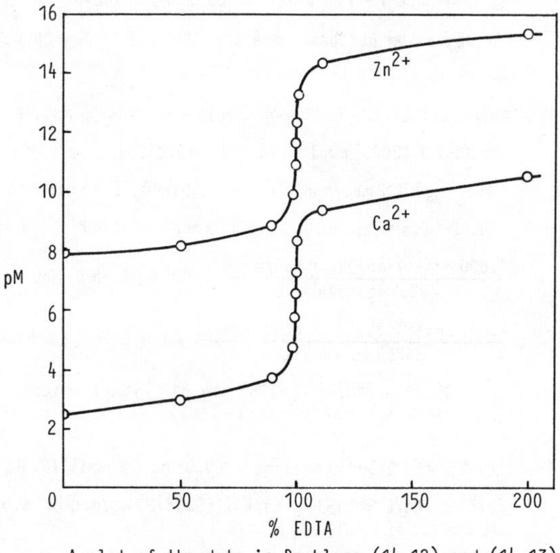

A plot of the data in Problems (14-12) and (14-13).

14-14. $[NiY^{2-}] = 0.0100 \times (99.99/100) = 9.999 \times 10^{-3}$ $\underline{M}$. $[BaY^{2-}] = 0.0100 \times (0.01/100) = 1.00 \times 10^{-6}$ $\underline{M}$ $\therefore$ $[Ba^{2+}] = 0.0100 - 1.00 \times 10^{-6} \simeq 0.0100$ $\underline{M}$.

Substituting in the formation constant expression for $[BaY]^{2-}$, we have

$K_{BaY} = 5.75 \times 10^{7} = 1.00 \times 10^{-6}/0.0100\,[Y^{4-}]$ or $[Y^{4-}] = 1.74 \times 10^{-12}$ $\underline{M}$.

Mass balance : $C_{EDTA} = [Y'] + [NiY^{2-}] + [BaY^{2-}] = 0.0300$ $\underline{M}$

$\therefore$ $[Y'] = 0.0300 - 9.999 \times 10^{-3} - 1.00 \times 10^{-6} \simeq 0.0200$ $\underline{M}$, and $\alpha_4 = [Y^{4-}]/[Y'] = 1.72 \times 10^{-12}/0.0200 = 8.60 \times 10^{-11}$. Interpolating in Table 14-1 gives a pH = 3.05 for this α_4 .

Similarly, we have

$K_{NiY} = 4.17 \times 10^{18} = 0.0100/1.00 \times 10^{-6}\,[Y^{4-}]$ or $[Y^{4-}] = 2.40 \times 10^{-15}$ $\underline{M}$

$\therefore$ $\alpha_4 = 2.40 \times 10^{-15}/0.0200 = 1.20 \times 10^{-13}$. Interpolating in Table 14-1 gives a pH = 2.03 for this α_4 . Hence, we should have $2.03 < pH < 3.05$.

14-15. $[Ca^{2+}] = (26.39\text{ mL} \times 0.01046\text{ mmol/mL})/50.00\text{ mL} = 0.00552$ $\underline{M}$

$[Zn^{2+}] = [(46.78 - 26.39)\text{ mL} \times 0.01046\text{ mmol/mL}]/50.00\text{ mL} = 0.00427$ $\underline{M}$

14-16. $T_{EDTA} = [250.0\text{ mg } CaCO_3 \times (25.00/500.0)]/31.25\text{ mL} = 0.4000\text{ mg } CaCO_3\text{/mL EDTA}$

$\therefore$ $30.00\text{ mL} \times 0.4000\text{ mg } CaCO_3\text{/mL} \times (100/25.00) = 48.0\text{ mg } CaCO_3\text{/100 mL water} \equiv 48.0\ F^{0}$

$48.0\text{ mg } CaCO_3\text{/100 mL water} \times 56.08\text{ mg CaO}/100.09\text{ mg } CaCO_3 = 26.89\text{ mg CaO/100 mL water} \equiv 26.89\ D^{0}$

$48.0\text{ mg } CaCO_3\text{/100 mL water} \times 1000\text{ mL/L} = 480\text{ mg } CaCO_3\text{/L} \equiv 480\text{ ppm } CaCO_3$

$\therefore$ magnesium hardness $\equiv 480 - 180 = 300$ ppm $CaCO_3$

14-17. Suppose that the 0.2184-g sample contains y mmol MgO and z mmol $NaHCO_3$. We have

$(25.00 \times 0.02000)\text{ mmol} = y\,(0.1092/0.2184)$, or $y = 1.000$

$y\text{ mmol MgO} \times 2\text{ meq/mmol} + z\text{ mmol } NaHCO_3 \times 1\text{ meq/mmol} = (2y + z)\text{ meq} = 2.000 + z = (20.00 \times 0.5000 - 30.00 \times 0.2000)\text{ meq} = 4.000$, or $z = 2.000$. Hence, the sample contains

$$\frac{1.000\text{ mmol} \times 40.31\text{ mg MgO/mmol}}{218.4\text{ mg sample}} \times 100 = 18.46\%\text{ MgO}$$

$$\frac{2.000\text{ mmol} \times 84.01\text{ mg } NaHCO_3\text{/mmol}}{218.4\text{ mg sample}} \times 100 = 76.93\%\ NaHCO_3$$

and $100.00 - (18.46 + 76.93) = 4.61\%$ inert materials.

14-18. $[(0.252\text{ mL} \times 0.00130\text{ mmol/mL} \times 40.08\text{ mg Ca/mmol})/0.100\text{ mL serum}] \times 100 = 13.1\text{ mg Ca/100 mL serum} \equiv 131\text{ mg Ca/L} \equiv (131\text{ mg Ca/L})/(40.08/2)\text{ mg/meq} = 6.5\text{ meq Ca/L}$

14-19. $\dfrac{30.04\text{ mL} \times 1.600\text{ mg } CaCO_3/\text{mL} \times 40.08\text{ mg Ca}/100.09\text{ mg } CaCO_3 \times (100.0/25.00)}{257.4\text{ mg sample}} \times 100 = 29.91\%$ Ca

$\dfrac{(32.75 - 30.04)\text{ mL} \times 1.600\text{ mg } CaCO_3/\text{mL} \times 24.30\text{ mg Mg}/100.09\text{ mg } CaCO_3 \times (100.0/25.00)}{257.4\text{ mg sample}} \times 100 =$

1.64 % Mg.

14-20. $(25.00 \times 0.0100)\text{mmol} \times 236.08\text{ mg } Ca(NO_3)_2{\cdot}4H_2O/\text{mmol} \times (100.0/25.00) = 236.1\text{ mg } Ca(NO_3)_2{\cdot}4H_2O$

$\therefore$ 736.2 - 236.1 = 500.1 mg NaCl + KCl. Suppose that the sample contains y mg NaCl, and consequently (500.1 - y) mg KCl. We have

$\dfrac{y\text{ mg NaCl}}{58.44\text{ mg/mmol}} + \dfrac{(500.1 - y)\text{mg KCl}}{74.56\text{ mg/mmol}} = (25.00 \times 0.1000 - 4.000 \times 0.1250)\text{ mmol} \times (100.0/25.00) = 8$

from which y = 150.6 . Hence, the sample contains

$(236.1/736.2) \times 100 = 32.07\%$ $Ca(NO_3)_2{\cdot}4H_2O$

$(150.6/736.2) \times 100 = 20.46\%$ NaCl, and

$[(500.1 - 150.6)/736.2] \times 100 = 47.47\%$ KCl

14-21. $\%\text{ Fe} = \dfrac{(32.00 \times 0.01250)\text{ mmol} \times 55.85\text{ mg Fe/mmol} \times (500.0/50.00)}{276.7\text{ mg sample}} \times 100 = 80.74$

$\%\text{ Zn} = \dfrac{(6.40 \times 0.01250)\text{ mmol} \times 65.37\text{ mg Zn/mmol} \times (500.0/50.00)}{276.7\text{ mg sample}} \times 100 = 18.90$

14-22. $\dfrac{77.7\text{ mg Pb}}{207.19\text{ mg/mmol}} = (50.00 \times 0.01000)\text{ mmol} - V\text{ mL} \times 0.01210\text{ mmol/mL}$, from which V = 10.33 mL.

14-23. (a) $M_{MgSO_4} = (25.00 \times 0.02004)\text{ mmol}/45.34\text{ mL} = 0.01105\text{ mmol/mL}$

(b) $\dfrac{(25.00 \times 0.02004 - 3.25 \times 0.01105)\text{ mmol} \times 142.04\text{ mg } Na_2SO_4/\text{mmol}}{145.5\text{ mg sample}} \times 100 = 45.4\%$ Na_2SO_4

14-24. (a) See Example 14-12.

Substituting in Equation (14-20), we have

$$pCa = 10.25 - \log \frac{10.00/1000}{50.00/1000} = 10.95$$

(b) When calcium is added, 1.20 mmol $[CaY]^{2-}$ is formed, and 50.00 - 1.20 = 48.80 mmol EDTA remain uncomplexed

$$\therefore\ pCa = 10.25 - \log \frac{11.20/1000}{48.80/1000} = 10.89$$

Hence, $\Delta pCa = 10.95 - 10.89 = 0.06$ units .

14-25. See Example 14-13.

(a) At pH 10.0, we have $\log K_{MgY'} = 8.69 - 0.45 = 8.24$, and $\log K_{MgIn'} = 5.44$. Substituting in Equation (14-17), we have $pM_{eq} = (8.69 - 0.45 + 2.70)/2 = 5.47$. From Equation (14-28), we have $pMg_{en} = 5.44 - \log(91/9) = 4.44 < 5.47 = pM_{eq}$

∴ we have a negative error, calculated by Equation (14-32), which becomes:

$$(1 - X) = \frac{10^{-4.44}}{2.00 \times 10^{-3}} - \frac{1}{10^{8.24} \cdot 10^{-4.44}} = 0.0180$$

Hence, we have a negative error of -1.80%.

(b) $pMg_{en} = 5.44 < 5.47 = pMg_{eq}$

$$\therefore (1 - X) = \frac{10^{-5.44}}{2.00 \times 10^{-3}} - \frac{1}{10^{8.24} \cdot 10^{-5.44}} = 0.000230$$

Hence, we have a negative error of -0.02%.

(c) $pMg_{en} = 5.44 - \log(9/91) = 6.44 > 5.47 = pMg_{eq}$ ∴ we have a positive error, calculated by Equation (14-33):

$$(X - 1) = \frac{1}{10^{8.24} \cdot 10^{-6.44}} - \frac{10^{-6.44}}{2.00 \times 10^{-3}} = 0.0157$$

Hence, we have a positive error of $+1.57\%$.

15-1. (a) Substituting in Equation (15-21a), we have

$$pH = 7.00 + (0.5250 - 0.3920)/0.05916 = 9.25$$

(b) $[OH^-] = \sqrt{(1.00 \times 10^{-14}/1.8 \times 10^{-5}) \times 0.100} = 7.45 \times 10^{-6}\ \underline{M}$

$\therefore\ pH = 14.00 - [-\log(7.45 \times 10^{-6})] = 8.87$

Hence, $8.87 = 7.00 + \dfrac{(E_{cell})_x - 0.3920}{0.05916}$ or $(E_{cell})_x = +0.5026\ V$

15-2. $+0.3595 = E_{SCE} - E_H = +0.2412 - (0.000 - \dfrac{0.05916}{2}\log\dfrac{1}{[H^+]^2})$

from which $[H^+] = 1.00 \times 10^{-2}\ \underline{M}\ \therefore\ pH = -\log(1.00 \times 10^{-2}) = 2.00$

15-3. $E_{cell} = E_{SCE} - E_H = +0.2412 - (0.000 - \dfrac{0.05916}{2}\log\dfrac{1}{[H^+]^2}) = +0.2412 + 0.05916\,pH$

15-4. Substituting in Equation (15-16), we have

$$K^{pot}_{A,B} = \frac{5.00 \times 10^{-3} \times [10^{(0.0040 - 0.017)/0.02958}] - (4.90 \times 10^{-4})}{4.90 \times 10^{-3}} = 0.27$$

$$\therefore\ 0.27 = \frac{5.00 \times 10^{-3} \times [10^{(0.0120 - 0.0170)/0.02958}] - a_{Ca^{2+}}}{5.00 \times 10^{-3}}$$

or $a = 2.04 \times 10^{-3}\ \underline{M}$

15-5. $K^{pot}_{Ca,Na} \cdot a^{2/1}_{Na^+} = 0.0016\,(0.50)^2 = 0.03\ [Ca^{2+}]_{min}$, from which $[Ca^{2+}]_{min} = 0.0133\ \underline{M}$

15-6. See Example 15-7.

For Cu^{2+} : $0.03\,(5.00 \times 10^{-3}) = 0.27 \times a^{2/2}_{Cu^{2+}}$ or $a_{Cu^{2+}} = 5.6 \times 10^{-4}\ \underline{M}$

For K^+ : $0.03\,(5.00 \times 10^{-3}) = 0.0001 \times a^{2/1}_{K^+}$ or $a_{K^+} = 1.22\ \underline{M}$

For Mg^{2+} : $0.03\,(5.00 \times 10^{-3}) = 0.01 \times a^{2/2}_{Mg^{2+}}$ or $a_{Mg^{2+}} = 0.015\ \underline{M}$

15-7. On the basis of Equation (15-9), we have

$$C_u = C_s = \frac{0.5 \times 0.40 \times 1.00}{50.00 - (50.00 + 1.00)\,10^{[(-0.4496) - (-0.4621)]/(-0.02958)}} = 6.51 \times 10^{-3}\ \underline{M}$$

15-8. Substituting the data in the relation

$$\%\ error = \frac{K^{pot}_{Ca^{2+},Na^+} \cdot a^{2/1}_{Na^+}}{a_{Ca^{2+}}} \times 100 \quad ,$$

we have $\%\ error = \frac{0.0016 \times 0.250^2}{0.00200} \times 100 = 5\%$

$\therefore\ [Ca^{2+}]_{theor} = 2.00 \times 10^{-3}\ \underline{M}$, $pCa_{theor} = 2.699$, $[Ca^{2+}]_{exp} = 2.00 \times 10^{-3} \times 1.05 =$ $2.10 \times 10^{-3}\ \underline{M}$, $pCa_{exp} = 2.678$. Hence, the relative error in the determination of pCa is $[(2.678 - 2.699)/2.699] \times 100 = -0.8\%$.

15-9. Let $y = [F^-]$ after adding NaF. We have

$$+0.1300 = E' - 0.05916 \log (1.00 \times 10^{-5}) \quad (1)$$

$$+0.0120 = E' - 0.05916 \log y \quad (2)$$

Subtracting Equation (2) from (1) we have

$+0.1180 = 0.05916 \log (y/1.00 \times 10^{-5})$, from which $y = 9.88 \times 10^{-4}\ \underline{M}$

$\therefore$ 100 mL $\times (9.88 \times 10^{-4} - 1.00 \times 10^{-5})$ mmol/mL $\times$ 41.99 mg NaF/mmol = 4.11 mg NaF were added.

15-10. (a) Substituting in Equation (16-11), we have

$\%\ error \simeq 4 \times 2 \times (\pm 0.1) = \pm 0.8\%$

(b) Let y be the maximum error in the potential. We have

1) for +1% error in $a_{Ca^{2+}}$:

$$E = E' + (0.05916/2) \log a_{Ca^{2+}} \quad (1)$$

$$E + y = E' + (0.05916/2) \log 1.01\, a_{Ca^{2+}} \quad (2)$$

Subtracting Equation (1) from (2) and solving for y gives y = +0.13 mV

2) for −1% error in $a_{Ca^{2+}}$:

$$E - y = E' + (0.05916/2) \log 0.99\, a_{Ca^{2+}} \quad (3)$$

Subtracting Equation (3) from (1) and solving for y gives y = −0.13 mV

Hence, the maximum permissible error in the potential is ±0.13 mV.

15-11. At pH 4.60 : $[CH_3COO^-]_A = \frac{K_a C_{HA}}{[H^+] + K_a} = \frac{(1.8 \times 10^{-5})(1.50 \times 10^{-3})}{2.51 \times 10^{-5} + 1.8 \times 10^{-5}} = 6.26 \times 10^{-4}\ \underline{M}$

At pH 5.30 : $[CH_3COO^-]_B = \frac{(1.8 \times 10^{-5})(1.50 \times 10^{-3})}{0.501 \times 10^{-5} + 1.8 \times 10^{-5}} = 1.17 \times 10^{-3}\ \underline{M}$

$$\therefore\ E_A = E' - 0.05916 \log (6.26 \times 10^{-4} + K^{pot}_{CH_3COO^-,Cl^-} \cdot 0.0100) = +0.1830 \quad (1)$$

$$E_B = E' - 0.05916 \log (1.17 \times 10^{-3} + K^{pot}_{CH_3COO^-,Cl^-} \cdot 0.0100) = +0.1739 \quad (2)$$

Subtracting Equation (2) from (1) and solving for $K^{pot}_{CH_3COO^-,Cl^-}$ gives

$K^{pot}_{CH_3COO^-,Cl^-} = 0.0654$

15-12. The potential of electrode A in a solution containing both ions A^+ and B^+ is

$$E_{AB} = E_A^{o\prime} + S\log(a_{A+} + K_{A,B}^{pot}a_{B+}) \qquad (1)$$

whereas in a solution containing only ion B^+ is

$$E_B = E_B^{o\prime} + S\log a_{B+} \qquad (2)$$

Equation (1) for a solution containing only ion B^+ becomes

$$E_B = E_A^{o\prime} + S\log K_{A,B}^{pot}a_{B+} = E_A^{o\prime} + S\log K_{A,B}^{pot} + S\log a_{B+} \qquad (3)$$

Combining Equations (2) and (3) we have

$$E_B^{o\prime} + S\log a_{B+} = E_A^{o\prime} + S\log K_{A,B}^{pot} + S\log a_{B+}$$

$$\text{or } \log K_{A,B}^{pot} = \frac{E_B^{o\prime} - E_A^{o\prime}}{S}$$

15-13. Let y be the final $[NH_4^+]$ and z the potential of the nitrate electrode after the bacterial action. We have

$$+0.0401 = E' + 0.05916\log(2.00 \times 10^{-3}) \qquad (1)$$

$$+0.0490 = E' + 0.05916\log y \qquad (2)$$

Subtracting Equation (2) from (1) and solving for y gives $y = 2.828 \times 10^{-3}$ $\underline{M}$ = $[NH_4^+]_{final}$

$$\therefore \Delta[NH_4^+] = 2.828 \times 10^{-3} - 2.00 \times 10^{-3} = 0.828 \times 10^{-3}\ \underline{M}$$

Hence, $[NO_3^-]_{final} = 2.00 \times 10^{-3} - 0.828 \times 10^{-3} = 1.172 \times 10^{-3}$ $\underline{M}$, whereupon we have for the nitrate electrode :

$$+0.0886 = E'' - 0.05916\log(2.00 \times 10^{-3}) \qquad (3)$$

$$z = E'' - 0.05916\log(1.172 \times 10^{-3}) \qquad (4)$$

Subtracting Equation (3) from (4) and solving for z gives $z = +0.1023$ V .

15-14.

$$+0.1286 = E' + 0.05916\log\left([2X/(142.04 + 18.02n)]/1000\right) \qquad (1)$$

$$+0.1675 = E' + 0.05916\log[2(2X/142.04)/1000] \qquad (2)$$

Subtracting Equation (1) from (2) and solving for n gives $n \simeq 10$

15-15 Let $y = [NO_3^-]$ in solution A. We have

$$+0.1269 = E' - 0.05916\log y \qquad (1)$$

$$+0.1134 = E' - 0.05916\log\left(\frac{20.00y + 10.00 \times 0.0100}{30.00}\right) \qquad (2)$$

Subtracting Equation (2) from (1) and solving for y gives $y = 0.003254$.

Hence, the sample contains

$$\frac{0.003254\ \text{mmol/mL} \times 250.0\ \text{mL} \times 0.10111\ \text{g}\ KNO_3/\text{mmol}}{0.1172\ \text{g sample}} \times 100 = 70.2\%\ KNO_3$$

15-16. Suppose that the 0.2436-g sample contains y mmol $NaNO_3$ and z mmol $NaNO_2$. We have

$$+0.2134 = E' - 0.05916 \log[(y + 0.021z)/100.0] \quad (1)$$

$$+0.2398 = E' - 0.05916 \log(y/100.0) \quad (2)$$

$$84.99y + 69.00z = 243.6 \quad (3)$$

Subtracting Equation (1) from (2) gives $0.0264 = 0.05916 \log(\frac{y + 0.021z}{y}) =$ $0.05916 \log(1 + 0.021 \cdot \frac{z}{y})$, from which

$$z/y = 85.44 \quad (4)$$

Solving the simultaneous Equations (3) and (4) gives

$y = 0.0407 \equiv 0.0407 \text{ mmol } NaNO_3 \times 84.99 \text{ mg/mmol} = 3.46 \text{ mg } NaNO_3$

Hence, the sample contains $(3.46/243.6) \times 100 = 1.42\%$ $NaNO_3$

15-17. $$E_1 = E' + S \log C_u \quad (1)$$

$$E_2 = E' + S \log \frac{C_uV_u - nC_sV_s}{V_u + V_s} \quad (2)$$

Subtracting Equation (1) from (2) we have

$$E_2 - E_1 = \Delta E = S \log \frac{C_uV_u - nC_sV_s}{(V_u + V_s)C_u}$$

or $$\frac{C_uV_u - nC_sV_s}{(V_u + V_s)C_u} = 10^{\Delta E/S}$$

or $$C_uV_u - nC_sV_s = C_u(V_u + V_s)10^{\Delta E/S}$$

or $$C_u[V_u - (V_u + V_s)10^{\Delta E/S}] = nC_sV_s$$

or $$C_u = \frac{nC_sV_s}{V_u - (V_u + V_s)10^{\Delta E/S}}$$

15-18. $pCa = -\log(2.00 \times 10^{-3}) = 2.700$

$\therefore$ substituting in Equation (15-22) we have

$$(pCa)_x = 2.700 + \frac{0.4532 - 0.4182}{0.02958} = 3.88$$

15-19. $E_{Na} = +0.0320 = E^{0\prime}_{Na} + 0.05916 \log 0.0100 = E^{0\prime}_{Na} - 0.1183$ or $E^{0\prime}_{Na} = +0.1503$ V

$\therefore E_{Na,K} = +0.0720 = +0.1503 + 0.05916 \log K^{pot}_{Na^+,K^+} \times 0.0100$, from which

$K^{pot}_{Na^+,K^+} = 4.7$

15-20. Let $y = [NO_3^-]$ after adding $NaNO_3$. We have

$+0.1194 = E' - 0.05916 \log (2.50 \times 10^{-3})$ (1)

$+0.0826 = E' - 0.05916 \log y$ (2)

Subtracting Equation (2) from (1) we have

$+0.0368 = 0.05916 \log (y/2.50 \times 10^{-3})$, from which $y = 1.047 \times 10^{-2}$ M.

$\therefore$ 500 mL X ($1.047 \times 10^{-2} - 2.50 \times 10^{-3}$) mmol/mL X 0.08499 g $NaNO_3$/mmol =

0.3387 g $NaNO_3$ was added.

CHAPTER 16

16-1.

λ, Å	λ, nm	λ, µm	λ, cm	ν, Hz	$\bar{\nu}$, cm^{-1}
5890	589	0.589	5.89×10^{-5}	5.09×10^{14}	1.70×10^{4}
4400	440	0.440	4.40×10^{-5}	6.81×10^{14}	2.27×10^{4}
6.54×10^{4}	6.54×10^{3}	6.54	6.54×10^{-4}	4.58×10^{13}	1.53×10^{3}
3.00	0.300	3.00×10^{-4}	3.00×10^{-8}	1.00×10^{18}	3.33×10^{7}
4.00×10^{8}	4.00×10^{7}	4.00×10^{4}	4.00	7.50×10^{9}	0.250
2.00×10^{4}	2.00×10^{3}	2.00	2.00×10^{-4}	1.50×10^{14}	5.00×10^{3}

16-2. $\% T = \frac{P}{P_0} \times 100$. Hence, $\frac{P_0}{P} = \frac{100}{\% T}$, and $\log \frac{P_0}{P} = A = 2.00 - \log \% T$.

16-3.

P/P_0	% T	A
1.00	100	0
0.100	10.0	1.00
0.0100	1.00	2.00

16-4. (a) $\varepsilon = \frac{A}{b\,c} = \frac{0.212}{1.00\text{ cm} \times 9.00 \times 10^{-5}\text{ mol/L}} = 2.36 \times 10^{3}\text{ L mol}^{-1}\text{ cm}^{-1}$

(b) $k = \frac{A}{b\,c} = \frac{0.212}{1.00\text{ cm} \times 9.00 \times 10^{-5}\text{ mol/L} \times 158.04 \times 10^{3}\text{ mg KMnO}_4\text{/mol}} = 1.49 \times 10^{-2}\text{ L mg}^{-1}\text{cm}^{-1}$

(c) $A = 2.36 \times 10^{3} \times 0.500 \times 9.00 \times 10^{-5} = 0.1062 \quad \therefore \quad T = 10^{-0.1062} = 0.783$

16-5. All relations but b are false.

16-6. The absorbance of X_1 is equal to $A_1 = -\log 0.450 = 0.3468$. The concentration of Fe^{2+} and consequently of ferroin in the mixture obtained by mixing 5.00 mL of 5.00 ppm Fe^{2+} with 5.00 mL of 1,10-phenanthroline is equal to (5.00 mL × 0.00500 mg Fe^{2+}/mL)/(55.85 mg/mmol × 10.00 mL) = 4.476×10^{-5} $\underline{M}$ ∴ its absorbance $A = 1.10 \times 10^{4} \times 1.00 \times 4.476 \times 10^{-5} = 0.4924$. Hence, absorbance of X_2 is equal to A_2 = [(10.00 × 0.3468) + (10.00 × 0.4924)]/20.00 = 0.4196 ∴ [ferroin] in X_2 = $0.4196/(1.10 \times 10^{4} \times 1.00) = 3.81 \times 10^{-5}$ $\underline{M}$.

16-7. After mixing, we have in solution B

$[FeL_3^{2+}]$ = (20.00 mL × 5.00×10^{-5} mmol/mL)/100.0 mL = 1.000×10^{-5} $\underline{M}$,
C_L = (20.00 mL × 5.00×10^{-3} mmol/mL)/100.0 mL = 1.000×10^{-3} $\underline{M}$

$\therefore [L]_{free} = 1.000 \times 10^{-3} - (3 \times 1.000 \times 10^{-5}) = 0.970 \times 10^{-3}$ M

Hence, $A = (2.24 \times 10^{4})(1.00)(1.00 \times 10^{-5}) + (12)(1.00)(0.97 \times 10^{-3}) = 0.236$

16-8. (a) $pH = pK_2 + \log \frac{[HPO_4^{2-}]}{[H_2PO_4^-]} = 7.21 + \log \frac{0.010}{0.050} = 6.51$

$\therefore \quad 6.51 = pK_{HX} + \log \frac{[X^-]}{[HX]} \quad$ or $\quad [X^-]/[HX] = 8.13 \qquad (1)$

$[X^-] + [HX] = C_{HX} = 2.50 \times 10^{-4} \qquad (2)$

Solving the two simultaneous equations gives $[HX] = 2.74 \times 10^{-5}$ M, $[X^-] = 2.23 \times 10^{-4}$ M.

From Example 16-12, we have $\varepsilon_{HX,460} = 0.210/2.50 \times 10^{-4} = 840$,

$\varepsilon_{X^-,460} = 0.025/2.50 \times 10^{-4} = 100$. Hence, $A_{460} = 840 \times 1.00 \times 2.74 \times 10^{-5} + 100 \times 1.00 \times 2.23 \times 10^{-4} = 0.045$.

(b) Similarly, from Example 16-12, we have $\varepsilon_{HX,680} = 0.060/2.50 \times 10^{-4} = 240$,

$\varepsilon_{X^-,680} = 0.260/2.50 \times 10^{-4} = 1040$. Hence, $A_{680} = 240 \times 1.00 \times 2.74 \times 10^{-5} + 1040 \times 1.00 \times 2.23 \times 10^{-4} = 0.238$.

16-9. See Example 16-11. Since L is in large excess over M, [L] remains practically constant. We have

$A = \varepsilon b [ML_2] \qquad (1)$

$C_M = [ML_2] + [M] \qquad (2)$

$K_f = [ML_2]/[M][L]^2 \qquad (3)$

Combining Equations (2) and (3), we have

$C_M = [ML_2] + \frac{[ML_2]}{K_f[L]^2} = [ML_2](1 + \frac{1}{K_f[L]^2}) \qquad (4)$

Combining Equations (1) and (4), we have

$A = \frac{\varepsilon b C_M}{1 + (1/K_f[L]^2)}$

16-10. $\%T_{real} = 30.8/0.90 = 34.2$

16-11. (a) Substituting in Equation (16-7), we have $\alpha = 340/10 = 34.0$

(b) $\varepsilon = \alpha \cdot MW = 34.0 \times 250 = 8.50 \times 10^{3}$

16-12. (a) $1 \longrightarrow 2$

(b) $1 \longrightarrow 4$

(c) For $T_1 = 0.100$, $A_1 = -\log 0.100 = 1.00$; for $T_2 = 2\,T_1 = 0.200$, $A_2 = -\log 0.200 = 0.70$

$\therefore$ required dilution is $7 \longrightarrow 10$

(d) For $T_3 = 4\,T_1 = 0.400$, $A_3 = -\log 0.400 = 0.398$ $\therefore$ required dilution is $3.98 \longrightarrow 10$

16-13. $(C_{Fe})_B = (C_{Fe})_D \times (100.0/25.00) = [-\log 0.792/(1.10 \times 10^4 \times 5.00)] \times 4 = 7.37 \times 10^{-6}$ $\underline{M} \equiv$
7.37×10^{-6} mol Fe/L $\times$ 55.85×10^3 mg Fe/mol = 0.412 mg Fe/L

$\therefore$ ppm Fe = (0.412 mg Fe/2451 mg sample) $\times 10^6$ = 168

16-14. Let C be the concentration of K in solution D. We have

$A = -\log 0.222 = 0.654 = \varepsilon \times 1.00 \times c$ (1)

$\varepsilon = -\log 0.178/(1.00 \times 3.31 \times 10^{-4}) = 2265$ (2)

Combining Equations (1) and (2), we find $c = 2.887 \times 10^{-4}$ $\underline{M}$. Hence, the sample contains

$$\frac{2.887 \times 10^{-4} \text{ mol/L} \times 0.500 \text{ L} \times 273 \text{ g K/mol}}{0.3122 \text{ g sample}} \times 100 = 12.62\% \text{ K}$$

16-15. $A = -\log T$ (1)

$A/3 = -\log 2T$ (2)

Combining Equations (1) and (2), we have $3 = \log T/\log 2T$ or

$A = -\log T = -3(\log 2 + \log T) = -0.9031 + 3A$ or $A = 0.4515 = 1.10 \times 10^4 \times 1.00 \times c$ or

$c = 4.10 \times 10^{-5}$ $\underline{M}$. Hence, solution B contains

4.10×10^{-5} mol/L $\times$ 55.85×10^3 mg Fe/mol = 2.29 mg Fe/L $\equiv$ 2.29 ppm Fe

16-16. For the 0.1% Fe sample, in order that the absorbance of solution X falls in the range 0.200 - 0.800 , its iron concentration should be between

$(0.200/1.10 \times 10^4 \times 1.00)$ mol/L $\times$ 55.85×10^3 mg Fe/mol = 1.015 mg Fe/L

and $(0.800/1.10 \times 10^4 \times 1.00)$ mol/L $\times$ 55.85×10^3 mg Fe/mol = 4.062 mg Fe/L

$\therefore$ y should lie between [1.015 mg/(0.1 mg Fe/100 mg sample)] and [4.062 mg/(0.1 mg Fe/100 mg sample)], that is, between 1,015 and 4,062 mg.

Similarly, for the 0.2% Fe sample, y should lie between [1.015 mg/(0.2 mg Fe/100 mg sample)] and [4.062 mg/(0.2 mg Fe/100 mg sample)] , that is, between 508 and 2,031 mg . Hence, for 0.1 - 0.2% Fe and A = 0.200 - 0.800, y should lie between 1,015 and 2,031 mg .

16-17. For solution D, we have $c = 0.515/(1.35 \times 10^4 \times 1.00) = 3.815 \times 10^{-5}$ $\underline{M}$. Hence, the sample contains

$$\frac{3.815 \times 10^{-5} \text{ mol/L} \times 73.14 \text{ g } C_4H_9NH_2\text{/mol} \times \frac{100.0}{10.00} \times \frac{100.0}{10.00} \times 0.250 \text{ L}}{0.0782 \text{ g sample}} \times 100 = 89.2\% \; C_4H_9NH_2$$

16-18. $[M^{3+}] = -\log 0.182/(450 \times 1.00) = 0.001644$ $\underline{M}$

$\therefore$ $E = +0.0558 + 0.2412 = +0.2970 = +0.402 - 0.05916 \log([M^{2+}]/0.001644$, from which $[M^{2+}] = 0.0979$ $\underline{M}$.

16-19. Let c be the concentration of solution B, in µg Mn/mL. We have

$0.326 = k\,b\,c$ (1)

$0.312 = k\,b\,[(10.00\,c + 1.00 \times 4.00)/11.00]$ (2)

Dividing Equation (1) and (2) and solving for c, we find $c = 7.58$ µg Mn/mL

16-20. (a)

Substance	A_{320}/A_{278}
B	0.840/0.360 = 2.33
C	0.480/0.432 = 1.11
Unknown	0.386/0.347 = 1.11

Hence, the unknown solution contains compound C.

(b) $c = 1.00 \times 10^{-4} (0.386/0.480) = 8.04 \times 10^{-5}$ $\underline{M}$

16-21. (a) The absorbance of solution A is equal to $A_A = -\log 0.565 = 0.2480$.
Similarly, $A_B = -\log 0.295 = 0.5302$, $A_D = -\log 0.500 = 0.3010$. Suppose that y mL of solution A should be mixed with z mL of solution B. We have

$y + z = 250.0$ (1)

$(0.2480\,y + 0.5302\,z)/250.0 = 0.3010$ (2)

Solving the two simultaneous equations gives y = 203.0 mL A, z = 47.0 mL B

(b) For solution D, we have $C_x = 0.3010/(6.85 \times 10^3 \times 1.00) = 4.394 \times 10^{-5}$ $\underline{M}$.
Hence, solution D contains

4.394×10^{-5} mmol/mL × 250.0 mL × 323.1 mg X/mmol = 3.55 mg X

16-22. $M_{KMnO_4} = N/5 = 2.00 \times 10^{-4}/5 = 4.00 \times 10^{-5}$. The absorbance of solution B is equal to $A_B = -\log 0.215 = 0.6676$, and of the standard $KMnO_4$ solution is equal to $A_{KMnO_4} = -\log 0.460 = 0.3372$. Hence, we have $[KMnO_4]_B/4.00 \times 10^{-5} = 0.6676/0.3372$ or

$[KMnO_4]_B = 7.92 \times 10^{-5}$ $\underline{M}$.

Hence the sample contains

$$\frac{7.92 \times 10^{-5}\ \text{mol/L} \times 1.000\ \text{L} \times 54.94\ \text{g Mn/mol}}{0.3421\ \text{g sample}} \times 100 = 1.27\ \%\ \text{Mn}$$

16-23. 1.62 ppm Fe $\equiv$ $(1.62\ \text{mg Fe/L})/(55.85 \times 10^3\ \text{mg/mmol}) = 2.901 \times 10^{-5}$ $\underline{M}$

$\therefore A = 1.10 \times 10^4 \times 1.00 \times 2.901 \times 10^{-5} = 0.3191$, $T = 10^{-0.3191} = 0.4796$

Hence, $T_{real} = 0.4796 - 0.02 = 0.4596$, $A_{real} = -\log 0.4596 = 0.3376$

$\therefore$ real % Fe = $5.25 \times (0.3376/0.3191) = 5.55$

16-24. The absorbance of sample a is equal to $A_a = 3.10 \times 10^3 \times 1.00 \times [0.3535 \times 0.01/(250 \times 0.500)] = 0.0877$. Similarly, we have

$A_b = 3.10 \times 10^3 \times 1.00 \times [1.6821 \times 0.01/(250 \times 0.500)] = 0.4172$, and

$A_c = 3.10 \times 10^3 \times 1.00 \times [5.0050 \times 0.01/(250 \times 0.500)] = 1.241$.

Hence, the second analysis (b) is expected to yield the most accurate result, because the absorbance of 0.4172 measured in this analysis is the closest to the value of 0.434 which corresponds to the minimum error (Figure 16-2).

16-25. $c_{min} = A_{min}/\varepsilon b = 0.01/(2.50 \times 10^3 \times 0.0100) = 4.0 \times 10^{-4}$ $\underline{M}$.

16-26. $A_u/A_s = 0.357/0.591 = C_u/3.00$, from which $C_u = 1.81$ ppm Fe

16-27. (a) $\varepsilon_{B,470} = 0.912/(1.00 \times 1.20 \times 10^{-4}) = 7.6 \times 10^3$

$\varepsilon_{C,470} = 0.132/(1.00 \times 1.50 \times 10^{-4}) = 8.8 \times 10^2$

$\varepsilon_{B,530} = 0.216/(1.00 \times 1.20 \times 10^{-4}) = \varepsilon_{C,530} = 0.270/(1.00 \times 1.50 \times 10^{-4}) = 1.80 \times 10^3$

$\varepsilon_{B,630} = 0.054/(1.00 \times 1.20 \times 10^{-4}) = 450$

$\varepsilon_{B,630} = 0.975/(1.00 \times 1.50 \times 10^{-4}) = 6.5 \times 10^3$

For solution (3), we have

$A_{470} = 0.607 = 7.6 \times 10^3 \times 1.00[B] + 8.8 \times 10^2 \times 1.00 \times [C]$ (1)

$A_{530} = 0.252 = 1.80 \times 10^3 \times 1.00\ ([B] + [C])$ (2)

Solving the two simultaneous equations gives $[B] = 7.2 \times 10^{-5}$ $\underline{M}$, $[C] = 6.8 \times 10^{-5}$ $\underline{M}$

(b) $A_{630} = 450 \times 1.00 \times 7.2 \times 10^{-5} + 6.5 \times 10^3 \times 1.00 \times 6.8 \times 10^{-5} = 0.474$

16-28. In order to achieve maximum accuracy, the absorbance A_B of the final solution should be 0.434, where the relative error is minimum (Figure 16-2) ∴ its concentration should be equal to $C_B = 0.434/(4.3 \times 10^3 \times 1.00) = 1.009 \times 10^{-4}$ $\underline{M}$. Hence, we have

$$\frac{1.009 \times 10^{-4}\ \text{mmol/mL} \times 250.0\ \text{mL} \times 0.160\ \text{g B/mmol}}{\text{g sample}} \times 100 = 1.10 \quad \text{, or} \quad \text{g sample} = 0.367$$

16-29. In solution B , $C_{Fe} = -\log 0.445/(1.10 \times 10^4 \times 1.00) = 3.197 \times 10^{-5}$ $\underline{M}$

∴ in solution A , $C_{Fe} = 3.197 \times 10^{-5} \times (500.0/2.00) = 0.007992$ $\underline{M}$. Hence, we have

$$\% \text{Fe} = \frac{0.007992\ \text{mol/L} \times 0.100\ \text{L} \times 55.85\ \text{g Fe/mol}}{6.8520\ \text{g sample}} \times 100 = 0.65$$

The 6.8520-g sample gives $0.0568 \times (100.0/25.00) = 0.2272$ g of $Fe_2O_3 + Al_2O_3$; it contains

$$6.8520\ \text{g sample} \times 0.0065\ \text{g Fe/g sample} \times \frac{159.69\ \text{g}\ Fe_2O_3}{(2 \times 55.85)\ \text{g Fe}} = 0.0637\ \text{g}\ Fe_2O_3 ,$$

and consequently $0.2272 - 0.0637 = 0.1635$ g Al_2O_3. Hence, the sample contains

$$\frac{0.1635\ \text{g}\ Al_2O_3 \times \dfrac{(2 \times 26.98)\ \text{g Al}}{101.96\ \text{g}\ Al_2O_3}}{6.8520\ \text{g sample}} \times 100 = 1.26\%\ \text{Al}$$

16-30. Curve 2 .

16-31. (a) For $C_{HX} = 5.00 \times 10^{-5}$ $\underline{M}$, using Equation (5-19a), we have

$$[H^+]^2 + 1.00 \times 10^{-5}[H^+] - 5.00 \times 10^{-10} = 0 \qquad (1)$$

Solving Equation (1) gives $[H^+] = 1.79 \times 10^{-5}$ $\underline{M} \simeq [X^-]$

∴ $[HX] = 5.00 \times 10^{-5} - 1.79 \times 10^{-5} = 3.21 \times 10^{-5}$ $\underline{M}$, whereupon

$A = (120 \times 1.00 \times 1.79 \times 10^{-5}) + (6.00 \times 10^3 \times 1.00 \times 3.21 \times 10^{-5}) = 0.195$

Similarly, for $C_{HX} = 1.00 \times 10^{-4}$ $\underline{M}$, $[H^+] = 2.70 \times 10^{-5}$ $\underline{M} \simeq [X^-]$, $[HX] = 7.30 \times 10^{-5}$ $\underline{M}$,

∴ $A = (120 \times 1.00 \times 2.70 \times 10^{-5}) + (6.00 \times 10^3 \times 1.00 \times 7.30 \times 10^{-5}) = 0.441$

For $C_{HX} = 2.00 \times 10^{-4}$ $\underline{M}$, $[H^+] = 4.00 \times 10^{-5}$ $\underline{M} \simeq [X^-]$, $[HX] = 1.60 \times 10^{-4}$ $\underline{M}$

∴ $A = (120 \times 1.00 \times 4.00 \times 10^{-5}) + (6.00 \times 10^3 \times 1.00 \times 1.60 \times 10^{-4}) = 0.965$

For $C_{HX} = 3.00 \times 10^{-4}$ $\underline{M}$, $[H^+] = 5.00 \times 10^{-5}$ $\underline{M} \simeq [X^-]$, $[HX] = 2.50 \times 10^{-4}$ $\underline{M}$

∴ $A = (120 \times 1.00 \times 5.00 \times 10^{-5}) + (6.00 \times 10^3 \times 1.00 \times 2.50 \times 10^{-4}) = 1.506$

From the four calculated absorbance values (or from a plot, $A = f(C_{HX})$),it can be seen that there is no linear relation between A and C_{HX} , and that the system shows an apparent positive deviation from Beer's law.

(b) At pH 4.00, $[HX] = \alpha_0 C_{HX} = \dfrac{[H^+]\ C_{HX}}{[H^+] + K_a} = \dfrac{1.0 \times 10^{-4} C_{HX}}{1.0 \times 10^{-4} + 1.00 \times 10^{-5}} = 0.909\ C_{HX}$,

$[X^-] = \alpha_1 C_{HX} = 0.091\ C_{HX}$

$\therefore$ for $C_{HX} = 5.00 \times 10^{-5}$ $\underline{M}$, $[HX] = 0.909 \times 5.00 \times 10^{-5} = 4.545 \times 10^{-5} \underline{M}$,
$[X^-] = 0.455 \times 10^{-5}$ $\underline{M}$. Hence,
$A = (120 \times 1.00 \times 0.455 \times 10^{-5}) + (6.00 \times 10^3 \times 1.00 \times 4.545 \times 10^{-5}) = 0.273$
Similarly, we find for $C_{HX} = 1.00 \times 10^{-4}$ $\underline{M}$, $A = 0.546$; for $C_{HX} = 2.00 \times 10^{-4}$ $\underline{M}$, $A = 1.092$, and for $C_{HX} = 3.00 \times 10^{-4}$ $\underline{M}$, $A = 1.638$. From the four calculated absorbance values (or from a plot, $A = f(C_{HX})$), it can be seen that there is no deviation from Beer's law. Actually, $A = k\,C_{HX}$ ($k = 5460$). This equation is also valid at pH 5.00, but k has a different value.

16-32. See Example 16-14. The real absorbance of sample D_1 is equal to $A_{1,r} = \log(100/4.0) = 1.40$, whereas its experimentally measured absorbance is equal to $A_{1,exp} = \log[(100+1.0)/(4.0+1.0)] = 1.305$. Hence, the % error in the concentration of D_1 is equal to $[(1.305 - 1.40)/1.40] \times 100 = -6.8\%$.
Similarly, for sample D_2 we have $A_{2,r} = \log(100/40.0) = 0.398$, $A_{2,exp} = \log[(100+1.0)/(40.0+1.0)] = 0.391_5$, and the % error in the concentration of D_2 is equal to $[(0.391_5 - 0.398)/0.398] \times 100 = -1.6\%$.

16-33. See Example 16-17. Since $\Delta T = 0.005$, whereas in Example 16-17 we have $\Delta T = 0.01$, using Equation (16-39) we find relative errors equal to one half of those calculated in Example 16-17. The corresponding curve is given below.

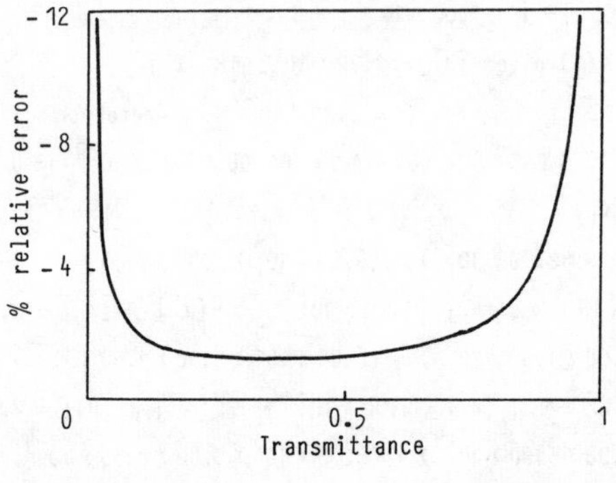

16-34. Let T_{exp} and A_{exp} be the experimental values of T and A, and T_r and A_r their corresponding real values. We have

	A_r	$T_r = 10^{-A_r}$	T_{exp}	$A_{exp} = -\log T_{exp}$	$\%\,error = \frac{A_{exp} - A_r}{A_r} \times 100$
a)	0.090	0.8128	0.8178	0.0874	-2.94
b)	0.450	0.3548	0.3598	0.4439	-1.36
c)	1.050	0.0891	0.0941	1.0264	-2.25

Conclusion. We have the smaller error in case b, in which the absorbance is close to 0.434, where the relative error is minimum.

16-35. See Example 16-19. Substituting the data in Equation (16-42), we have

$$0.165 = \varepsilon b\,(1.150 \times 10^{-4} - 1.000 \times 10^{-4}) \quad (1)$$

$$0.550 = \varepsilon b\,(c_x - 1.000 \times 10^{-4}) \quad (2)$$

Dividing Equations (1) and (2) and solving for c_x, we find that $c_x = 1.500 \times 10^{-4}$ $\underline{M}$.

16-36. (a) As long as Beer's law is obeyed, the absorbances of the two solutions will always differ by $(1.210 - 0.660) = 0.550$ $\therefore$ when the absorbance of the standard is 0, the absorbance of the unknown solution D will be 0.550.

(b) Classical spectrophotometry: For standard, $\%T = 10^{-A} \times 100 = 10^{-0.660} \times 100 = 21.88$; for unknown, $\%T = 10^{-1.210} \times 100 = 6.17$ $\therefore$ difference in $\%T = 21.88 - 6.17 = 15.71$

High absorbance method: For standard, $\%T = 10^{-0} \times 100 = 100.00$; for unknown, $\%T = 10^{-0.550} \times 100 = 28.18$ $\therefore$ difference in $\%T = 100.00 - 28.18 = 71.82$

Note. From the calculated values of the differences in %T, it can be seen that the scale of the spectrophotometer is expanded when using the high absorbance method.

16-37. Substituting the data in Equations (16-4) and (16-42), we have

$$0.236 = \varepsilon b\,(1.000 \times 10^{-4}) \quad (1)$$

$$0.223 = \varepsilon b\,(c_x - 1.000 \times 10^{-4}) \quad (2)$$

Dividing Equations (1) and (2), we have

$$c_x = 1.000 \times 10^{-4}\,[(0.223 + 0.236)/0.236] = 1.945 \times 10^{-4}\ \underline{M}\ KMnO_4 \equiv$$

$$1.945 \times 10^{-4}\ \text{mol/L} \times 54.94 \times 10^{3}\ \text{mg Mn/mol} = 10.69\ \text{mg Mn/L} \equiv 10.69\ \text{ppm Mn}$$

16-38. (a) See Example 16-20. The data are plotted below. From the plot, it can be seen that M^{2+} and L^- react at a 1:1 ratio. Hence, the formula of the complex is $[ML]^+$.

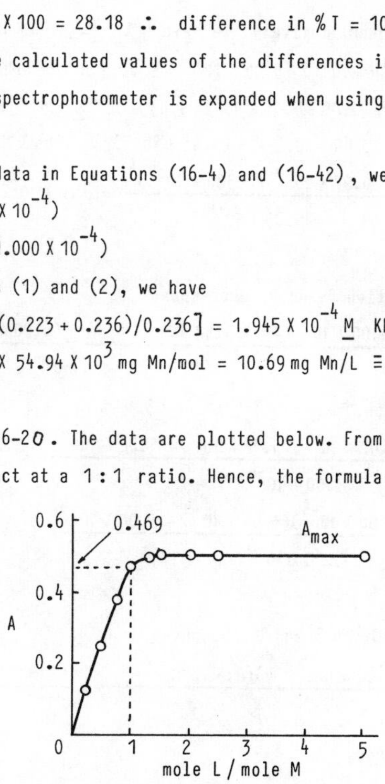

Mole - ratio plot

(b) A_{max} corresponds to practically quantitative complexation of M^{2+}

$\therefore$ $[ML^+] \simeq 2.50 \times 10^{-4}$ $\underline{M}$ and $\varepsilon_{ML^+,495} = 0.499/2.50 \times 10^{-4} \simeq 2.00 \times 10^3$

(c) Substituting the data corresponding to the stoichiometric point in Equation (16-48), we have

$$K_{inst} = \frac{[1 - (0.469/0.499)]^2 \times 2.50 \times 10^{-4}}{0.469/0.499} = 9._6 \times 10^{-7}$$

16-39. Since M^{n+} is complexed quantitatively, we have $[ML_3^{n+}] = 5.00 \times 10^{-6}$ $\underline{M}$ and $\varepsilon_{ML_3^{n+}} = 0.315/(1.00 \times 5.00 \times 10^{-6}) = 6.30 \times 10^4$. Hence, in the other solution of the complex we have $[ML_3^{n+}] = 0.565/(1.00 \times 6.30 \times 10^4) = 8.97 \times 10^{-6}$ $\underline{M}$, $[M^{n+}] = 1.00 \times 10^{-5} - 8.97 \times 10^{-6} = 1.03 \times 10^{-6}$ $\underline{M}$ and $[L] = 5.00 \times 10^{-5} - 3(8.97 \times 10^{-6}) = 2.31 \times 10^{-5}$ $\underline{M}$

$$\therefore K_f = \frac{[ML_3^{n+}]}{[M^{n+}][L]^3} = \frac{8.97 \times 10^{-6}}{(1.03 \times 10^{-6})(2.31 \times 10^{-5})^3} = 7.1 \times 10^{14}$$

16-40. Since M^{n+} is complexed quantitatively, we have $[ML_4^{n+}] = 1.00 \times 10^{-5}$ $\underline{M}$ and $\varepsilon_{ML_4^{n+}} = 0.515/(1.00 \times 1.00 \times 10^{-5}) = 5.15 \times 10^4$. Hence, in the other solution of the complex we have $[ML_4^{n+}] = 0.465/(1.00 \times 5.15 \times 10^4) = 9.03 \times 10^{-6}$ $\underline{M}$, $[M^{n+}] = 1.00 \times 10^{-5} - 9.03 \times 10^{-6} = 0.97 \times 10^{-6}$ $\underline{M}$ and $[L] = 5.00 \times 10^{-5} - 4(9.03 \times 10^{-6}) = 1.388 \times 10^{-5}$ $\underline{M}$

$$\therefore K_{inst} = \frac{[M^{n+}][L]^4}{[ML_4^{n+}]} = \frac{(0.97 \times 10^{-6})(1.388 \times 10^{-5})^4}{9.03 \times 10^{-6}} = 4.0 \times 10^{-21}$$

16-41. Let $y = [ML^{n+}]$ in solution B and D, whereupon

$$K_{inst} = \frac{[M^{n+}][L]}{[ML^{n+}]} = \frac{(4.00 \times 10^{-4} - y)(3.12 \times 10^{-4} - y)}{y} = \frac{(6.00 \times 10^{-4} - y)(3.04 \times 10^{-4} - y)}{y}$$

or $y = 3.00 \times 10^{-4}$. Hence, $\varepsilon_{550} = 0.375/(1.00 \times 3.00 \times 10^{-4}) = 1.25 \times 10^3$, and

$$K_{inst} = \frac{(4.00 \times 10^{-4} - 3.00 \times 10^{-4})(3.12 \times 10^{-4} - 3.00 \times 10^{-4})}{3.00 \times 10^{-4}} = 4.0 \times 10^{-6} \quad \text{or}$$

$$K_{inst} = \frac{(6.00 \times 10^{-4} - 3.00 \times 10^{-4})(3.04 \times 10^{-4} - 3.00 \times 10^{-4})}{3.00 \times 10^{-4}} = 4.0 \times 10^{-6}$$

16-42. Let $y = [ML^{n+}]$, in solution B and D. We have

$$K_{inst} = \frac{[M^{n+}][L]}{[ML^{n+}]} = \frac{(3.60 \times 10^{-4} - y)(2.48 \times 10^{-4} - y)}{y} = \frac{(2.80 \times 10^{-4} - y)(2.62 \times 10^{-4} - y)}{y}$$

or $y = 2.412 \times 10^{-4}$. Hence,

$$K_{inst} = \frac{(3.60 \times 10^{-4} - 2.412 \times 10^{-4})(2.48 \times 10^{-4} - 2.412 \times 10^{-4})}{2.412 \times 10^{-4}} = 3.3 \times 10^{-6}$$

or $$K_{inst} = \frac{(2.80 \times 10^{-4} - 2.412 \times 10^{-4})(2.62 \times 10^{-4} - 2.412 \times 10^{-4})}{2.412 \times 10^{-4}} = 3.3 \times 10^{-6}$$

16-43. We have $[H^+] = 10^{-5.30} = 5.0 \times 10^{-6}$ $\underline{M}$, and $[X^-] = 0.444/(3.36 \times 10^4 \times 2.00) = 6.61 \times 10^{-6}$ $\underline{M}$

$$\therefore K_a = \frac{[H^+][X^-]}{[HX]} = \frac{(5.0 \times 10^{-6})(6.61 \times 10^{-6})}{(2.00 \times 10^{-5} - 6.61 \times 10^{-6})} = 2.5 \times 10^{-6}$$

16-44. pK_{HX} can be found from the plot given below, $A = f(pH)$. When $[X^-] = [HX]$, we have $pH = pK_{HX}$, and $[X^-]/[HX] = (A_{max} - A)/(A - A_{min}) = 1$ or $A = (A_{max} + A_{min})/2$. From the plot, we have $A = (0.599 + 0.001)/2 = 0.300$ at $pH = 5.00$ $\therefore$ $pK_{HX} = pH = 5.00$. Hence, $K_a = 1.0 \times 10^{-5}$.

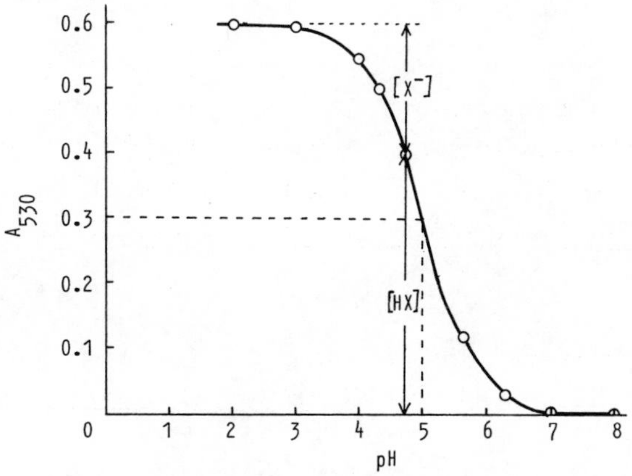

Note. pK_{HX} can also be found by substituting any pair of data in Equation (20-52). For example, for $pH = 4.00$, $A_{530} = 0.545$, we have

$$pK_{HX} = 4.00 - \log \frac{0.599 - 0.545}{0.545 - 0.001} = 5.00 \quad \therefore K_a = 1.0 \times 10^{-5}$$

16-45. Substituting the data in Equation (16-51), we have

$$pK_{HX} = 4.70 - \log \frac{0.285 - 0.090}{0.675 - 0.285} = 5.00 \quad . \text{ Hence, } K_{HX} = 1.0 \times 10^{-5}$$

16-46. a) b) c)

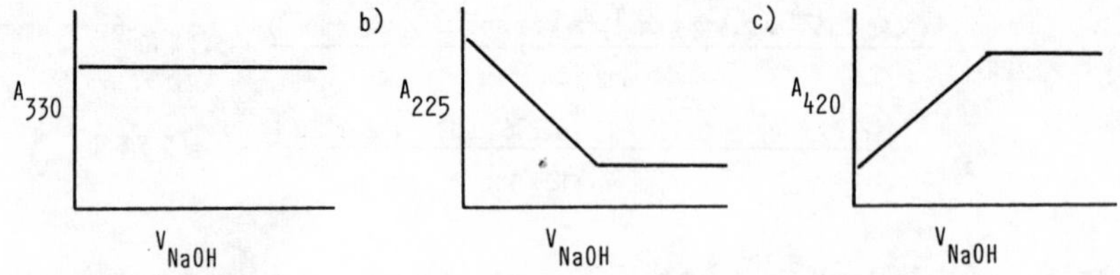

The determination of the equivalent point from the titration curve is impossible in case (a).

CHAPTER 17

17-1. (a) The weights of ZrO_2 and HfO_2 are related to the corresponding initial quantities of the metals in the sample by the expressions

$$W_{ZrO_2} = \frac{ZrO_2}{Zr}(Q_{Zr})_o = 1.3508\,(Q_{Zr})_o$$

$$W_{HfO_2} = \frac{HfO_2}{Hf}(Q_{Hf})_o = 1.1793\,(Q_{Hf})_o$$

(the terms of the fractions refer to atomic and molecular weights).

Substituting the above values in Equation (17-9), where $Q_A = (Q_A)_o$ and $Q_B = (Q_B)_o$, because no separation is carried out, we have

$$E_r = \frac{\varkappa_B}{\varkappa_A}\,\frac{(Q_B)_o}{(Q_A)_o} = \frac{1.1793}{1.3508} \times \frac{0.8}{15} = +0.466 \quad \text{or} \quad +4.66\,\%$$

(b) Substituting in Equation (17-10), we have

$$E_r = (0.99 - 1) + \frac{1.1793}{1.3508} \times \frac{0.8}{15} \times 0.12 = -0.0044 \quad \text{or} \quad -0.44\,\%$$

17-2. Let $W_{Fe_2O_3}$ and $W_{Al_2O_3}$ be the weight of Fe_2O_3 and coweighted Al_2O_3. Since a relative error smaller than 0.1% is required, we have

$$0.001 \geq \frac{W_{Al_2O_3}}{W_{Fe_2O_3}} = \frac{\frac{Al_2O_3}{2Al}\,Q_{Al}}{\frac{Fe_2O_3}{2Fe}\,(Q_{Fe})_o} = \frac{1.8895}{1.4297} \cdot \frac{Q_{Al}}{(Q_{Fe})_o} \tag{1}$$

In the worst case, we have

$$\frac{(Q_{Al})_o}{(Q_{Fe})_o} = \frac{15}{20} \quad \text{or} \quad (Q_{Fe})_o = 1.3333\,(Q_{Al})_o \tag{2}$$

Combining Equations (1) and (2), we have

$$0.001 \geq \frac{1.8895}{1.4297} \cdot \frac{Q_{Al}}{1.3333\,(Q_{Al})_o} = 0.99123 \cdot \frac{Q_{Al}}{(Q_{Al})_o}$$

$$\text{or} \quad \frac{Q_{Al}}{(Q_{Al})_o} \leq 0.0010088 \quad \text{or} \quad \frac{Q_{Al}}{(Q_{Al})_o} \leq 0.101\,\%$$

17-3. (a) Let R_{Cl} and R_{Br} be the recovery coefficients of Cl^- and Br^-, and $S_{Br,Cl}$ the separation coefficient. The weights of AgCl and AgBr are related to the corresponding initial quantities (mol) of the halides in the solutions by the expressions

$$W_{AgCl} = k \cdot 143.32\,(\text{mol } Cl^-)_o \tag{1}$$

$$W_{AgBr} = k \cdot 187.77\,(\text{mol } Br^-)_o \tag{2}$$

Substituting the data in Equations (1) and (2) and combining the results with Equation (17-10), we have

$$-0.0145 = (R_{Cl} - 1) + \frac{187.77}{143.77} \times \frac{0.100}{0.150} \times R_{Br} \quad (3)$$

$$+0.0405 = (R_{Cl} - 1) + \frac{187.77}{143.32} \times \frac{0.200}{0.050} \times R_{Br} \quad (4)$$

Solving the simultaneous Equations (3) and (4) gives $R_{Cl} = 0.9745$, $R_{Br} = 0.01259$.

Hence, we have $S_{Br,Cl} = 0.01259/0.9745 = 0.0129$

(b) Substituting in Equation (17-10), we have

$$E_r = (0.9745 - 1) + \frac{187.77}{143.32} \times \frac{1}{1} \times 0.01259 = -0.00901$$

Hence, the expected percent analytical error is -0.90% .

17-4. (a) The volume of nitrogen, V_{N_2}, is related to the corresponding initial quantities of H_2NCONH_2 and $(NH_4)_2SO_4$ in the sample by the expressions

$$V_{N_2} = k \cdot \frac{W_{H_2NCONH_2}}{H_2NCONH_2} = k \cdot \frac{W_{H_2NCONH_2}}{60.06} = k \cdot 0.016651 \cdot W_{H_2NCONH_2}$$

$$V_{N_2} = k \cdot \frac{W_{(NH_4)_2SO_4}}{(NH_4)_2SO_4} = k \cdot \frac{W_{(NH_4)_2SO_4}}{132.14} = k \cdot 0.007568 \cdot W_{(NH_4)_2SO_4}$$

Substituting the above values in Equation (17-10), we have

$$0.03 \geq (1 - 1) + \frac{W_{(NH_4)_2SO_4}}{W_{H_2NCONH_2}} \times \frac{0.007568}{0.016651} \times 0.05 \quad \text{or} \quad \frac{W_{(NH_4)_2SO_4}}{W_{H_2NCONH_2}} \leq 0.0660$$

(b) Substituting in Equation (17-10), we have

$$0.03 \geq (1 - 1) + \frac{W_{(NH_4)_2SO_4}}{W_{H_2NCONH_2}} \times \frac{0.007568}{0.016651} \times 0.05 \quad \text{or} \quad \frac{W_{(NH_4)_2SO_4}}{W_{H_2NCONH_2}} \leq 1.32$$

17-5. Substituting in Equation (17- 2), we have

$$S_{B/A} = S_{Co/Ni} = \frac{Q_{Co}/Q_{Ni}}{(Q_{Co})_o/(Q_{Ni})_o} = \frac{0.15/100}{1/0.05} = 7.5 \times 10^{-5}$$

17-6. (a) See Example 17-2.

The molar ratio of A and B is mol A/mol B = (20/55.85)/(1/95.94) = 34.36

Substituting in Equation (17-9), where $Q_A = (Q_A)_o$ and $Q_B = (Q_B)_o$, since no separation is carried out, we have

$$E_r = \frac{\varkappa_B(Q_B)_o}{\varkappa_A(Q_A)_o} = \frac{5650 \times 1}{2850 \times 34.36} = +0.0577 \quad \text{or} \quad +5.77\%$$

(b) Substituting in Equation (17-10), we have

$$E_r = (0.99 - 1) + \frac{5650}{2850} \times \frac{1}{34.36} \times 0.18 = +0.00038 \quad \text{or} \quad +0.04\%$$

(c) Since the recovery coefficient of A, R_A, is practically equal to 1, substituting in Equation (17-10) we have

$$\frac{0.3}{100} \geq (1.00 - 1) + \frac{5650}{2850} \cdot \frac{1}{34.36} \cdot R_B$$

or $R_B \leq 0.0520$

17-7. See Example 17-4.

Substituting the data in Equation (17-14), we have

$$\frac{W_n}{W_0} = \frac{100 - 99.5}{100} = \left(\frac{100}{(8 \times 50.0) + 100}\right)^n$$

$\frac{1}{200} = (\frac{1}{5})^n$ or $n = 3.3$. Hence, at least four extractions are required.

For $n = 1$, $W_1 = \left(\frac{100}{(8 \times 50.0) + 100}\right) W_0 = 0.200\, W_0$. Hence, 80% of substance A, that is 0.6000 g is removed with the first extraction. In a similar way, it is found that 0.1200, 0.0240, and 0.0048 g of substance A is removed with the second, third, and fourth extraction, respectively.

17-8. The aqueous solution contains 50.0 mL X 0.0200 g X/mL = 1.000 g X.

$\therefore W_1 = \left(\frac{50.0}{(5.00 \times 50.0) + 50.0}\right) 1.000 = 0.167$. Hence, 0.167 g of X will remain in the aqueous phase.

17-9. It is assumed that HX does not dissociate in the presence of the strong acid HCl (flask A), whereas it dissociates completely in the presence of NaOH (flask B). Since the extract from flask B contained no HX or X^-, it is concluded that X^- is insoluble in the organic solvent. In all flasks, before the extractions, $C_{HX} = (0.400 \times 25.0)/100 = 0.100$ M. If $[HX]_o$ and $[HX]_w$ are the concentrations of HX in the organic and aqueous phase, respectively, we have

$$K_D = \frac{[HX]_o}{[HX]_w} = \frac{0.0580}{0.100 - 0.0580} = 1.38$$

Since $[HX]_o = 0.0370$ M, $[HX]_w = 0.0370/1.38 = 0.0268$ M, and $[X^-]_w = 0.100 - 0.0370 - 0.0268 = 0.0362$ M. We have $[X^-]_w = [H^+]_w + [OH^-]_w \simeq [H^+]_w$. Hence, $K_a = (0.0362)^2/0.0268 = 0.0489$.

17-10. Using Equation (17-18), we have for HA :

At pH = 4.0 , $D_{HA} = 10\,(1.00 \times 10^{-4})/(1.00 \times 10^{-4} + 1.0 \times 10^{-3}) = 0.909$,

at pH = 5.0 , $D_{HA} = 10\,(1.00 \times 10^{-5})/(1.00 \times 10^{-5} + 1.0 \times 10^{-3}) = 0.099$,

at pH = 6.0 , $D_{HA} = 10\,(1.00 \times 10^{-6})/(1.00 \times 10^{-6} + 1.0 \times 10^{-3}) = 0.010$,

at pH = 7.0 , $D_{HA} = 10\,(1.00 \times 10^{-7})/(1.00 \times 10^{-7} + 1.0 \times 10^{-3}) = 0.001$, and

at pH = 8.0 , $D_{HA} = 10\,(1.00 \times 10^{-8})/(1.00 \times 10^{-8} + 1.0 \times 10^{-3}) = 0.0001$.

Similarly, we have for HB :

At pH = 4.0 , $D_{HB} = 1000\,(1.00 \times 10^{-4})/(1.00 \times 10^{-4} + 1.0 \times 10^{-9}) = 1000$,

at pH = 5.0 , $D_{HB} = 1000\,(1.00 \times 10^{-5})/(1.00 \times 10^{-5} + 1.0 \times 10^{-9}) = 1000$,

at pH = 6.0 , $D_{HB} = 1000\,(1.00 \times 10^{-6})/(1.00 \times 10^{-6} + 1.0 \times 10^{-9}) = 999$, at pH = 7.0 , $D_{HB} = 1000\,(1.00 \times 10^{-7})/(1.00 \times 10^{-7} + 1.0 \times 10^{-9}) = 990$, and

at pH = 8.0 , $D_{HB} = 1000\,(1.00 \times 10^{-8})/(1.00 \times 10^{-8} + 1.0 \times 10^{-9}) = 909$

From the calculated values of the distribution ratios, it can be seen that the requested value of pH is about 6. At pH = 6 , $D_{HB}/D_{HA} = 999/0.010 = 10^5$, the extraction of HB is quantitative (> 99.9%), whereas the coextraction of HA is negligible (~1%). At pH > 6, the coextraction of HA decreases, but simultaneously the extraction of HB becomes smaller than 99.9%. At pH < 6 , the extraction of HB becomes even larger, but simultaneously the coextraction of HA increases.

17-11. See Example 17-9.

We have the expressions

$$K_f = \frac{[ML_2]}{[M][L^-]^2} \qquad (M = Cu \text{ or } Zn) \tag{1}$$

$$[L^-] = \frac{K_a C_{HL}}{[H^+] + K_a} \tag{2}$$

$$D = \frac{(C_{ML_2})_o}{(C_{ML_2})_w} = \frac{[ML_2]_o}{[M^{2+}]_w + [ML_2]_w} \tag{3}$$

Combining Equations (1), (2), and (3) we have

$$D = \frac{[ML_2]_o}{\dfrac{[ML_2]_w}{K_f [L^-]_w^2} + [ML_2]_w} = \frac{[ML_2]_o}{[ML_2]_w} \cdot \frac{1}{\dfrac{1}{K_f [L^-]_w^2} + 1} = \frac{K_D}{\dfrac{([H^+] + K_a)^2}{K_f K_a^2 C_{HL}^2} + 1} \tag{4}$$

If W_0 is the initial weight of complex ML_2 in volume V_w of water, W_1 is the weight of ML_2 remaining in the aqueous phase after its extraction with volume V_o of the organic solvent and %E is the percent of the extracted metal, we have the expressions

$$\frac{W_1}{W_0} = \frac{V_w}{DV_o + V_w} \qquad \text{(see Equation 4-21)} \tag{5}$$

$$\%E = \left(\frac{W_0 - W_1}{W_0}\right) 100 \tag{6}$$

Combining Equations (5) and (6) we have

$$\%E = \left(1 - \frac{W_1}{W_0}\right) 100 = \left(1 - \frac{V_w}{DV_o + V_w}\right) 100 = \left(\frac{DV_o}{DV_o + V_w}\right) 100 \tag{7}$$

For $V_o = V_w = 20$, Equation (7) becomes

$$\%E = \left(\frac{D}{D + 1}\right) 100 \tag{8}$$

Values of D for any given pH are calculated using Equation (4) and then substituted in Equation (8). Calculated values of D at various pH's and their corresponding percentages of the extracted metal are tabulated below :

pH	2.0	3.0	4.0	5.0
D_{Cu}	0.32	29.1	347	398
% Cu	24.2	96.7	99.7	99.7
D_{Zn}	0.0025	0.245	19.6	244
% Zn	0.25	19.7	95.1	99.6

17-12. We have the expressions

$$\frac{[H^+][A^-]}{[HA]_w} = K_a \qquad (1)$$

$$[HA]_o/[HA]_w = K_D \qquad (2)$$

Mass balance : $V_w C = V_w [A^-] + V_w [HA]_w + V_o [HA]_o \qquad (3)$

Electroneutrality (aqueous phase) : $[H^+] + [Na^+] = [OH^-] + [A^-] \qquad (4)$

$$\text{or}\quad [H^+] + C = \frac{K_w}{[H^+]} + \frac{K_a [HA]_w}{[H^+]} \qquad (4a)$$

Combining Equations (1), (2), and (3), we have

$$V_w C = \frac{V_w K_a [HA]_w}{[H^+]} + V_w [HA]_w + V_o K_D [HA]_w \qquad (5)$$

$$\text{or}\quad [HA]_w = \frac{V_w C}{\dfrac{V_w K_a}{[H^+]} + V_w + V_o K_D} \qquad (5a)$$

Combining Equations (4a) and (5a) we have

$$[H^+] + C = \frac{K_w}{[H^+]} + \frac{K_a V_w C}{V_w K_a + [H^+] V_w + [H^+] V_o K_D} \qquad (6)$$

or, dividing by V_w the numerator and the denominator of the second fraction in Equation (6), we obtain

$$[H^+] + C = \frac{K_w}{[H^+]} + \frac{K_a C}{K_a + [H^+] + \dfrac{[H^+] V_o K_D}{V_w}} = \frac{K_w}{[H^+]} + \frac{K_a C}{K_a + [H^+](1 + \dfrac{V_o K_D}{V_w})} \qquad (7)$$

Substituting λ for $1 + (V_o/V_w)K_D$ in Equation (7) we have

$$[H^+] + C = \frac{K_w}{[H^+]} + \frac{K_a C}{K_a + [H^+]\lambda} \qquad (8)$$

from which we obtain the sought for equation

$$[H^+]^3 + (K_a + \lambda C)[H^+]^2 - \lambda K_w [H^+] - K_w K_a = 0 \qquad (8a)$$

17-13. See Solution 17-12.

Initially, $[OH^-]_1 = \sqrt{(1.00 \times 10^{-14}/5.0 \times 10^{-5})\, 0.0100} = 1.41 \times 10^{-6}$ M $\therefore$ $[H^+]_1 = 1.00 \times 10^{-14}/1.41 \times 10^{-6} = 7.09 \times 10^{-9}$ M, $pH_1 = -\log(7.09 \times 10^{-9}) = 8.15$

After the extraction, using Equation (8a) of problem 17-12 and taking into account that $\lambda = 1 + (V_o/V_w)K_D = 1 + (50/100)1000 = 501$, we obtain

$$501\,[H^+]_2^3 + 5.01\,[H^+]_2^2 - 5.01 \times 10^{-12}\,[H^+]_2 - 5 \times 10^{-19} = 0 \qquad (1)$$

Solving Equation (1) by the method of successive approximations, we have

$[H^+]_2 = 3.16 \times 10^{-10}$ M $\therefore$ $pH_2 = -\log(3.16 \times 10^{-10}) = 9.50$, and $\Delta pH = 9.50 - 8.15 = 1.35$

17-14. If K is the equilibrium constant, C_A is the initial concentration of A in the aqueous solution, and V_w and V_o are the volumes of the aqueous and organic phases, we have the expressions

$$K_D = [A]_o/[A]_w \qquad (1)$$

$$K = [A_2]_o/[A]_o^2 \qquad (2)$$

Mass balance (A): $V_w C_A = V_w[A]_w + V_o[A]_o + 2\,V_o[A_2]_o$ (3)

or, since $V_w = V_o$, $C_A = [A]_w + [A]_o + 2\,[A_2]_o$ (4)

$$D = \frac{(C_A)_o}{(C_A)_w} = \frac{C_A - [A]_w}{[A]_w} \qquad (5)$$

from which $[A]_w = C_A/(D+1)$ (5a)

Combining Equations (1), (2), and (4), we have

$$C_A = [A]_w + K_D[A]_w + 2\,K[A]_o^2 = [A]_w + K_D\,[A]_w + 2\,K\,K_D^2\,[A]_w^2 \qquad (6)$$

Combining Equations (5a) and (6) we have

$$C_A = \frac{C_A}{D+1} + \frac{K_D\,C_A}{D+1} + \frac{2\,K\,K_D^2\,C_A^2}{(D+1)^2} \qquad (7)$$

Multiplying all terms of Equation (7) by $(D+1)/C_A$ we have

$$K_D + \frac{2\,C_A\,K\,K_D^2}{D+1} = D \qquad (8)$$

Substituting the data in Equation (8), we have

$$K_D + 0.08163\,K\,K_D^2 = 3.9 \qquad (9)$$

$$K_D + 0.00606\,K\,K_D^2 = 2.3 \qquad (10)$$

Solving the system of Equations (9) and (10) we find $K_D = 2.17$, $K = 4.50$

17-15. Substituting the data in Equation (17-14), we have

$$0.05 = \left(\frac{100}{25\,D + 100}\right)^4$$

from which $D = 4.46$ $\therefore$ in the second case we have

$$0.05 = \left(\frac{100}{4.46\,V + 100}\right)^2$$

from which $V = 77.9$ mL $CHCl_3$

17-16. (a) Proceeding as in Solution 17-1, we obtain

$$W_{Ta_2O_5} = \frac{Ta_2O_5}{2\,Ta}(Q_{Ta})_o = 1.2211\,(Q_{Ta})_o \quad (1)$$

$$W_{Nb_2O_5} = \frac{Nb_2O_5}{2\,Nb}(Q_{Nb})_o = 1.4843\,(Q_{Nb})_o \quad (2)$$

Substituting in Equation (17-10), we have

$$E_r = (1-1) + \frac{1.2211}{1.4843} \times \frac{1}{5} \times 1 = +0.1645 \text{ or } +16.45\%$$

(b) $$R_{Nb} = \frac{W_1}{W_0} = \left(\frac{50}{(25 \times 0.040) + 50}\right)^n \quad (3)$$

$$R_{Ta} = \frac{W_1}{W_0} = \left(\frac{50}{(25 \times 2.1) + 50}\right)^n \quad (4)$$

Combining Equations (1), (2), (3), (4), and (17-10), we have

$$E_r = \left[\left(\frac{50}{(25 \times 0.040) + 50}\right)^n - 1\right] + \frac{1.2211}{1.4843} \times \frac{1}{5} \times \left(\frac{50}{(25 \times 2.1) + 50}\right)^n \quad (5)$$

from which we find, for

$n = 1$, $E_r = +0.0607$ or $+6.07\%$

$n = 2$, $E_r = +0.0003$ or $+0.03\%$

$n = 3$, $E_r = -0.0386$ or -3.86%

17-17. If M' is the molarity of HA after extraction, we have

$25.0 \text{ mL} \times M' \text{ mmol/mL} = 10.00 \text{ mL} \times 0.1000 \text{ mmol/mL}$, or $M' = 0.0400$.

Hence,

$100 \text{ mL} \times (0.100 - 0.0400) \text{ mmol/mL} = 6.00 \text{ mmol}$ HA was extracted into 50.0 mL of CCl_4

$$\therefore \; D = \frac{6.00/50.0}{4.00/100} = 3.00$$

17-18. Substituting in Equation (17-18), we have

$$D = \frac{25}{100 - 25} = \frac{40 \times (1.00 \times 10^{-7})}{1.00 \times 10^{-7} + K_a}$$

from which $K_a = 1.19 \times 10^{-5}$

17-19. Substituting in Equation (17-14), we have

$$0.0100 = \left(\frac{100}{45\,D + 100}\right)^2 \text{ or } \sqrt{0.0100} = 0.100 = \frac{100}{45\,D + 100}$$

from which $D = 20.0$

17-20. (a) Substituting in Equation (17-14), we have

$$\frac{0.00200}{2.00} = 0.00100 = \left(\frac{100}{(20 \times 20) + 100}\right)^n = (0.200)^n$$

from which $n = 4.3$ $\therefore$ 5 extractions or 100 mL CCl_4 are required

(b) Similarly,

$$0.00100 = \left(\frac{100}{(20 \times 10) + 100}\right)^n$$

from which $n = 6.3$ ∴ 7 extractions or 70 mL CCl_4 are required

17-21. (a) Substituting in Equation (17-14), we have

$$\frac{0.00100}{0.100} = 0.0100 = \left(\frac{100}{20\,D + 100}\right)^2 \quad \text{or} \quad \sqrt{0.0100} = 0.100 = \frac{100}{20\,D + 100}$$

from which $D = 45$

(b) Similarly,

$$0.0100 = \left(\frac{100}{10\,D + 100}\right)^4$$

from which $D = 21.6$

17-22. Substituting in Equation (4-20), we have

$$0.00100 = \left(\frac{25}{25\,K_D + 25}\right)^4$$

from which $K_D = 4.62$

17-23. Let y be the fraction of A remaining in the aqueous phase, after five consecutive extractions. Substituting in Equation (17-14), we have

$$0.100 = \left(\frac{V_1}{D\,V_2 + V_1}\right)^2 \quad \text{or} \quad \frac{V_1}{D\,V_2 + V_1} = \sqrt{0.100} \qquad (1)$$

$$y = \left(\frac{V_1}{D\,V_2 + V_1}\right)^5 \qquad (2)$$

Combining Equations (1) and (2), we have

$y = (\sqrt{0.100})^5 = 0.00316$

∴ $(1 - 0.00316)\,100 = 99.7\%$ A extracted

17-24.

pH	2.0	2.5	3.0	3.5	4.0
log D	-3.62	-2.12	-0.62	0.88	2.38

$$\log D = \log K'_{ex} + n \log [HL]_o + n\,pH \qquad (17\text{-}44a)$$

∴ A plot of log D vs pH (when $[HL]_o$ is constant) should be a straight line with a slope of n. Hence, $n = \dfrac{2.38 - (-3.62)}{4.0 - 2.0} = 3$

At pH 2.0 (other pH values can also be used), we have $\log D = -3.62 = \log K'_{ex} + 3 \log(0.020) + (3 \times 2.0)$ or $\log K'_{ex} = -4.52$ ∴ $K'_{ex} = 10^{-4.52} = 3.0 \times 10^{-5}$

17-25. See Example 17-6

We have the expressions

$$D = \frac{(C_B)_o}{(C_B)_w} = \frac{[B]_o}{[B]_w + [BH^+]_w} \tag{1}$$

$$K_D = [B]_o / [B]_w \tag{2}$$

$$K_b = \frac{[BH^+]_w [OH^-]_w}{[B]_w} \tag{3}$$

Combining Equations (1), (2) and (3) we have the sought for expression

$$D = \frac{[B]_o}{[B]_w + \frac{[B]_w K_b}{[OH^-]_w}} = \frac{[B]_o}{[B]_w(1 + \frac{K_b}{[OH^-]_w})} = \frac{K_D [OH^-]_w}{[OH^-]_w + K_b} = \frac{K_D \frac{K_w}{[H^+]_w}}{\frac{K_w}{[H^+]_w} + K_b} = \frac{K_D K_w}{K_w + [H^+]_w K_b}$$

17-26. (a) $p = \frac{D}{D+1} = \frac{3.0}{3.0+1} = 0.75$, $q = 1 - p = 1 - 0.75 = 0.25$

$(p + q)^n = (0.75 + 0.25)^{20} = (0.75)^{20} + 20(0.75)^{19}(0.25) + \ldots = 0.00317 + 0.0211 + \ldots$

$\therefore$ fraction of A remaining in the first two tubes 0.00317 + 0.0211 = 0.243 or 2.43%

(b) $(p + q)^{50} = (0.75 + 0.25)^{50} = (0.75)^{50} + 50(0.75)^{49}(0.25) + \ldots = 0.000000566 + 0.00000944$ $\therefore$ fraction remaining 0.000000566 + 0.00000944 0.00001 or 0.001%

17-27. $p = \frac{4.0}{4.0+1} = 0.8$, $q = 1 - 0.8 = 0.2$

$(p+q)^n = (0.8 + 0.2)^4 = (0.8)^4 + 4(0.8)^3(0.2) + 6(0.8)^2(0.2)^2 + 4(0.8)(0.2)^3 + (0.2)^4$

$= 0.4096 + 0.4096 + 0.1536 + 0.0256 + 0.0016$

$\therefore$ 0.4096 X 0.0200 = 0.008192 g A in tubes 0 and 1,

0.1536 X 0.0200 = 0.003072 g A in tube 2,

o.0256 X 0.0200 = 0.000512 g A in tube 3, and

0.0016 X 0.0200 = 0.000032 g A in tube 4.

17-28. See Example 17-11.

Substituting the data in Equation (17-55) we have the following results which are also represented in a diagram.

Tube number	Fraction of substance A	Fraction of substance B
0	$(f_{5,0})_A = \frac{5!}{0!(5-0)!}\frac{1.0^0}{(1.0+1)^5} = 0.03125$	$(f_{5,0})_B = \frac{5!}{0!(5-0)!}\frac{2.0^0}{(2.0+1)^5} = 0.00411$
1	$(f_{5,1})_A = \frac{5!}{1!(5-1)!}\frac{1.0^1}{(1.0+1)^5} = 0.15625$	$(f_{5,1})_B = \frac{5!}{1!(5-1)!}\frac{2.0^1}{(2.0+1)^5} = 0.04115$
2	$(f_{5,2})_A = \frac{5!}{2!(5-2)!}\frac{1.0^1}{(1.0+1)^5} = 0.3125$	$(f_{5,2})_B = \frac{5!}{2!(5-2)!}\frac{2.0^2}{(2.0+1)^5} = 0.16461$

3 $(f_{5,3})_A = \frac{5!}{3!(5-3)!}\frac{1.0^3}{(1.0+1)^5} = 0.3125$ $(f_{5,3})_B = \frac{5!}{3!(5-3)!}\frac{2.0^3}{(2.0+1)^5} = 0.32912$

4 $(f_{5,4})_A = \frac{5!}{4!(5-4)!}\frac{1.0^4}{(1.0+1)^5} = 0.15625$ $(f_{5,4})_B = \frac{5!}{4!(5-4)!}\frac{2.0^4}{(2.0+1)^5} = 0.32922$

5 $(f_{5,5})_A = \frac{5!}{5!(5-5)!}\frac{1.0^5}{(1.0+1)^5} = 0.03125$ $(f_{5,5})_B = \frac{5!}{5!(5-5)!}\frac{2.0^5}{(2.0+1)^5} = 0.13169$

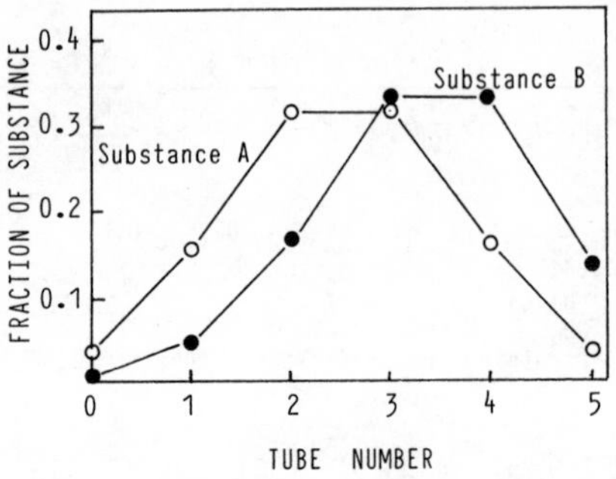

17-29 (a) See Example 17-15.

On the basis of Equation (17-77a), we have

$$[Na^+] = \frac{(2.00 \times 10^{-3})^2}{1.50\left(\frac{1.75 \times 2.00}{100} - 2.00 \times 10^{-3}\right)} = 8.08 \times 10^{-5}$$

$(8.08 \times 10^{-5} < 0.05 \times 2.00 \times 10^{-3} = 1.0 \times 10^{-4}$ $\therefore$ we correctly selected the simplified Equation (17-77a) instead of (17-76). Consequently,

$$\left(\frac{2.00 \times 10^{-3} - 8.08 \times 10^{-5}}{2.0}\right) 100 = 96.0\%$$

of sodium ions will be adsorbed by the resin.

(b) For 1.00 g of resin, on the basis of Equation (17-77a) we have

$$[Na^+] = \frac{(2.00 \times 10^{-3})^2}{1.50\left(\frac{1.75 \times 1.00}{100} - 2.00 \times 10^{-3}\right)} = 1.72 \times 10^{-4}$$

$1.72 \times 10^{-4} > 0.05 \times 2.00 \times 10^{-3} = 1.0 \times 10^{-4}$ $\therefore$ we incorrectly selected the simplified Equation (17-77a). Instead, we should use Equation (17-76), whereupon we have

$$(1.50 - 1)[Na^+]^2 + \left[\frac{1.50 \times 1.75 \times 1.00}{100} + 2.00 \times 10^{-3}(2 - 1.50)\right][Na^+] - (2.00 \times 10^{-3})^2 = 0$$

or $0.50[Na^+]^2 + 0.02725[Na^+] - 4.00 \times 10^{-6} = 0$

from which $[Na^+] = 1.46 \times 10^{-4}$ M.

After the removal of the initial resin from the solution and the addition of the remaining 1.00 g of resin, on the basis of Equation (17-77a) we have

$$[Na^+] = \frac{(1.46 \times 10^{-4})^2}{1.50\,(\frac{1.75 \times 1.00}{100} - 1.46 \times 10^{-4})} = 8.18 \times 10^{-7}$$

Consequently,

$$(\frac{2.00 \times 10^{-3} - 8.18 \times 10^{-7}}{2.00 \times 10^{-3}})\,100 = 99.96\,\%$$

of sodium ions will be adsorbed by the resin.(We find the same result, 99.96%, using the precise Equation (17-76).)

17-30. Suppose that the mixture contains y% KCl (w/w) and z% KNO_3. We have

$$y + z = 100 \qquad (1)$$

$$\frac{y}{100} \cdot \frac{140.1}{74.56} + \frac{z}{100} \cdot \frac{140.1}{101.11} = 16.30 \times 0.0997 \qquad (2)$$

Solving the system of Equations (1) and (2), we find that y = 48.56% KCl and z = 51.44% KNO_3

17-31. Solving Equation (15-75) for W, we have

$$W = \frac{V}{C}\left[\frac{([M^+]_0 - [M^+])^2}{K_X^M\,[M^+]} + [M^+]_0 - [M^+]\right] \qquad (1)$$

Substituting the data in Equation (1), we have

$$W = \frac{100}{3.50}\left[\frac{(2.00 \times 10^{-3} - 2.00 \times 10^{-5})^2}{2.70\,(2.00 \times 10^{-5})} + 2.00 \times 10^{-3} - 2.00 \times 10^{-5}\right] = 2.13\ g$$

17-32. (a) We have the expressions

$$K_H^{Cs} = 2.56 = \frac{[H^+][Cs^+]_r}{[H^+]_r\,[Cs^+]} \qquad (1)$$

$$K_D = \frac{[Cs^+]_r}{[Cs^+]} = \frac{2.56\,[H^+]_r}{[H^+]} \qquad (2)$$

Assume that practically all Cs enters the resin, so that

$[Cs^+]_r = (100 \times 0.00100)/2.0 = 0.050$, $[H^+]_r = [4.00 - (100 \times 0.00100)/2.0] = 3.95$,

and $[H^+] = 0.00100$. Substituting in Equation (2), we have

$$K_D = (2.56)(3.95)/0.00100 = 10112$$

At equilibrium, we have

$$\frac{\text{amount of Cs in resin}}{\text{amount of Cs in solution}} = \frac{[Cs^+]_r \times \text{g resin}}{[Cs^+] \times \text{mL solution}} = \frac{10112 \times 2.0}{100} = 202$$

Hence,

$$\text{fraction of Cs remaining in solution} = (\frac{1}{1 + 202})\,100 = 0.49\,\%$$

Thus, at equilibrium the 2.0 g of resin has removed 99.51% of Cs from solution. The result shows that the assumption of practically complete exchange of Cs is valid.

(b) Assume that practically all Cs enters the 1.0 g of resin, so that

$[Cs^+]_r = (100 \times 0.00100)/1.0 = 0.10$, $[H^+]_r = [4.00 - (100 \times 0.00100)/1.0] = 3.90$,

and $[H^+] = 0.00100$. Substituting in Equation (2), we have

$K_D = (2.56)(3.90)/0.00100 = 9984$

$$\therefore \frac{\text{amount of Cs in resin}}{\text{amount of Cs in solution}} = \frac{9984 \times 1.0}{100} = 99.84$$

Hence,

$$\text{fraction of Cs remaining in solution} = \left(\frac{1}{1 + 99.84}\right) 100 = 0.99\%$$

After the removal of the initial 1.0 g of resin, we have $[Cs^+] = (0.00100 \times 0.99)/100 = 1.0 \times 10^{-5}$. After the addition of the remaining 1.0 g of resin, practically all Cs enters the resin, so that

$[Cs^+]_r = (100 \times 1.0 \times 10^{-5})/1.0 = 1.0 \times 10^{-3}$, $[H^+]_r = [4.00 - (100 \times 1.0 \times 10^{-3})/1.0] \simeq 4.00$, and $[H^+] = 1.0 \times 10^{-5}$ $\therefore K_D = (2.56)(4.00)/(1.0 \times 10^{-5}) = 1024000$, and

$$\frac{\text{amount of Cs in resin}}{\text{amount of Cs in solution}} = \frac{1024000 \times 1.0}{100} = 10240$$

Hence,

$$\text{fraction of Cs remaining in solution} = \left(\frac{1}{1 + 10240}\right) 100 = 0.01\%$$, that is

$(0.01/100) \times (0.99/100) = 0.000001\%$ of the initial amount.

17-33. $$\frac{(10.82\ \text{mL})(0.1002\ \text{meq NaOH/mL})(1\ \text{meq cation/meq NaOH})}{100.0\ \text{mL sample}} \times 1000\ \frac{\text{mL}}{\text{L}} = 10.84\ \frac{\text{meq cation}}{\text{L}}$$

17-34. $30.70\ \text{mL} \times 0.0998\ \text{meq/mL} = 50.00\ \text{mL} \times y\ \text{mmol/mL} \times 2\ \text{meq/mmol}$,

from which $y = 0.0306$

17-35. $$\frac{(11.85\ \text{mL})(0.1004\ \text{mmol NaOH/mL})(1\ \text{mmol HCl/mmol NaOH})}{50.00\ \text{mL A}} = 0.02379\ \frac{\text{mmol HCl}}{\text{ml A}}$$

$$\frac{(15.64\ \text{mL})(0.1004\ \text{meq NaOH/mL})}{20.00\ \text{mL A}} = 0.07851 = \frac{\text{meq HCl + meq } CaCl_2}{\text{mL A}}$$

$\therefore$ meq $CaCl_2$/mL A = 0.07851 - 0.02379 = 0.05472

Hence,

$M_{CaCl_2} = (0.05472\ \text{meq } CaCl_2/\text{mL A})(1\ \text{mmol } CaCl_2/2\ \text{meq } CaCl_2) = 0.02736\ \text{mmol } CaCl_2/\text{mL A}$

CHAPTER 18

18-1. Combining Equations (18-3) and (18-21), we have

$h = L/n = \sigma^2/L \quad \therefore \quad n = L^2/\sigma^2$

18-2. From Equation (18-23a), since $K_A < K_B$, we have $t_{R_A} < t_{R_B}$ $\therefore$ A will be be eluted first

18-3. Substituting the data in Equation (18-23b), we have

$V_{R_A} = 2.1 + (10.0 \times 1.3) = 15.1$ mL

$V_{R_B} = 2.1 + (40.0 \times 1.3) = 54.1$ mL

Substituting these values in Equation (18-15), we have

$24 = 16\,(15.1/w_A)^2$, from which $w_A = 12.33$ mL,

$24 = 16\,(54.1/w_B)^2$, from which $w_B = 44.17$ mL

$\therefore$ peak A is from $[15.1 - (w_A/2)]$ to $[15.1 + (w_A/2)]$, that is from $(15.1 - 6.17)$ to $(15.1 + 6.17)$ or 8.9 to 21.3 mL, whereas peak B is from $(54.1 - 22.08)$ to $(54.1 + 22.08)$ or 32.0 to 76.2 mL . Hence, the separation is satisfactory, because peaks A and B do not overlap

18-4. (a) $n = 16\,(t_R/w)^2 = 16\,(6.05/0.58)^2 = 2343 \simeq 2.34 \times 10^3$

(b) $N = 16\,(t'_R/w)^2 = 16\,[(6.05 - 1.29)/0.50]^2 = 1737 \simeq 1.74 \times 10^3$

(c) $h = L/n = 248/2343 = 0.106$ cm

18-5. Combining Equations (18-15) and (18-3), we have

$16\,(t_R/w)^2 = L/h$

$\therefore$ $t_R/w \propto \sqrt{L}$. since $t_R \propto L$, then $w \propto \sqrt{L}$. Hence, t_R increases by $\sqrt{3} = 1.73$

18-6. (a) Since $w_A \simeq w_B$, Equation (17-18) becomes

$$R = \frac{2(t_{R_B} - t_{R_A})}{w_A + w_B} = \frac{2(t_{R_B} - t_{R_A})}{2\,w} = \frac{t_{R_B} - t_{R_A}}{w} = \frac{(t_{R_B}/t_{R_A}) - 1}{w/t_{R_B}} = \frac{\alpha - 1}{w/t_{R_B}} \qquad (1)$$

Since $t_M \ll t_R$, Equation (17-13) becomes

$$\alpha = \frac{t_{R_B} - t_M}{t_{R_A} - t_M} \simeq \frac{t_{R_B}}{t_{R_A}}$$

$$\text{or} \quad t_{R_B} = \alpha\, t_{R_A} \qquad (2)$$

Combining Equations (1) and (2), we have

$$R = \left(\frac{\alpha - 1}{\alpha}\right)\left(\frac{t_{R_A}}{w}\right) \qquad (3)$$

From Equation (18-15),

$$t_{R_A}/w = \sqrt{n}/4 \qquad (4)$$

Combining Equations (3) and (4), we have

$$R = (\frac{\sqrt{n}}{4})(\frac{\alpha - 1}{\alpha}) \qquad (5)$$

(b) Since $R \propto \sqrt{n}$ (Equation 5), and $n = L/h$ (Equation 18-3), then $R \propto \sqrt{L}$

$\therefore\ R_2 = R_1 \sqrt{L_2/L_1} = 0.90 \sqrt{40/20} = 1.27$

18-7. Since $t_{R_B} \propto R^2$ (Equation 18-26), to double the resolution, t_{R_B} should be increased by a factor of $2^2 = 4$

18-8. (a) On the basis of Equation (18-19), for the original set of conditions, we have

$$R_{or} = (\frac{\sqrt{3136}}{4})(\frac{1.20 - 1}{1.20})(\frac{1.80}{1 + 1.80}) = 1.50$$

When N is decreased to 1394, the resolution becomes equal to

$$R = (\frac{\sqrt{1394}}{4})(\frac{1.20 - 1}{1.20})(\frac{1.80}{1 + 1.80}) = 1.00 ,$$

that is the resolution deteriorates

(b) When k' is decreased to 0.75 , the resolution becomes equal to

$$R = (\frac{\sqrt{3136}}{4})(\frac{1.20 - 1}{1.20})(\frac{0.75}{1 + 0.75}) = 1.00 ,$$

that is the resolution deteriorates

18-9. From Equation (18-23b), $V_R = 8.0(1 + k')$ or $k' = 11$

$\therefore$ from Equation (18-19), $1.50 = (\frac{\sqrt{N}}{4})(\frac{1.20 - 1}{1.20})(\frac{11}{1 + 11})$ or $N = 1542$, and from Equation (18-17), $n = 1542\,(\frac{1 + 11}{11})^2 = 1835$, whereupon from Equation (25-3), $L = h\,n = 0.110 \times 1835 = 202$ cm

18-10. Column C_1 (Equation 18-15) : $w_A = \frac{4t_{R_A}}{\sqrt{n}} = \frac{4\,(21.0 + 2.0)}{\sqrt{4900}} = 1.314$, $w_B = \frac{4\,(22.0 + 2.0)}{\sqrt{4900}} =$ 1.371

$\therefore$ from Equation (18-18), $R_1 = \frac{2\,(24.0 - 23.0)}{1.314 + 1.371} = 0.7449 \simeq 0.79$

Column C_2 : $w_A = \frac{4\,(0.40 + 0.12)}{\sqrt{19600}} = 0.01486$, $w_B = \frac{4\,(0.40 + 0.13)}{\sqrt{19600}} = 0.01514$

$\therefore\ R_2 = \frac{2\,(0.53 - 0.52)}{0.01486 - 0.01514} = 0.67$

Although $n_2 = 19600 > 4900 = n_1$, column C_2 ($R = 0.67$) shows less resolution than column C_1 ($R = 0.74$), because of the very large value of t_M for column C_2, relative to t'_{R_A} and t'_{R_B} , which results in a small effective plate number N for column C_2 . Thus,

$$\overline{N}_2 = \frac{16(t'_{R_A}/w_A)^2 + 16(t'_{R_B}/w_B)^2}{2} = \frac{16(0.12/0.01486)^2 + 16(0.13/0.01514)^2}{2} = 1112 =$$

$(1112/19600)\,n_2 = 0.057\,n_2$,

whereas for column C_1 we have

$$\overline{N}_1 = \frac{16\,(21.0/1.314)^2 + 16\,(22.0/1.371)^2}{2} = 4103 = (4103/4700)\,n_1 = 0.84\,n_1$$

18-11. Since h is expressed in cm, and $h = A + (B/\upsilon) + C\upsilon$ (Equation 18-27), the terms A, B/υ, and $C\upsilon$ should also be expressed in cm ∴ constant A is expressed in cm. Since B/υ (cm/s) = cm, then B is expressed in cm^2/s; also, since $C\upsilon$ (cm/s) = cm, C is expressed in s.

18-12. Values of h, calculated by Equation (18-27), are tabulated below:

υ, cm/s	0.5	1	2	3	4	5	6	8	10
h, cm	1.09	0.61	0.40	0.357	0.355	0.37	0.393	0.453	0.52

From a plot of h vs. υ, we find υ_{opt} = 3.5 cm/s, h_{min} = 0.35 cm. On the basis of Equation (18-28), we have $\upsilon_{opt} = \sqrt{0.50/0.04}$ = 3.5 cm/s, whereas using Equation (18-29), we find $h_{min} = 0.07 + 2\sqrt{0.50 \times 0.04}$ = 0.35 cm

18-13. (a)

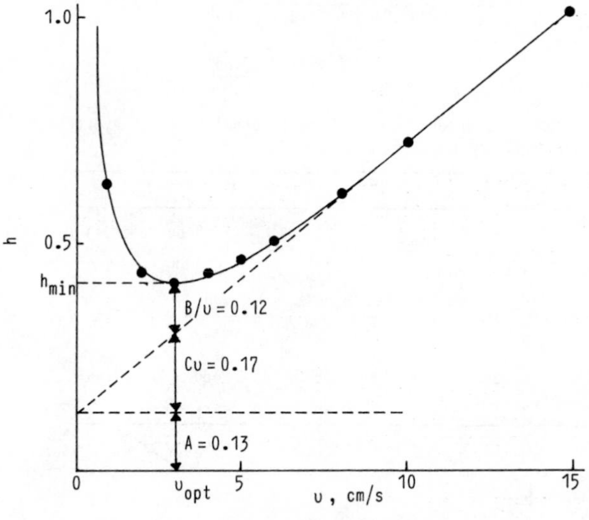

From the above plot we find υ_{opt} = 3.0 cm/s, h_{min} = 0.42 cm

(b) From the plot we find A = 0.13 cm, B = 0.36 cm^2/s, C = 0.06 cm. We also find that h = 0.44 for υ = 2 or 4, and h = 0.47 for = 5 ∴ on the basis of Equation (18-27), we have

for υ = 2, $h = A + 0.5\,B + 2\,C = 0.44$ (1)

for υ = 4, $h = A + 0.2\,B + 4\,C = 0.44$ (2)

for υ = 5, $h = A + 0.2\,B + 5\,C = 0.47$ (3)

Solving the three simultaneous equations gives A = 0.14 cm, B = 0.40 cm^2/s, C = 0.05 s.

There is satisfactory agreement between the two sets of values for A, B, and C

18-14. (a) Substituting the data in Equation (18-27), we have

$h_1 = 0.10 + (0.40/1.0) + (0.06 \times 1.0) = 0.56$

$h_2 = 0.13 + (0.32/1.0) + (0.13 \times 1.0) = 0.58$

Since $h = L/n$ (Equation 18-3) and L is the same for both columns, we have $n_1/n_2 = (L/h_1)/(L/h_2) = h_2/h_1 = 0.58/0.56$ or $n_1 = 1.04\, n_2$, that is column 2 gives the larger number of theoretical plates.

(b) Substituting the data in Equation (18-28), we have

$(\upsilon_{opt})_1 = \sqrt{0.40/0.06} = 2.58$ cm/s

$(\upsilon_{opt})_2 = \sqrt{0.32/0.13} = 1.57$ cm/s

18-15. Substituting the data in Equation (18-33), and taking into account that the two paraffins given differ by 2 carbon atoms, we have

$$\text{for A}: \quad I = 100\,\frac{2\log[(85.4-5.6)/(48.7-5.6)]}{\log[(103.0-5.6)/(48.7-5.6)]} + 100 \times 4 = 555$$

$$\text{B}: \quad I = 100\,\frac{2\log[(152.0-5.6)/(48.7-5.6)]}{\log[(103.0-5.6)/(48.7-5.6)]} + 100 \times 4 = 700$$

Since $I \neq 100z$, compound A cannot be a normal paraffin hydrocarbon.

18-16.

Compound	t_R, min	$\log t_R'$	I
Ethane	0.20	-0.70	200 by definition
n-Pentane	1.48	0.17	500 " "
n-Octane	11.2	1.05	800 " "
Ethylene	0.11	-0.96	110 from plot
Butene-1	0.66	-0.18	380 " "
Benzene	3.31	0.52	615 " "

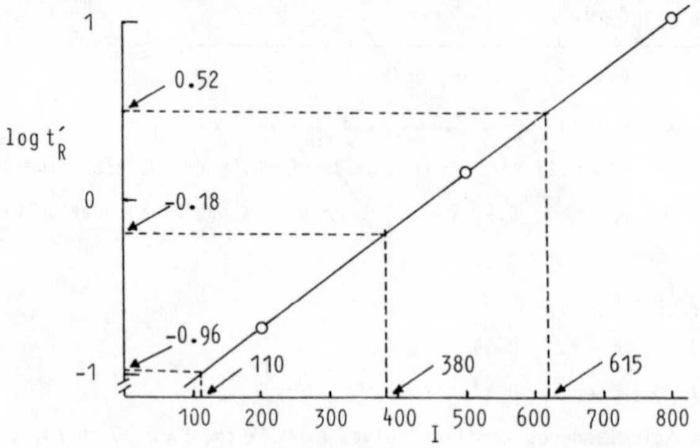

By definition, I = 200, 500, 800 for ethane, n-pentane, and n-octane, respectively. From a plot of $\log t'_R$ vs. I for these compounds, we find I = 110, 380, 615 for ethylene, butene-1, and benzene, respectively.

18-17. See Example 18-8

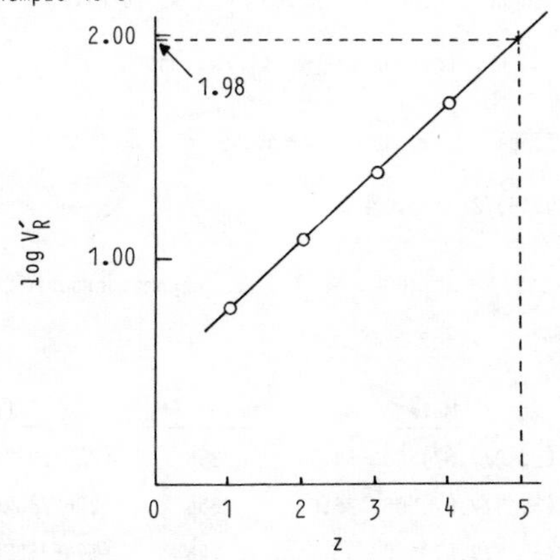

From plot, for z = 5 we find $\log V'_R = 1.98$ ∴ $V'_R = 10^{1.98} = 95.5$ mL

18-18.

Compound	t_R	t'_R	$\log t'_R$
A (z = 5)	1.98	1.48	0.17
B (z = 8)	11.7	11.2	1.05
X_1	0.7	0.2	0.46
X_2	3.4	2.9	-0.70

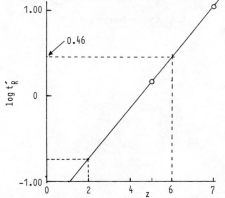

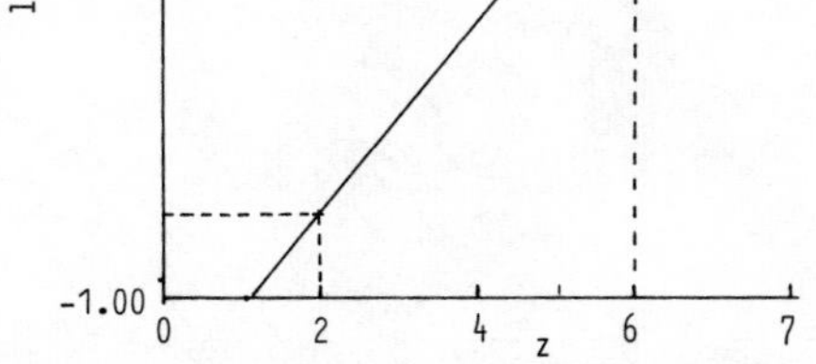

From above plot, we find z = 6 for compound X_1 and z = 2 for X_2

18-19. Ratio of peak areas:

for A : (2.20/1.21) : (5.86/1.21) : 1 or 1.818 : 4.843 : 1

B : (1.82/1.05) : (6.90/1.05) : 1 or 1.733 : 6.571 : 1

C : (1.97/1.10) : (5.90/1.05) : 1 or 1.791 : 5.364 : 1

Suppose that C contains y% B and consequently (100.00 − y)% A. We have

$$\frac{1.818\,(100.00-y) + 1.733\,y}{100.00} = 1.791\text{, from which } y = 31.76\text{, and}$$

$$\frac{4.843\,(100.00-y) + 6.57\,y}{100.00} = 5.364\text{, from which } y = 30.15$$

∴ C contains $\overline{y} = (31.76 + 30.15)/2 = 31.0\%$ B

18-20. Sample A contains [3.0 (0.50/4.17)/10.0] 100 = 3.6% B ∴ chromatographic purity of A is equal to 100.0 − 3.6 = 96.4% A.

18-21 (a)

Compound	MW	Area	Mole %	Mole % X MW	% (w/w)
n-Pentane	72.15	2.40	(2.40/7.67)100 = 31.3	2258	(2258/8870)100 = 25.5
1-Hexanol	102.18	2.15	(2.15/7.67)100 = 28.0	2864	(2864/8870)100 = 32.3
Toluene	92.14	3.12	(3.12/7.67)100 = 40.7	3748	(3748/8870)100 = 42.3
		7.67	100.0	8870	100.0

(b)

Compound	Area	Area X WF	% (w/w)
n-Pentane	2.40	2.40 X 0.87 = 2.088	(2.088/8.398)100 = 24.9
1-Hexanol	2.15	2.15 X 1.15 = 2.472	(2.472/8.398)100 = 29.4
Toluene	3.12	3.12 X 1.23 = 3.838	(3.838/8.398)100 = 45.7
	7.67	8.398	100.0

18-22.

$$\frac{1.525}{1.525 + \left(\frac{15.41/18.32}{13.98/12.12}\right)1.783} \times 100 = 54.0\%\text{ cyclohexane}$$